Augustus Smith, aged 51, in his Tresco garden with an aloe
Enlarged print from original plate, William Jenkyns, April 1856

VIEWS AND LIKENESSES

EARLY PHOTOGRAPHERS AND THEIR WORK IN CORNWALL AND THE ISLES OF SCILLY 1839–1870

CHARLES THOMAS

FOUNDED 1818

ROYAL INSTITUTION OF CORNWALL

TRURO

1988

First published 1988

Royal Institution of Cornwall
River Street, Truro, Cornwall TR1 2SJ, UK

British Library Cataloguing in Publication Data.

THOMAS, Charles
(1928) −

    Views and Likenesses:
    Early Photographers and Their Work in Cornwall and the Isles of Scilly 1839−1870

    1. Cornwall & Isles of Scilly.
       Photography 1839−1870.

    i. Title

    ii. Royal Institution of Cornwall.

770' 9423' 7

ISBN 1 871294 00 2

Printed by Cornwall Lithographic Printers Ltd., Redruth, Cornwall

Cover design, by author, is based on a view of St Michael's Mount by William Jenkyns, about 1856

CONTENTS

6

Appendixes

LIST OF ILLUSTRATIONS

FOREWORD

AT A TIME when public interest in old photographs has never been greater, the publication of *Views and Likenesses* is particularly welcome. It will doubtless come as a surprise to many people that Cornwall played such a leading part in the development of photography, and that so many photographers, both professional and amateur, were working in Cornwall in the nineteenth century. The Royal Institution of Cornwall has the good fortune to possess a particularly rich collection of early photographs, and in the present volume, the first of a series, Professor Thomas traces the development of photography in Cornwall. He has not only selected for our interest and enjoyment a remarkable collection of photographs of people, places and events in Cornish life, but also an illustrated gazetteer of the photographers themselves. The choosing of photographs from the wealth of material in the Royal Institution of Cornwall and from other sources must have been a very difficult task, but one which has obviously given the author a great deal of pleasure, and he writes about them with scholarship, technical expertise and humour. Fascinating subjects for the camera include a study by William Jenkyns of Augustus Smith in his garden at Tresco, the Royal party descending into Botallack Mine in 1865 taken by Robert Preston, and a sensitive and thoughtful portrait of the antiquary and author John Thomas Blight, also by Preston. The views of Cornwall surprise and enchant us. We see two identical photographs of houses in Falmouth taken by Robert Hunt FRS in 1841 and by the author in 1987 in which, except for the absence of iron railings and the growth of a yew tree, the only significant change in 136 years is the ugly forest of television aerials sprouting from the roof-tops. A photograph taken by John Beringer of the Tolmen in Constantine, which was destroyed in 1869, reminds us of the important part that early photographic records have played in local history. The author gives us intriguing anecdotes about some of the sitters, such as Grace Briney, photographed by a professional called James Chenhall at Redruth, who at the age of 91 walked 50 miles from Redruth to St Dominick to collect a load of cherries! And who could imagine ostriches at Tresco in 1862? They were there, and were photographed by Archibald Coke, a visiting professional. The biographical details of the phtographers themselves make fascinating reading. Many of them followed other occupations at the same time, and there were watchmakers, printers and grocers among them.

When one considers the lack of scientific and technical aids available to the early photographers in Cornwall, it is all the more remarkable that they were able to produce photographs of such beauty and excellence as many of those illustrated in this volume. We all owe Charles Thomas our deepest gratitude for *Views and Likenesses,* and who better than he with his vast knowledge of Cornwall and Cornish life to afford us a glimpse into a vanished age? The past always seems to take on a certain enchantment, perhaps more so now because of these harsh and violent times. How fortunate we are therefore to be able to share with Professor Thomas a precious mine of valuable and fascinating information about Cornwall's early photographers, their sitters and the places themselves. I look forward greatly to our next volume.

DIANA COLVILLE
President, Royal Institution of Cornwall

AUTHOR'S INTRODUCTION

This book is not a history of photography in Cornwall. In writing it, I have had four separate aims. Intending readers and users may find it helpful to know what these are.

First of all, *Views and Likenesses* is meant as a foretaste of the collection of prints, plates, negatives and slides, ranging in date from the 1850s to the present day, which has been built up at the Royal Institution of Cornwall, Cornwall's County Museum and the home of its premier learned society (founded in 1818). This collection is widely used but in a piecemeal fashion. The decision to treat it as an historical archive – which is what it is – was taken in 1986. This led to the idea of a series of volumes, the first of which could form an introduction to the whole collection and also cover the early years up to 1870, a convenient break-point. The R.I.C. as a society has always managed to inspire a genuine affection from its members, staff and officers, who seek to maintain it as a service for everyone. As the Institution's Courtney Librarian, the task of compiling this first volume fell to me; the compilation has however been a labour of love, and a fascinating exercise in local history.

My second aim, which arose from the discovery that so much material existed, is to publicise the existence in Cornwall and Scilly from about 1845 to 1870 of a school of regional photography, apparently quite unknown to photographic historians outside the county and not particularly well known within it because, so far, no single work has described it. One could go further and say that none of the photographers apart from Robert Hunt has ever been discussed, except in footnotes. I hope that the importance of this school will become apparent. Early by national standards, photography in Cornwall before 1870 involved nearly a hundred people whose names and outline histories are known. About half of them have left us identifiable work. I think it unlikely that lists of comparable size could be put together in respect of other counties, because special factors operated in the case of Cornwall. There was the lead given by the Royal Cornwall Polytechnic Society founded in 1833 at Falmouth. There was the growth from about 1850 of a tourist industry, and the attraction of Cornwall for artists professional and lay, photographers among them. During the last century, too, there was an involvement in technical and scientific invention – a localised, indigenous, Industrial Revolution – making Cornwall and the Cornish anything but marginal. Art, science, public and private activity, intelligent visitors and inventive natives all came together, in the right place and at the right moment, to provide a unique seed-bed for the development of photography.

Thirdly, I have tried to bring a new approach to the theme of photographic history, much worked-over in larger areas of this subject. One would want to bring exactitude to any study of local history, or archaeology, or the history of art. The examination of photography before 1870 in any region is something that also deserves the closest attention to dates, identities, connections and explanations. I make no pretence at all to the technical history of photography (processes or cameras); this is more than covered in a score of available books, and should in any case be explored on a national or international footing. On the other hand, a local historian with an intimate knowledge of 19th-century sources, those for Cornwall in particular, is perhaps better equipped than most photographic experts to explore the human links, the immediate background and the hard evidence for dates; in short, to make visible the wood rather than single trees.

These remarks lead on to the fourth and last aim, one that is implied in the book's sub-title. *Views and Likenesses* is as much, perhaps slightly more, a study of the photographers themselves, than of the images they made. We already have biographies of many famous early cameramen – Fox Talbot, Roger Fenton, Francis Frith, Frank Meadow Sutcliffe, *et al*. One is very hard put to find the briefest mentions of hundreds of other lesser-known men (and women), busily photographing during the same period. Yet they included artists alongside tradesmen; artists untrained, but with real gifts for composition and texture, and people whose careers it is just as important to describe. Passing references are made to photographers who were involved in more than one kind of livelihood; but what kinds, and why? A bird's-eye view of this 'multiple occupation' aspect is provided here in *Appendix IV*. Its existence point to another topic about which almost nothing seems to be known, or published; the economics of the photographic world, by areas of Britain, during the last century. Today (1988) Truro, where I write this, is Cornwall's principal town, a city whose permanent population (city limits only) is about 17,000. Truro can support four studio photographers, one of whom doubles up as a taxi firm, and three camera shops. In 1865, when the town's population was about one-quarter the size of today's, it supported five, possibly six, separate photographers, engaged mostly in making portraits. Market forces are at work, but precisely what sort of forces? For every private camera-owner in 1865, there must now be a hundred or more. It is because the historian, whose business it is to look for explanations behind the facts, always needs still more facts, that the historical enquiry now shifts from the photographers' products and techniques to the photographers themselves. In human terms, the harvest is rich. Many of the early cameramen were lifelong enthusiasts and consequently never died of boredom – they lived for years and years. The least successful failed in business, went bankrupt, assaulted people and tried to swindle insurance companies; the best of them became mayors and magistrates, amassed wealth, provided for their families and were active citizens. They issued boastful advertisements, opened sea-side branches in the summer, took part in competitions, and admitted their sons to partnerships. They were as human as all of us. It is high time that we wrote their history, as humans.

Four aims, then, with four explanations or justifications. An enthusiast hardly needs to justify this kind of research. Any good early photograph is a successful theft from that greatest thief of all, Time. In bringing together within one book so colourful a plunder, instantly evoking a Cornwall (and Scilly) that none of us can see for ourselves, we must go a stage further and use these riches to illuminate, if only for a moment, a vanished society.

ACKNOWLEDGEMENTS

This compilation of text and illustrations is largely due to the help and support of a great many friends, old and new. Within the Royal Institution of Cornwall's own circle, I am especially grateful to Mr H.L. Douch (past Curator), Mr Roger Penhallurick (present Curator), Miss Angela Broome (Assistant Librarian) and Mr Rex Hall, a stalwart regular in the Courtney Library, for helping to choose and to identify images and photographers and for a quite invaluable supply of key references from our newspaper files. Mr Peter Pool and Mr John Stengelhofen, both past Presidents of the Institution, have freely given information, advice and technical aid, and I am also most grateful to Mrs Diana Colville (President) for her gracious Foreword. Thanks go, too, to our friends at Camera Craft, Truro — Mr and Mrs E.A. Earl-Davies, Mr Steven Earl-Davies and Mr Andrew Garner — who service our photographic collection and have patiently made all the copies, new negatives and prints.

As for all those who have generously assisted with facts and dates, family trees, the details of subjects and locations, and above all with gifts or loans with ready permission to copy, it seems only right to start with the descendants 'unto the fourth and fifth generations' (as indeed they all are) of some of the early cameramen, named in brackets below. They are: Mr Geoffrey L. Smith, JP, of Messrs Beringer's (Fidelis and John Beringer); my old friend Mr Francis E. (Frank) Gibson in Scilly (John Gibson); Mr Christopher Gutch, Maidenhead, Mr Richard Gutch, Chiswick, and Rev Nigel Nicholson, Guildford (John Gutch); Dr Francis Hambly of Camborne (S.S. Hambly); Mr Edward Richards, Penzance (William Jenkyns and William Richards); my cousin Mrs Marjorie Jenkin, Illogan (William Piper); Mrs Evelyn Batty of Oxford (Robert Preston); and all the Thorn gentlemen of Bude, notably Mr Roy and Mr Spencer Thorn (Harry, Samuel and Sarah Thorn).

From other institutions and societies I desire to record our thanks to: Dr Ian Kinnes (The British Museum), Mr Stephen Croad (National Monuments Record, R.C.H.M. England), Mr Winfrith Scutt (City of Plymouth Museums & Art Gallery), Mr John S. Williams (Acting City Archivist, Bristol) and Mrs Christine North (County Archivist, Cornwall County Records Office, Truro) — and especially also to Miss Frances Dymond (Curator, Photographic Collection, Royal Archives, Windsor Castle) and Mr John Ward (Curator, Photography & Cinematography Collections, The Science Museum) for their time, keen and expert interest, and kindness in arranging the reproduction of prints.

The Institution, as well as myself, would want to express its gratitude to all those (members included) who have lent items for copying and have permitted reproduction. They include: Mr Justin Brooke, Mr and Mrs L. Hewitt, Mr and Mrs R.G. Jenkin, Mr Martin, Mr Eric Quayle and Mr A.G. Stirling. Very special thanks go to Miss Brenda Pye of St Mawes for her active support, and for allowing reference to, and extensive copying from, her own fine collection, and to Mr and Mrs Bernard Crumpler of Victoria, Australia, for their kindness and trouble in connection with the Levick Album. We also include here all the friends who have materially assisted with information, otherwise unknown photographers, and references — Mr Cedric Appleby, Mr Clive Carter, Mr Andrew Lanyon, Mr Douglas Lobb, Mr Alan Pearson, Mr and Mrs Peter Pool, Mr John Rapson, Rev Thomas Shaw and Mr David Thomas.

I am personally indebted to my brother Mr Nicholas Thomas and my aunt Mrs A.L. Thomas, Polstrong, for kindly letting me use family items; to Mr Robin Fenner of Tavistock, for so much help with photographers in Devon — details taken from his own archive, increasing our eagerness to see his companion work on that county; and to the modest but expert enthusiast for Victorian photography and its sidelines, Mr Bernard Howarth-Loomes, for his encouragement, tuition in the history of stereoscopy, and above all his unprompted gift of some superb images to the Institution.

Finally — with apologies to any friend whose name is inadvertently neglected here — in my immediate family, thanks to my wife and children for their understanding and patience when part of our home had to become a photographic depot, and to my elder daughter Susanna for the likeness on the back cover.

1833 – THE ROYAL CORNWALL POLYTECHNIC SOCIETY, FALMOUTH

The story of the 'Polytechnic', as it has always been generally called throughout Cornwall and is so referred to in these pages, is not easily separable from that of the Fox family; certainly not in the years before 1870. Unrelated to George Fox, 1624–90, founder of the Society of Friends (or Quakers), these Foxes – who were themselves Quakers – traced their descent from one Francis Fox of Wiltshire who settled in the east of Cornwall after the Civil War. In the mid-18th century George Croker Fox came west to Falmouth, founding the ancient and respectable firm of G.C. Fox & Co. In Victorian times various branches of the family made up a compact distribution, at large houses in and around Falmouth. Liberal-minded, intellectual and philanthropic, and deservedly prosperous, they contributed much to Cornish affairs. The most interesting facet of a notably interesting clan was perhaps the extent of their contacts, national and international, outside the county.

Best known to posterity has been the immediate family of Robert Were Fox, F.R.S., who lived at Penjerrick just south of Falmouth. His eldest child was Anna Maria (born in 1815), and the journals of two other children – Caroline (1819–71) and Robert Barclay (1817–55) – have been published in part.[1] Caroline's journal and letters, in particular, have been a considerable source for social and literary sidelights during her lifetime.

Among the Fox concerns was the large Perran Foundry, situated at Perranarworthal between Falmouth and Truro. According to the definitive account by her cousin Wilson Lloyd Fox,[2] Anna Maria became anxious to find some way of encouraging clever workmen, then in Fox employ at the foundry, who were constantly bringing their inventions and models to her father Robert for his inspection. If this sounds in any way too good to be true, it should be remembered firstly that the Foxes were, like most of the Quaker industrialists, model employers, eager to seek out technological merit; secondly, that anything tending to contribute to the common good was equated with moral progress; and thirdly, that such activity was to some extent characteristic of Cornwall in the early 19th century. The Cornish, far from regarding themselves as occupying some remote province where native industry might be up-dated through advances brought about elsewhere, were principally interested in what was going on in Cornwall. Mindful of Trevithick, Humphry Davy, Gilbert and other compatriots, the Cornish were

Fig.1 The Royal Cornwall Polytechnic Society's autumn meeting, 1859, at the Polytechnic Hall, Falmouth; mid-day at the opening of the Exhibition, Wednesday 28 September, when 'prior to the commencement of the proceedings, a photographic artist introduced the apparatus of his art' and then took a view of the hall and its occupants. In the chair, Sir Charles Lemon, F.R.S.; on his right, Sydney Hodges the Secretary (?) standing, Lord Vivian, Caroline and Anna Maria Fox; on his left his niece Louisa Ann Dyke, Robert Fox or John Jope Rogers (standing), and unidentified dignitaries. Probably by John Counsell Stephens. (Courtesy A.G. Stirling, Esq.)

leading an industrial revolution of their own making, and well knew it.[3] Anna Maria Fox, her sister Caroline, their father Robert and various relations and friends founded the Cornwall Polytechnic Society at Falmouth in 1833. The name 'Polytechnic' is believed to have been proposed (on the French model) by Caroline. Sir Charles Lemon, F.R.S., of Carclew *(Figs. 1 and 129)* agreed to become president, and remained so until his death in 1868. In 1835 William IV, 'Sailor Billy', consented to be named Patron, and permitted the addition of the prefix *Royal* to the society's official title.

The opening aims were grandiose, but practicable, and in large part they were met. They were to promote the useful and fine arts, to encourage industry, and to elicit the ingenuity of a community distinguished for its mechanical skill. The officers and the very large Central Committee together extended the thrust of the society, by calling the attention of Cornwall's public to the greatest desiderata in art and science, 'especially as connected with the permanent interests of the

Jubilee Meeting, Sept. 5, 1882.

Fig.2 The Polytechnic's 1882 50th Jubilee meeting at the Polytechnic Hall, Falmouth, 5 September, when 'at the conclusion of the President's speech, Mr Gael took a couple of Memorial Photographs of the platform, which will be highly prized in days to come' (50 RCPS, 35). The President, the Reverend Canon Rogers, is in the chair. Sepia-toned copies of this print, 95 by 150 mm, were pasted as frontispieces into the Annual Reports issued to subscribers.

1882; Edgar Gael, Falmouth

(R.I.C.)

county'.[4] This wide phraseology allowed the Polytechnic to interest itself in almost everything happening at the time. By 1836 the Polytechnic Hall, intended as a permanent home, was ready for use. It was certainly much needed. While the Polytechnic might otherwise have been content to pursue its aims by conventional methods − the lecture, the conversazione, the odd summer excursion − another and more important innovation was introduced in December 1833. On the two days before Christmas, the Polytechnic mounted its inaugural Exhibition at Falmouth.

In subsequent years this annual (autumn) exhibition was expanded to occupy nearly a week; it involved an Annual Meeting, a series of lectures, visitors from all over Cornwall and from further afield, and appropriate coverage by the local newspapers. The Exhibition was saved from being what it might have become, merely an exercise in self-congratulation, because − far-sightedly − endeavour was categorised. There were classes of entries in Fine Arts, Mechanical Inventions, Schools Productions, and so on, and competitive premiums were awarded in the shape of cash prizes, medals and certificates; the names of all the winners

and entrants were fully publicised. From 1833, too, *Annual Reports* were promptly published and, as these were the records of a learned and Royal body, exchanged with those of many organisations at home and abroad. Earlier in this century the Annual Exhibition − that is, the whole week-long meeting with displays and lectures − was sometimes staged in other Cornish towns, reaching considerable size when taken to a mining centre like Camborne (1908).

W.L. Fox's invaluable memoir was compiled directly from the Society's own full records, and much more material could be adduced; but, so far, nobody has written a proper history of the Polytechnic. Two important papers[5] have examined its role in a specific direction, that of 19th-century technical and adult education. Another huge topic, that of the Polytechnic's part in encouraging the fine arts in Cornwall and, partly, in Devon and thus paving the way for various later movements, has hardly been appreciated and certainly not fully discussed. Treatment of just one component of this theme − the art of photography − is emphasised throughout the present book. In so doing, it becomes apparent that (as was the case in the

Polytechnic's support for mechanical inventiveness) there was a very special, if fortuitous, contribution to the society's success; perhaps most markedly so in the case of photography. This was the good luck, or sound judgement, that secured the services of Thomas Brown Jordan and Robert Hunt as successive Secretaries or paid executive officers at Falmouth. Through the teachings, enthusiasm and devotion to the Polytechnic's ideals of Robert Hunt, and later that of such men as William Brooks, Falmouth from about 1840 was more closely in contact with the birth and rapid growth of photography than were virtually all the large English cities outside London. The crucial channel for inculcating this awareness was the annual competitive exhibition (discussed below in a separate essay), coupled with Hunt's lectures and demonstrations.

What was the eventual fate of the Polytechnic, here examined mainly up to 1870? It still exists; it still issues much-reduced *Annual Reports;* but its decline can be placed as far back as the last quarter of the 19th century. Depression in all of Cornwall's heavy industries was, as Stephens and Roderick have shown, one factor. Oddly another factor, which Anna Maria Fox and her family could not have foreseen, may have been the Polytechnic's success in fulfilling many of its original aims, and then inevitably in a changing social world 'the replacement of many of its roles by government institutions'.[6] Was it perhaps a shade too harsh to write that[7] 'by 1900, with the government and local authorities fully awake to their responsibilities and anxious to take over existing educational provision . . . there was no room for such organisations as the Royal Cornwall Polytechnic Society'? The comment would be fair insofar as the Polytechnic did take an active part in forms of technical education, but missed the chance to sponsor its own technical college in Falmouth. The other face of the society's work, the promotion of culture in its widest and most liberal sense, was also gradually eclipsed by the rise of art

societies, commercial galleries, and finally state sponsorship of the arts. Yet the present existence of the Polytechnic — described a little unkindly as being centred on 'amateur dramatics for the rich retired English around the Fal and Helford' (!) — shows that, bereft of the Hall, museums, library and social purpose, the society swings from a thread of continuity that remains cultural, not technological.

Progress can be unintentionally destructive. The wind-up gramophone is now a rare fossil; television and video-recording have overtaken the cinema, the music-hall is long dead, and live theatre is maintained only with subventions and minority support. The graphic arts in Cornwall, however, would — if exhibited today in the original Polytechnic Hall — swamp the entire exhibition, and photography is an art (or technique) followed by almost everybody. What might Anna Maria and Caroline Fox make of their beloved Falmouth, a century and a half later? But none of this is to decry the long history and attainments of the Polytechnic, nor the vision of its founding circle; nor, least of all where photography is concerned, with the society's status and accomplishments in the period between 1833 and 1870.

1. Pym, Horace N., *Memories of Old Friends — being extracts from the Journals and Letters of Caroline Fox etc.* (new and rev. edn., 1883); Harris, Wilson, *Caroline Fox* (1944); Brett, R.L., *Barclay Fox's Journal* (1979).

2. W.L. Fox 1915.

3. Cf. Rowe, J., *Cornwall in the Age of the Industrial Revolution* (Liverpool, 1953); Todd, A.C., *Beyond the Blaze — A Biography of Davies Gilbert* (Truro, 1967).

4. W.L. Fox 1915, 3–4.

5. Stephens, M.B. and Roderick, G.W., *The Royal Cornwall Polytechnic Society — a history of the origins, aims, etc. in relation to 19th century adult education* (Earle, Redruth, 1970); 'Private enterprise and technical education — the Royal Cornwall Polytechnic Society' in: Roderick, G.W. and Stephens, M.D., *Scientific and Technical Education in 19th Century England* (Newton Abbot, 1972), 119–133.

6. Stephens and Roderick (*op.cit.,* 1970), 20.

7. Roderick and Stephens (*op.cit.,* 1972), 133.

EARLY PHOTOGRAPHIC EXHIBITIONS IN CORNWALL

As a part of the 1851 Great Exhibition in London, itself a vast announcement of all conceivable kinds of artistic and scientific endeavour, there was a display of photographic images. From 1840 to 1850, pioneers in both England and France had had to confine themselves to correspondence and to the interchange of photographic specimens, with only small meetings within those few intellectual circles where the New Art was being nurtured. The Great Exhibition was the first public statement of progress. As the Gernsheims have commented,[1] 'For many, it was an eye-opener to the isolation in which they had been working, for they saw

specimens of processes about which they had so far read but had been unable to employ'. Practical manuals of photography existed;[2] but, reading any of them today, one appreciates just how such processes, simple to a trained chemist like Hunt, would have daunted the novice and the beginner.

In 1847 a small group of distinguished amateur calotypists, private followers of the photographic process on paper invented by Fox Talbot, began to meet in London as the Photographic Club. Under the stimulus of the Great Exhibition and, in the same year,

Scott Archer's publication of his (unrestricted) collodion or wet-plate process, conditions existed for a much larger photographic body. In July 1852 Fox Talbot was at last persuaded to abandon his patent rights for the calotype process (the later expiry in 1853 of Daguerre's protected monopoly of the daguerreotype was by then less relevant). The Photographic Society was formed on 20 January 1853, but its foundation-meeting was preceded by a Christmas and New Year public exhibition at the Society of Arts.[3] Just over a year later (January 1854), the Photographic Society held its own first show at Suffolk Street, W., an event attended with keen enthusiasm by Queen Victoria and Prince Albert. Roger Fenton, photographer of the Crimean War and a man in close contact with the Prince Consort, had persuaded him and the Queen to become patrons of the Society in May 1853; the Royal Photographic Society was fully launched, as indeed was the House of Windsor's own long and active involvement with photography.

Given this rapid and Royally-patronised start, it is extraordinary to discover that events in Cornwall were scarcely behind those in London. The earliest recorded public display in the county of any form of photograph, daguerreotypes, took place as part of the Royal Cornwall Polytechnic Society's autumn meeting at Falmouth in 1843.[4] It may have been among the earliest anywhere — certainly before another landmark, D.O. Hill's and Robert Adamson's public showing of ten of their 1844 calotypes at the 1845 exhibition of the Royal Scottish Academy.[5] And, to pursue the claims of Cornwall, early in 1839 at both Falmouth and Truro there had been exhibited at meetings the photogenically-recorded weather observations invented by Mr T.B. Jordan, using paper prepared according to Fox Talbot's instructions.[6] Meetings of the Polytechnic were occasions on which surprises were commonplace; in 1841, for example, a whole album of Fox Talbot's calotypes was passed around for general admiration.[7]

We move to 1853, a year of the Photographic Society's show in London. In that year Robert Hunt, no longer Secretary of the Falmouth Polytechnic but always welcomed as a visitor and mentor, brought down to the Polytechnic's meeting 'a beautiful series of specimens of photography', which he displayed non-competitively.[8] The items either belonged to, or had been lent, to Hunt; the contributors included Sir William Newton, R.A., Frederick Berger and Hugh Owen, all friends of Robert Hunt's since the original 1847 Photographic Club, and Messrs Ross and Thompson from Edinburgh, who had just published their helpful pamphlet *A few plain answers to common questions regarding photography*.[9]

At Penzance, the Regent House School of Art had been founded in 1853, and the next year the annual showing of pupils' work, arranged by the head of the School, Mr H.M. Geoffroi,[10] included 'a fine collection of photographs'. The Polytechnic's 1854 exhibi-

Fig.3   Portrait of Robert Hunt, F.R.S.

This, one of a group depicting leading figures in the photographic world and taken about 1851 (Stirling, A.G., 'Early Photography: 1839–53', *Royal Society of Arts Journal, 129* (1981), 737–40), shows Hunt in his forties as a professor at the School of Mines, London. Though he had left Falmouth he was still a familiar figure in Cornwall, the object of great respect and affection. If the high forehead — not unlike Charles Darwin's — suggests the remarkable intellect behind it, the warmth of his character is obvious in the generous mouth and the set of the head. With the partial exception of William Brooks, no-one played a greater part in the development and the encouragement of photography in Cornwall than Robert Hunt.

Unascribed.   (Courtesy, and copyright, of A.G. Stirling)

tion at Falmouth was also enriched by photography, items now being classified as 'Art' instead of (as previously) 'Mechanical Inventions'.[11] It was at Falmouth that the principal interest was maintained. Robert Hunt lectured to the Polytechnic in 1855, drawing attention to Mrs Glaisher's fine photographs of magnified snow-crystals,[12] and again in 1856, when the members were able to hear one of Hunt's typically sweeping orations on recent theoretical advances in light, optics, and photographic science.[13]

In 1859 the Polytechnic's opening meeting was itself made the subject of a historic photograph (*Fig. 1*, attributable to John Counsell Stephens).

Outside Falmouth, Penzance and Truro the lesser Cornish towns had their own 'Literary and Scientific Institutions'; most of them founded in the early 1800s, as combinations of reading-rooms, small libraries, debating clubs, and avenues of self-improvement for the younger men and skilled artisans. These institutions all held frequent winter meetings, and were circles in which the proponents of photography could expect to get sympathetic audiences. In the spring of 1854 Edwin Docton from Padstow, self-taught operator of Daguerre's process, spoke and showed examples of his work at the Wadebridge Institution.[14] At Camborne, a Society for the Promotion of Useful Knowledge, founded very humbly in 1829, became a larger Institution when it moved into more commodious premises in 1842. This institution fixed upon 1859 for its fiftieth anniversary celebrations. Robert Hunt, who in one of his numerous capacities was a champion of mining education and had many friends and admirers in Camborne as a mining centre, readily agreed to give a special lecture. For the occasion he brought with him his travelling exhibition of photographic art and equipment. Since Hunt permitted the members of the Institution and their guests to inspect 'upwards of 50 Photographic Views and specimens of photo-galvanography and an equally valuable collection of chromolithographs sent down from London', Camborne was indeed honoured.[15]

When the decade from 1861 to 1870 dawned, then, many urban centres in Cornwall had already been made aware of the considerable advances in photography. It was still something of a novelty, but a fully accepted one, and (see *Appendix I*) a nucleus of both professional and amateur photographers existed in the county. Robert Hunt (*Fig. 3*) — emitting new ideas like sparks, as much a prey to his nerves as poor Charles Darwin, yet renowned for his kindness and helpfulness to enquirers humble or great — continued to be a dominating figure. His opinions on photography, as on a good many other technical subjects, commanded universal respect throughout Cornwall. Photography under all of its numerous names and variable synonyms had arrived; be it art or science, Professor Hunt could be relied upon to explain it, at the Falmouth Polytechnic or elsewhere.

As commercial photography grew in Cornwall, responding to the local demands for likenesses and the visitors' demands for views, so too did the artistic and competitive aspects. The Polytechnic stepped into the lead. The 1859 announcement of the list of 'premiums' (the prizes in the annual competitive exhibitions) for 1860 included, for the first time, a new category in the already large class of 'Fine Arts'. This was One Pound 'for the best series of not less than 12 photographs'.[16] The Reverend Gutteres, a talented amateur, was the winner.[17] In 1861 there was an outcome that the Polytechnic's Committee may not have fully foreseen, despite their custom of circulating the competition announcements widely outside Cornwall. Mr Gutteres entered more of his images, but they were eclipsed in public attention by a major display submitted by 'Mr H.P. Robinson of Leamington' (Henry Peach Robinson, rapidly becoming one of Victorian England's leading romantic photographers).[18] The fact was that this attractive annual competition (a week's duration, much publicity, medals and cash prizes) could not expect to remain purely local. Hunt had his well-placed London photographic friends, the Fox family were closely in touch with artistic and intellectual circles far beyond Cornwall, and the Polytechnic itself was constantly electing national figures to honorary positions.

H.P. Robinson was only the first of many who found it worth their while to participate each autumn at Falmouth. From about 1863, London and Bristol names occur frequently in the lists. In 1866 both Francis Bedford and O.G. Rejlander sent work — the spelling of the latter's name gave rise to difficulties. Lt. Col. Stuart Wortley, a prominent London photographer who remained an exhibitor for years, appeared in 1863 with his 'fine collodion photographic views of the scenery around Naples', and was promptly invited to give a lecture.[19] By the later 1860s, William Brooks[20] as well as Hunt was responsible for suggesting invitations to distinguished non-Cornish exhibitors. This catchment was kept up for many years. We note that, in 1875, a Mr F.M. Sutcliffe of Whitby was welcomed as a new entrant.[21] In 1876 there was another first; Cornwall produced its first two ladies in the 'Professional' class, Miss Emma Bligh of Fowey with her portraits and Lady Graves Sawle of Penrice with her portfolio of Egyptian views.[22]

It was not until 1864 that, in the announcement of the rules and premiums for the following year's competition, photography was finally rescued from its matrix of Fine Arts and permitted to stand as a section on its own. This decision reflected the sheer volume of photographic entries, a week-long display of which required a good deal of wall-space. The ethos of the Polytechnic, placing as it did equal values on competing and winning, required that competitors should be treated with every consideration; there was more than a hint of Alice, the Caucus-Race, and the Dodo's ruling. Schoolchildren and young persons had their own classes, and amateurs were not generally matched against professionals. By 1864 the nice distinctions in the photographic world between the (commercial) professional and the amateur, actually a decade old, had to be faced. The rules for 1865 failed to mention this directly, but the standard entry condition (£1 prize for twelve photographs) was re-phrased as 'For amateurs only, residing in the county'. This gave the Cornish enthusiast a fairer chance against the Henry Peach Robinsons. Subsequently the range of prizes — medals or graded cash awards — for photography was increased and, as far as can be made out from the loosely-worded rules issued each year, a clear division of the photographic competitors into categories of 'Professional' and 'Amateur' was introduced in 1868.

In summary, then, we find that in Cornwall these public and semi-public photographic exhibitions were virtually coeval with photography itself. Easily the most significant factor was the encouragement afforded by the Polytechnic at Falmouth. Partly through the influence of Hunt's teaching, partly because of the intellectual calibre of those who led the society, and partly too because of the unusually rapid growth of photography in the county, the displays of every sort of photographic image in the end escaped from what had been their marginal position alongside the oils, water-colours and lithographs. They were re-structured as specific art exhibitions in their own right. The annual Falmouth meetings were noticed, at length, in all the Cornish papers. Robert Hunt and other speakers ensured that Cornish audiences were as much *au fait* with developments in photography as any London audiences could have been. In the entire story of early exhibited photography in this country, Cornwall's part retains this major importance. Well might Wilson Lloyd Fox come to write, of the year 1863, that by then 'the photographic art had received a very large amount of patronage and encouragement from the [Polytechnic] Society', and in later retrospect he concluded that 'it is no vain boast to say that as a provincial exhibition it has ranked second to none.'[23]

1. Gernsheims 1954, 7 ff.
2. Including Hunt 1841.
3. Stirling 1981, Stirling 1982.
4. 11 RCPS, xxx.
5. Stevenson, Sara, *David Octavius Hill and Robert Adamson; catalogue of their calotypes (etc)*, Nat. Gall. Scotland, Edinburgh, 1981, 11.
6. See p. 81 below.
7. W.L. Fox 1915, 11.
8. 21 RCPS, xxv.
9. Gernsheim 1984, no. 717.
10. See p. 50 below.
11. 22 RCPS, xxi.
12. 23 RCPS, xliii ff.
13. 24 RCPS, xxxvii.
14. See pp. 21 and 48 below.
15. Report in RCG 9 Sept 1859.
16. 27 RCPS, end-pages.
17. See p. 60 below.
18. 29 RCPS, xxxiii.
19. 31 RCPS, xxiv, 47 ff.
20. See p. 41 below.
21. 43 RCPS, cat. p. 24.
22. 44 RCPS, cat. pp. 19 and 21.
23. W.L. Fox 1915, 21.

SUPPORTING ROLES: THE ART UNION OF CORNWALL, AND SCHOOLS OF ART

The Art Union, according to Wilson Lloyd Fox,[1] was established at Falmouth in 1852 'in connection with the Polytechnic'. Its aim was to promote the sales of both pictures and photographs.

The vigour (and size) of the Polytechnic's annual competitive show depended, where arts and crafts as opposed to mechanical inventions and industrial items were concerned, on the input of amateurs. These enthusiasts were from the Falmouth, Helston and Lizard area, but people in other parts of Cornwall, regular visitors and schoolchildren were also repre-sented. Amateurs liked to see their work on show and the allocation of cash prizes, certificates and public acclaim was generous enough to keep people satisfied. The professional or 'pure' artists and, for that matter, some of the more gifted amateur artists could, it was thought, tend to be discouraged because the competitions were not primarily intended as sales. Pictures might bear prices, but a sale would then be a matter of luck.

The formation of the Art Union, a scheme pre-sumably copied from elsewhere,[2] was designed to remedy this want and to ensure that artists would continue to compete. It was, in effect, a kind of genteel annual raffle, and as such it had to be licensed by the Board of Trade.[3] Printed rules must have been issued, but no set has survived. The precise mode of operation can be reconstructed from mentions in the Poly-technic's Annual Reports.

The Committee at Falmouth appointed two officers to the Art Union of Cornwall, an Honorary Secretary and a Manager. These positions were held for five or six years at a time, by people who were closely involved with the Polytechnic. The photographer J.C. Stephens, for instance, acted as 'Manager' in the early 1860s,[4] and in 1866 succeeded Mr Sydney Hodges (General Secretary of the Polytechnic) as the Art Union's 'Hon. Secretary'.[5] The manager's job was to make all the arrangements. Shilling tickets were sold throughout the year, up to the Annual Draw held in conjunction with the annual autumn meeting. In 1863, 1605 tickets were sold, raising the sum of £80 5s. 0d. From this, the manager deducted printing costs and running expenses, which came to £16 17s. 6d.

For the actual draw, two small boys in the hall were chosen to pick out the numbers. One boy drew the prize-numbers from one bag, the other the numbered shilling ticket stubs from another bag. Seven prizes in 1863 were in cash (£15, £10, £5 and so on), in this respect the 'Annual Art Union Prize Draw' being no more than a lottery. The manager's job, however, had been to lay out the balance of the income on the purchase of works of art from competitors, at stated values. These constituted all the other prizes and, though this is not mentioned, one suspects that a cash-prize winner could choose to take the equivalent in art items. Photographs, as well as small oils and water-colours, could be and were purchased by the manager, giving an important stimulus to the amateur photographer. In 1863 (remembering that the manager was himself a photographer), ten original photographs were among the prizes. Uniquely, that year's Annual Report gives details of the titles and the names of all the photographers,[6] some but not all of whom were Polytechnic members.

Clearly the system gave a useful boost to photography, if a minor one. The Art Union of Cornwall was still in existence in 1912, [7] but in a less prominent way. Occasional references, near the end of the last century, to a 'West Cornwall Art Union' suggest that the scheme was adopted separately at Penzance.

References to 'Schools of Art' in 19th-century Cornwall are not particularly informative, no full account of the topic exists, and what follows has been inadequately pieced together; it must be included, because quite a few early Cornish photographers were involved in these establishments.

By the time of the 1851 Great Exhibition, a new interest in industrial art and design − pedantically regarded as separated from fine art − led to the notion that the designer or craftsman might be given formal artistic training, so that he could carry back improved taste and skill to his trade or craft.[8] The foundation in 1853 of the Department of Science and Art, parent with its 1852 predecessor the Department of Practical Art of the various South Kensington Museums (Victoria and Albert, Science, Geological, etc), was the essential basis for putting so worthy an aim on a proper national basis. The 'South Kensington scheme', as it was popularly known for decades, provided a standard of examinations, validation, syllabuses, certificates and diplomas; under its auspices visiting teachers could take classes locally organised, and under the same umbrella local learned societies and committees could proceed to set up training-schools.

Nearer the end of the century, by which time the Science and Art Department had become the Board of Education (half-way towards its present representative the Department of Education and Science), a growing conviction of the inadequacy of these Science and Art schools led to the establishment of new technical schools; after the 1902 Education Act, rate-supported. We are here concerned with the pre-1870 position. In Cornwall as in most other areas there was a risk that schools might be diverted from the specific purpose for which they were founded − artistic training for the designer and craftsman, art-and-design education on fixed lines for the young − and become filled by students of another kind; leisured amateurs in search of artistic accomplishment, young ladies with time on their hands, and the would-be 'pure' artist after a training with commercial value. Inevitably this happened, and there was a system of fees. Where classes (at first in 'science and trade') were grant-aided and had teachers approved by South Kensington, committees were urged to charge the middle classes as high a fee as the market would stand, at the same time entitling the artisans to attend without payment.

Three, at least, such schemes in Cornwall are relevant. The Penzance School of Art was founded in 1853, the date alone suggesting the Department of Science and Art as the root-cause. How soon it became, in essence, a fee-paying art school for young ladies and for the 1850s−1860s equivalent of the extra-mural student we do not know; it was certainly well along these lines when, in the 1880s, a larger School was built at the top of Morrab Road, Penzance. In Truro there are confusing references to both a 'School of Art' known to have been in Lemon Street, and a 'School of Design'; the latter was usually the official designation, the former the one most often found in newspapers. The two may or may not have started as the same thing. The Art aspect probably disappeared when Truro's Technical School was founded in Union Place. Falmouth offers a different instance; the Polytechnic was, understandably, in complete sympathy with the 1853 aims of the Department of Science and Art and allowed its rooms to be used for classes. In the 1880s and 1890s, the Polytechnic was closely associated with craft and industrial classes in the area. It did not however found its own school. (Falmouth School of Art, happily still flourishing as a degree-level institution, has other origins.)

Among Cornwall's pre-1870 photographers − professional and amateur, certain or suspected − H.M. Geoffroi was the master of the Penzance School of Art and, on a visiting basis, also of that at Truro. Both Richard Price Griffiths and John Gill taught at Truro, the former being a 'certificated art master' and therefore we suppose approved by South Kensington, the latter being connected with Design classes. At Falmouth, Thomas Hart had art pupils; the period, the connection with the Polytechnic and the improbability of Hart running classes at his own home suggest that such 'art classes' were Science and Art events supervised by the Polytechnic. None of this precluded other parallel careers. Griffiths (and family) were in business as shopkeepers and photographers, Hart as a straight commercial painter.

Fuller discussion must be left to historians of education; the accessible material hardly allows it at the moment. Photography in its earlier years, occupying a position that straddled both art and science, formed an obvious component of art instruction in the 1850s and − even on the reduced scale of happenings in Cornwall − must have entered into the activities of Schools of Art and Design. We see this imperfectly. Once again, though, the Polytechnic played some part, in the juncture between photography and education.

1. W.L. Fox 1915, 17.
2. Probably London, but the writer has been unable to confirm this.
3. Cf. advertisement; Wa 1864, 29.
4. *Ibidem.*
5. W.L. Fox 1915, appendix vii, 46.
6. 31 RCPS, xliii−xliv.
7. See n. 5; E.J. Moseley became Secretary that year. The last mention noted occurs in the 1935, Penzance, Exhibition Catalogue, when prizes were drawn on the evening of the fourth day.
8. Article 'Art Teaching' (by Walter Crane), *Encyclopaedia Britannica* (11th edn., 1910−11), is an excellent summary by an artist.

THE DAGUERREOTYPE ERA IN CORNWALL

In August, 1839, the French inventor and pioneer of photography Louis Daguerre announced details of his superior new process for making images. They could now be fixed with great clarity and fidelity on the polished silvered surface of a copper plate, sensitised with iodine fumes and then developed. Exploitation of the technique in Britain was, however, checked almost at once, when Daguerre's British agent Miles Berry took out a patent (14 August 1839), and promptly showed that he was prepared to support a monopoly through court injunctions. There was nothing particularly secret nor arcane about the process itself — Robert Hunt, who described it in 1841 in his own book,[1] would have been able to reproduce it — but the legal monopoly was of potential value and was upheld.

During June 1841 Richard Beard, a Devonshire man who had become a successful London merchant and had opened London's first commercial photographic studio for portrait-taking on 23 March 1841,[2] secured what amounted to a subsidiary monopoly. He purchased the English patent rights from Louis Daguerre, covering England, Wales and Berwick-on-Tweed. Over the next few years Beard, for fairly large payments, issued licences to others for the opening of daguerreotype portrait studios in particular towns and cities.[3] The first of these, hard on the heels of Beard's own metropolitan operation, was started in Plymouth in June 1841. Throughout the 1840s, and until the general change towards using the Scott Archer wet-plate process (in which no patented monopoly was claimed), the more expensive daguerreotype form of portraiture continued. The 1841 patent did not expire until 1853.

Where Cornwall was concerned, anyone who chose to visit Plymouth after the middle of 1841 could have obtained a daguerreotype likeness. Further licensed studios opened in Bath and Bristol. Certain Cornish landowners still possessed houses in Bath, where a residence for the season had been a considerable draw in the Regency period, and many Cornish people used the regular sea-route from Hayle to Bristol, eventually superseded by the railway system.

We are poorly informed on the currency and quantity of pre-1853 daguerreotype portraits of Cornish people. The better-off, enjoying seasons in London and Bath, and those whose lives involved travelling, probably did include quite a few who commissioned likenesses; but from studios outside Cornwall. The products were, for some time, the *dernier cri* in elegant likenesses. Influenced by the style of miniatures, the studios presented the finished daguerreotypes glazed and framed in ornate mounts and special embossed boxes (these, too, are collectors' items today). Almost invariably the photographic images lack dates, photographers' names or labels, and identifications. Plenty of them survive in Cornwall among older settled families, but unless some far-sighted relative in the past

Fig.4   Captain Charles Thomas, senior, of Camborne

Prolonged examination and comparisons force the conclusion that this mounted Ambrotype (c. 1860) was copied from an earlier daguerreotype. Charles Thomas, for many years an agent at Dolcoath Mine, was born in 1772 at Bolenowe, Camborne; married in 1794; and lived in a large thatched house at Knavegobye (*see Fig.90*). He died aged 74, at home, on 31 March 1847. The implication is that the original, lost, was a studio daguerreotype of 1845–46, possibly made by J.C. Stephens or J. Trebilcock. The sitter's son Charles Thomas junr., managing agent from 1844 of Dolcoath, was a friend and associate of Robert Hunt's for many years and could well have been advised on copying earlier likenesses. The copyist was probably William Piper, after his marriage to Elizabeth Mayne, one of the sitter's numerous grandchildren. This explanation is both chronologically and technically acceptable, and no other seems to fit.

Unascr. daguerreotype, c. 1845–46, copied.   (Private colln.)

chose to affix a label, the details are lost for ever. The Royal Institution of Cornwall has a whole box of extremely fine cased daguerreotypes, some hand-coloured with great skill. Believed to be from a Cornish family in the Helston area, these are all devoid of names and dates.

The first-known public display of daguerreotypes took place at Falmouth, during the Polytechnic's annual meeting of 1843.[4] A certain Monsieur Nollet, a French artist whom it has not been possible otherwise to trace, showed some examples of his art. They won a Fourth Prize, not as 'Art', but in the 'Mechanical Inventions' part of the competition. There was plenty of contact between Falmouth and the Continent at this time — young Barclay Fox, for instance, was in France and Italy during early 1843[5] — and unless Nollet's entry was prompted by Robert Hunt, his introduction

Fig.5 At Home − Joseph Passingham Dunstan and Friend

The sitter − 'Uncle Joe' to his descendants − was youngest of three children of Joseph Brailey Dunstan, an officer in the Falmouth Packet service, and his wife Julia Vivian of Camborne *(see Fig.86)*. When Dunstan was lost at sea in 1836, the family moved to what is now 13 Chapel Street, Camborne, home of Julia Vivian's brother Nicholas, a wealthy entrepreneur bachelor. Joe became a clerk with the town's new Gas Company (1851) and then a purser's clerk at Dolcoath mine; Josiah, son of Dolcoath's managing agent Capt. Charles Thomas, was courting Joe's sister Charlotte Augusta *(see Fig.88)*. In June 1855 Joe Dunstan joined the Miners' Bank, Truro; by 1866 he was managing its branch at St Columb and after 1873 Newquay. He retired in 1902, lived at St Columb and died in 1925.

J.P. Dunstan was born on 12 December 1833; the image shows a lad surely not more than 14 or 15. In later life Uncle Joe was a sharp dresser, much-photographed, and the identification is certain. The daguerreotype, and the chair on which he sits, are owned by Julia Dunstan's great-great-grandson. The informal setting implies a home portrait at 13 Chapel Street, which still houses the firm of solicitors (Daniell & Thomas) commenced by the widowed Julia Dunstan's second husband, W.C.B. Yewens.

Unascr. daguerreotype, c. 1848−49.

(Courtesy of N.D. Thomas)

may have come through a Fox contact. Two years later the firm evidence for Cornish daguerreotype portraiture begins. In 1845, Mr J. Trebilcock submitted specimens to the Polytechnic, as he did the following year.[6] In the 1846 competition, he was joined by William Michell of St Austell, first appearance of this interesting photographer.[7] In the years 1849, 1851 and 1852 a third photographer, a man closely associated with the Polytechnic, James Counsell Stephens,[8] submitted specimens of his daguerreotypes, some of them 'single', others in 'frames' (placed, like miniatures, in a temporary framed display). It is far from clear how Messrs Trebilcock, Michell and Stephens managed to get around the patented monopoly, of which no mention is made.

After the expiry of Daguerre's and Miles Berry's patents in 1853, anyone could exploit the art with legal impunity. It was at this date that Edwin Docton of Padstow — a skilled amateur — taught himself how to do it, and in autumn of 1853 we find Hugh Thomson, probably a travelling portraitist from outside the county, and William Jenkyns of Penzance, on the verge of his professional career, making on-the-spot daguerreotypes at Hayle.[9] These were however the last stages. For Cornish photographers who needed to make a living, cheaper processes like the non-patented wet-plate, or wet collodion, technique invented in 1851 by Frederick Scott Archer offered greater profit margins.

One interesting sidelight must be mentioned. Good, early, daguerreotype likenesses, of which a family might possess a single prized specimen, could be converted into other kinds of photographs if the original image was sufficiently sharp. Daguerreotypes could also be used as the bases for purely graphic images. In July 1855, J.C. Stephens was advertising for sale[10] a portrait of the late William Richards (a very popular Redruth surgeon) 'drawn on stone'. Inspection of a surviving copy shows that this was copied directly from a photograph, presumably a Stephens daguerreotype. In the later 1850s and the 1860s, photographers not infrequently advertised themselves as willing to copy daguerreotypes and 'old likenesses', and the demand obviously warranted this.

The illustrations shown here (*Figs. 4 and 5*) have been chosen because, through the accident of having been preserved in the same family, they are rare cases when the sitters can be identified and the dates quite closely estimated. Given the locality (Camborne), J.C. Stephens at nearby Redruth is a good guess as the artist for one of them, though if J. Trebilcock was working in Falmouth he is equally possible as the photographer of young Dunstan (*Fig. 5*). More identifiable daguerreotypes are bound to come to light, eventually. Without the most prodigious search, almost a door-to-door quest at the dwindling number of homes where Cornwall's *haute bourgeoisie* of the 1840s are still in place today, those further instances will emerge only by chance. We content ourselves with making the point that daguerreotype likenesses *were* made and shown in Cornwall from 1845 (perhaps from 1841, if Robert Hunt included examples in his displays at lectures), and can thus be discussed within the early stages of Cornish photographic history.

1. Hunt 1841, 53−71; cf. also Tong 1973, xx−xxi.
2. Pritchard (11−14) summarises Beard's career.
3. Map; Pritchard 15, fig. 3.
4. 11 RCPS, xxx.
5. Barclay Fox, 303−7.
6. 13 RCPS, xviii.
7. See p. 90 below.
8. See p. 122 below.
9. See pp. 74 and 125 below.
10. RCG 20 July 1855, p. 4 col. 6.

CORNWALL AND THE STEREOSCOPIC IMAGE

The word *stereoscopy* was made up, supposedly in 1838, from the Greek, and means (more or less) 'viewing solid'. The optical and mathematical principles are extremely complex; one can read them, not necessarily with comprehension, in any good encyclopaedia. A specially-built camera makes twin images from slightly differing viewpoints, through appropriate lenses. The resulting twinned prints, placed side by side, are *stereographs* — they were sometimes called 'binocular pictures' — and when they are viewed through a pair of lenses or fixed eyepiece mounted in a special viewer (a *stereoscope*), at the correct distance, the single image then seen has an illusion of solidity or depth of field. It is not, and could not be, fully three-dimensional. It consists of a series of receding planes, but the effect is usually pleasing and can be striking. It is quite possible to feel giddy when peering into a stereograph of the Grand Canyon, or to be personally involved in a Boer War skirmish or Dickensian London.

Commercially-produced, indeed mass-produced, stereographs were published in their hundreds of thousands. Most consist of twin albumen prints 3 inches square, the top corners often rounded, mounted carefully on 'slides', yellow or white cards 3¼ by 6¾ inches. The black-and-white or sepia-tone images were accompanied by hand-coloured versions (optically less successful) and by comic, facetious and juvenile scenes. Stereoscopic photography was a very early device and it was perfectly feasible to have daguerreotype pairs. The introduction of cheap prints on paper in the 1850s opened the gates. Sir David Brewster's famous manual *The Stereoscope* appeared in 1856[1] and most photographic textbooks gave practical instructions. Of particular importance was the London Stereoscopic Company, established at 54 Cheapside and 313 Oxford Street by 1856,[2] and issuing in that and in subsequent years an ever-growing catalogue of stereographs. The Company's own popular *A.B.C. of Photography* had by 1890 gone into twenty-five editions.[3]

Almost as intriguing nowadays as the pictures are the viewers or stereoscopes, ranging from cheap though neatly-made hand-held jobs to the *de luxe* varieties, on stands, intended for boudoir tables; a fine assortment may be seen at London's Science Museum. It goes too far to claim that the home stereoscope was the mid-Victorian equivalent of a television set, but a marginal parallel does exist. Just as every town now has its complement of video shops renting out tapes for nightly viewing, so it was possible to consult stereographic catalogues, and from them to hire sets of slides to wonder at in the privacy of the home. Slides could also be bought, usually at a shilling each. In areas like Cornwall, where the permissible range of activities for Sunday leisure could be restricted in the Methodist home, a quiet half-hour with the stereoscope was approved. Much could be learned. There were of course wildly pornographic stereographs to be found, in London as well as in more obvious sinks of vice like Paris and Alexandria, but the prevalent tone of stereoscopy followed what Sir David Brewster called 'its application to the fine and useful arts and to education'.[4]

The commercially-inspired choices of scenery, in the period from the late 1850s to 1870 (if not later), were far from random. City scenes — the Heart of London, St Paul's, the Crystal Palace — allowed the returning traveller to share what he had seen with the stay-at-homes. A new and patriotic interest in Scotland, the once barbaric north, was kindled by Victoria and Albert and affirmed in Helps's sycophantic edition of the Queen's *Leaves from the Journal of Our Life in the Highlands* (1868). Slides of photogenic Edinburgh led to many more of Dee-side and the Highland regions. The early tourist areas of Ireland, like Killarney and its lakes, followed. Stereographs of American scenery, the mountains and forests of the expanding Wild West and the many part-conquered regions of the mining camps, had both an appeal and a steady currency in Devon and Cornwall. They showed the acceptable side of a New World to which thousands of men had gone in search of mineral riches. Saloon interiors, Eastern women and rough graveyards were not included in the repertoire.

Cornwall itself entered the field as early as the late 1850s, overtly pointing at the new tourist market. By 1858 the Truro printing and bookselling house of J.R. Netherton was a local agency for the London Stereoscopic Co., advertising[5] the receipt of 'a new supply of slides' at 1s. each. An alternative was to join Saunder's Universal Circulating Library of Stereoscopic Slides, 37 Ludgate Street, London, where one

guinea a year allowed subscribers to borrow and to exchange slides continuously.[6] By 1860 most of the better Cornish photographers were able to advertise stereoscopic portraits as an alternative, actually less popular than carte or cabinet ones, which could be put in albums; and photographers and stationers alike were busy selling stereographs.

This trade led to a division of effort, one not always grasped by collectors and historians. Those who 'published', i.e., sold, stereoscopic views had not necessarily taken the original photographs themselves. The slides frequently omitted to show the names of those who had taken them, since the rights to market the views may have been sold. The system did not prevent photographers who owned shops from selling their own products, with their own named labels; but even then their original images might also be going out in someone else's range at the same time.

In Cornwall and Devon, a popular series was that put out by the artist-lithographer William Spreat. Mr Spreat had been a prize-winning entrant at the Polytechnic's competitions in 1848 and 1851.[7] His lithographic business, which was widely known and successful, began in Exeter at No. 229 High Street and No. 27 Gandy Street,[8] later moving to other premises at No. 254 High Street and No. 4 Castle Street.[9] In 1862, he was advertising[10] 'To Tourists and Visitors . . . First-Class Photographs and Stereographs . . . the list at present contains more than 300'. Stereoscopic slides of the 1860s show two imprints, both of 'W. Spreat, 229 High Street, Exeter', the earlier having this legend within a circlet marked 'Stereoscopic Treasures' and a later one being headed by 'New Series of Stereographs of Cornwall'. Mr Spreat's Cornish range was supplied by a whole variety of hands. None are identified on the imprint; the practised eye can identify many of the makers with near-certainty. At the same period, Richard Yeo's brother Stanley B. Yeo of Plymouth was issuing both Devon and Cornwall stereographs (recognisable by a small 'S.B.Y.' in ink on the back), some sold by himself, others through W.H. Luke's Stereoscopic Depot, Bedford Street, Plymouth. From further afield came A. Pumphrey's Stereographs of English Scenery, the Cornish slides numbered from 966 to 1034 and including views by (certainly) Beringer and (probably) Brooks, or Preston, or both. The cards bear no address; was Mr Pumphrey one of the 'Pumphrey Bros.' of Birmingham who issued photographic booklets in 1872?[11]

The early 1860s saw the viewing craze at its peak. William Jennings Clyma, bookseller of St Nicholas Street in Truro,[12] had 'a very large and extensive Assortment of Stereoscopic Views of Cornish Scenery, Groups, &c., &c.', and the list of these on the back of his cards contains no less than 112, all at one shilling. It is possible to work out that the list began with views of Truro and district (by R.P. Griffiths), then had a long range taken in west Cornwall and The Lizard

(John Beringer, interspersed with Charles Lobb), and ended with views in the east of Cornwall (some by Richard Yeo). None of these artists is identified by name. For Cornwall's smaller towns, one could single out St Columb Major. Here the local bookseller George S. Drew[13] was marketing stereographs of North Cornwall taken for him by W. May of Devonport; publishing the 'Drew' series for visitors, but including May's name on his slides.

The present book includes, among its illustrations, a sample of pre-1870 Cornish stereographs. Ascriptions are not always easy to spot; many photographers hand-wrote the locations on the back and dispensed with printed labels, and others used inconspicuous 'blind-stamps' (tiny lettering, impressed or pin-pricked). The total range for Cornwall must have been enormous and there were contributors from outside. Scottish photographers like A.L. Coke and G.W. Wilson had Cornish views in their series, their own products rather than bought-in items. Treating the Plymouth and Devonport photographers along with their Cornish colleagues, here is a provisional list:

Fidelis Beringer Own (amateur) series; possibly included in his nephew John's commercial list.

John Beringer Own series (as J. Beringer & Son), many included in W. Spreat's series, also in A. Pumphrey's.

William Brooks Own series; also marketed by Robert Preston and perhaps included in Preston labelling.

John Gibson Own (occasional?) stereographs, Land's End area.

Richard Griffiths Included in Spreat's series.

Revd. F.E. Gutteres Own (amateur) Falmouth views.

William Heath Own series, Devon and Cornwall.

Charles Lobb Own series; also in Clyma's series and possibly sold to others as well.

William May Own series, Plymouth area(?) and Cornwall; also in Drew's series, named.

William Piper Own small series, Camborne area, hand-labelled.

Robert Preston Own series; catalogue admittedly contained William Brooks's series (named?).

William Richards Own series, probably unlabelled.

Harry Thorn Own series, continued by Samuel Thorn, possibly sold to other series.

Richard Yeo Own series, probably included in general series marketed by his brother Stanley.

Stanley Yeo Own series(?), but in partnership with his brother.

This list has to exclude for the moment several other photographers who, here and there, seem to have advertised their capacity to make stereoscopic views or portraits, but whose slides are not represented in any known collection. Instances may of course come to hand. One notable aspect of all the series mentioned, whether published by the photographers themselves or sold by booksellers, is the degree of repetition. There must be dozens of well-nigh identical scenes of the Land's End, or St Michael's Mount from the low ground approach. That is why an unusual picture like William Heath's nice 'Empacombe' (*Fig. 50*) comes as a surprise and as a slight relief.

1. Gernsheim 1984, 104 (no. 757).
2. Pritchard, 65; Gernsheim 1984, 104−5.
3. Gernsheim 1984, 105 (no. 767).
4. See n.1 above.
5. RCG 18 Jun 1858.
6. Info. Mr Bernard Howarth-Loomes, London.
7. 16 RCPS − picture by him, xvi; portfolio of his lithographs, xviii; second prize awarded, xix. See also 19 RCPS − third prize for his lithographic drawing, xxi-xxii.
8. H 1862, 63 and advert.
9. K Devon 1873, 175.
10. In H 1862 (extended advert).
11. Gernsheim 1984, no. 544; William Pumphrey of Osbaldwick, York, in the 1850s (*ibid.*, nos. 16 and 39) seems far less relevant.
12. K 1856, 172; K 1873, 917.
13. S 1852, 53 (and in later directories).

AN ILLUSTRATED GAZETTEER OF PHOTOGRAPHERS AND THEIR WORK IN CORNWALL AND THE ISLES OF SCILLY, 1839–1870

Scope

The individual entries from 'Argall' to 'Yeo' follow a standard pattern. The heading gives the name(s) of each photographer, with an indication of status (see *Definitions,* below) and the town or place principally concerned. Concise biographies give dates and details, supported by entry footnotes (for which see *Abbreviations,* p.159), and there are cross-references with page numbers when other photographers are mentioned. Some of the entries are extended, either because the persons named are of special importance in the history of photography in Cornwall, or because extra information is available. All the photographers are listed in a concise, quick-reference, summary with useful details as *Appendix I* (p.145), in itself a pocket regional directory for the period to December 1870. *Appendix II* is a provisional check-list confined to professional photographers for the later period 1871 to 1900, arranged by decades; the people here are not individually discussed, but some are mentioned in the entries in the gazetteer and for the last few years we are within the era of the pictorial postcard. *Appendix III* is a preliminary examination, with maps, of the geographical distribution by dates of the various photographers; and *Appendix IV* summarises another interesting topic, that of early photographers who began in other trades and professions, or who continued to earn a living in areas other than photography.

Definitions

To define an amateur as 'One who cultivates anything as a pastime' is simply to beg the question of the definition of 'pastime'; we all know the difficulties met, today, in distinguishing between amateurs and professionals in such realms as international sport. For early photography a similar distinction has to be formulated, but care must be taken when one seeks to impose present-day criteria upon conditions as they really were in the 1860s.

In the south-west, Devon, Cornwall and the Isles of Scilly, an identifiable class of full-time photographers trading as such did not emerge until approximately 1860–65. Before those dates, as *Appendix IV* suggests, photography was an exciting new art and people were increasingly ready to pay for specimens of art, but in the main the practitioners had to support themselves through other skilled crafts and established businesses. The steady rise of tourism was one, obviously important, factor in encouraging photography as an exclusive commercial occupation. Summer visits to Cornwall, with the hire of a 'studio' or the short-time lease of a shop, held out promise of a reward to photographers outside the region, men whose year-round businesses were sited in areas of denser population and higher average incomes. Within Cornwall, the middle-class tourists were becoming conditioned to buy views that they could send to friends or paste into souvenir albums, and to look for stereographs that they could take home and gaze at in winter months. Having one's likeness or portrait made had long been a fashionable craze in London and other centres and, like every fashion, it spread slowly but irreversibly to the far corners of Britain and Ireland. Additional factors were at work in Cornwall, too. One could in theory show a correlation between the incidence of emigration and an increased demand for personal portraits as mementos; several hundred thousand Cornish people went overseas in the last century.[1] One could also suggest that tourism, then as now, could be promoted by influential guidebooks, and Cornwall was well served in this respect.[2] While daguerreotypes had been expensive, glass collodion positives were less so, and from about 1859–60 the new multiple processes like albumen prints on paper were cheap enough to stimulate consumer and producer alike.

For the purposes of this book, a careful attempt has been made to go beyond mere listings, and to provide evidence of distinctions not only between professional and amateur photographers, but also between resident and visiting photographers of both types. The attempt is dependent on the information available. More to the point, all the categories require to be fully defined at the outset. If the definitions seem lengthy, ambiguities have to be avoided. They have been constructed as follows:

Professionals (P)

Persons, whether or not Cornish by origin, resident permanently or for a significant period in Cornwall or Scilly who —

i. advertised prices for any of their photographic work;

ii. are known to have sold any such work, and to have been named in print as 'photographers' or 'photographic artists' in a context reasonably interpreted as indicating trade;

iii. are known to have sold any such work through the agency of another person; and/or —

iv. exhibited any such work within, or competed within, an exclusively 'Professional' class at exhibitions and competitions.

Visiting Professionals (VP)

Professional photographers, as just defined, but who —

i. can only be shown to have been present in Cornwall or Scilly for short periods, usually less than one year, in the pursuit of their trade; and/or —

ii. can be shown, explicitly or implicitly, to have

been carrying on a photographic business elsewhere.

Amateurs (A)

Persons, again whether or not Cornish by origin, resident permanently or for a significant period of years in Cornwall or Scilly who —

i. were at the time described, or described themselves, as 'amateurs', 'enthusiasts', or words of similar force;

ii. cannot be shown to have been involved in professional or commercial photography, as implied in the definition of Professionals, above; and/or —

iii. exhibited or competed within an exclusively 'Amateur' class.

Visiting Amateurs (VA)

Amateur photographers, as just defined, but who —

i. were normally resident outside Cornwall or Scilly; and —

ii. made photographs in Cornwall or Scilly only in the contexts of holidays and short visits.

However carefully one sets out these categories, individual cases remain open to debate. The distinctions refer to a bygone age. In this century, certainly since the 1920s, visiting amateurs have made up by far and away the largest group of all those engaged in photography in Cornwall and Scilly; before 1870, they may have been present rather rarely but — in the nature of things — it would now be almost impossible to identify their photographs save by chance. Before 1850, too, are the distinctions valid? Was Robert Hunt a 'professional' because he published a commercial handbook, tried to market a brand of photographic paper and included some of his own images in lecture-displays that must have promoted sales of his book? (The strict answer to the question seems to be 'Yes', though Hunt was by profession a scientist and a scientific administrator.)

Choosing the illustrations

Ideally one would wish to include here at least one example of the work of each named photographer. That ideal is, alas, unattainable. Nevertheless a prolonged search, and the generosity of many people, have made it possible to show photographs made by just over half the persons listed in the gazetteer.

In selecting the illustrations, certain guidelines have been followed, and they can be given briefly in case they prove helpful to anyone else contemplating a similar book about the photographic history of a comparable region. This volume is not meant to be a scientific treatise. Its subject is that of the photographers themselves — artists, merchants or enthusiasts — working and living in mid-Victorian Cornwall. That community, and area, was experiencing many changes and innovations, fortunately for us well-documented. Photographic images form a very special archive in

their own right. Likenesses of most of the Cornish middle-class technocrats exist because it was during the period in question, after a phase of national reform and at the start of the emergence of devolved local government, that a technocratic middle class consolidated its position in what, for Cornwall, had previously been a somewhat old-fashioned society. Wealth was being created, better education could be purchased, and leisure formed a seed-bed for new interests, one of them being a romanticised view of Cornwall's past. That past — Celtic, Druidic, folkloristic and even linguistic — embraced the visible remnants of what we would now call field-archaeology.[3] When John Gutch made his series of one hundred views in west Cornwall in 1858, with an emphasis on picturesque antiquities,[4] he must have been aware that the demand (from residents rather than tourists) would justify his time and outlay. These are just some of the aspects that the images chosen for inclusion here, with descriptive captions, do their best to mirror.

Secondly, a balance has been sought between pictures of scenery (views) and pictures of people (likenesses), if only to bear out the title of the volume. The balance is needed because, in Cornwall as elsewhere, before 1870 the overwhelming majority of all photographic images made under all and any circumstances *were* portraits. One can have too many of these, but when the sitters or subjects can be identified there may be an extra dimension of interest. For a lot of the smaller-scale professional workers, carte-sized portraits were the bread and butter of the trade and consequently formed virtually the entire product; if their work is to be reproduced at all, then it must be portraits or nothing.

Yet here again the lack of technical skill can be redeemed by a human touch, or by the interpretation of some faded and undistinguished photograph as a genuine social and historical footnote. We have the unstudied composition of Edwin Mayell's picture of a matronly lady (*Fig. 72*) and the human interest of William Piper's of his formidable mother-in-law (*Fig. 84*). As for the claim that photography mirrored Society, it is fortunate that the rise of the new art — carte and cabinet portraiture in particular — happened to coincide with rapid social change in distant Cornwall. It is all there, frozen for us. Success through merit and endeavour is precisely marked in Piper's likeness of Dr George Smith (*Fig. 85*). Matthew Row's crowded group with Captain Athanasius Pryor and Family (*Fig. 105*) depicts the mountaineers at rest upon the peak they have finally managed to scale. Study the nuances of differences between the portrait of Mr Loam, inventor, engineer and a man still better a friend than an enemy (*Fig. 78*), and that of Mr Jeremiah Reynalds, one-time Mayor of Truro — pretty warm, bursting with importance, but when all was said and done only a retail grocer. The unskilled artisans of Cornwall, the working miners and the 'labbuts' or agricultural labourers, were less often portrayed (or, if photographed, can less often be named and identified), and the occasions would have been special ones; marriage, or the eve of departure for the mining camps overseas. Photographers were of necessity more interested in customers with money. Tourists from outside were seen as potential spenders, and the Englishman's view of the native Cornish had certain peculiar tinges − in the 18th century, Devonshire children were taught that Cornish people had tails.[5] There is a distasteful hint of unwitting exploitation in the portrayal of less affluent Cornish folk as curiosities; An Old Fishwife (*Fig. 95*), The Town Crier, The Aged Madman, The Ranting Preacher (*Fig. 7*), even poor old Gracey Briney (*Fig. 26*). This, too, has to be accepted as life as it was. All in all, we find that, in the process of choosing likenesses to place alongside the scenic views, the range of selection has already been narrowed by circumstance.

Thirdly, since this book is also conceived as an introduction to Cornwall's own photographic history, special emphasis has been placed on establishing firm dates. In its turn, that must dictate a concentration on those photographs that present the best chances of so doing. Techniques for dating exist, and should be used. They are, unfortunately, seldom if ever exercised by the compilers of those numerous 'Historic Views of . . .' books and albums now on the market, in which the attributions to photographers are generally omitted and the quoted dates are unsupported and often wrong by a decade or more. This stricture is not meant in an unkindly way. The necessary research is time-consuming and difficult; it may be familiar to the historian, palaeographer and archaeologist but, understandably, not to the postcard-collector or local antique-dealer.

The sheer wealth of the photographic material, a potential archive so rarely intercepted on its brief passage from the family attic to the auction room or flea-market, deserves the best possible handling. Under the low-powered microscope, early prints and plate-negatives can yield such details as shopkeepers' names. Shops, like inns, changed their owners and tenants, and those changes can be winkled out of directories and forgotten newspapers. In Cornwall, the mines opened, did well or badly, closed and fell into ruins − closely dated stages within dated processes. Cartes de visite were made to be sent around in connection with visits, engagements, marriages, baptisms and funerals. Which is implied? All are potentially fixed in time. Deaths, marriages and baptisms are recorded on a national basis and the ten-year Census for the period (1841, 1851, 1861, 1871) is free for inspection on microfilm. And quite apart from the sitters, we have the photographers themselves. Their imprints, their combined trading titles and self-advertisements, began to occupy the reverse of card-mounted images from the late 1850s. The imprints were always being changed and up-dated. Addresses were included, any awards of prizes and medals were added as soon as possible. Surprisingly little attention has been paid to this vital strand of photographic history.

Historians and archaeologists make a useful distinction between what they know as *absolute* and *relative* datings. In so far as all pre-1870 photographic images could be described as 'the archaeology of time-fixed visual reproductions'; which is what in fact they are, the same distinction can be applied. Absolutely dated photographs are those with dates independently attached to them by external happenings; for instance, William Brooks's record of a lifeboat being launched on 10 September 1867 (*Fig. 23*) or Preston's capture of a Royal descent at Botallack on 24 July 1865. Now since on the backs of the mounted prints of these Brooks and Preston views we can find the imprints of the respective photographers, we know precisely the imprint details (wording, ornament, address) each was using at the stated date. This will not tell us, by itself, how long previously this imprint had been employed nor how long afterwards it continued to be employed. But as, in this case (notably so in Preston's), other imprints were used, some of them on the backs of other more or less absolutely dated images, it is possible to place them in order of time. In other words, they can be arranged as a *relatively* dated series. Then a newly-found Preston carte might be described as having a 'before 1865' and an 'after 1862' imprint, and thus, without any clue as to absolute date, be provisionally assigned to 1862−65. With care, it is also possible to extract clues from the pictures. In the case of William Piper of Camborne, many of whose portrait sitters happen to be known, his carte imprints changed regularly, and so apparently did the patterned carpet visible in the same studio room. An absolutely (or near-absolutely) dated group like the one entitled 'Three Generations' (*Fig. 86*) therefore helps us to build up, for Piper likenesses, a relatively-dated series. The method is quite straightforward and not in the least mysterious. Taking these aids to dating into consideration, those illustrations in the book that show how sequences can be worked out have − other things being equal − been chosen in preference to others.

Documented sources

As far as possible the biographical and personal details of the individual photographers are brought together in the gazetteer text entries, leaving the captions to the illustrations for explanations of what is portrayed and any special evidence for dates.

For the 19th century, individuals in commercial, professional and official life can usually be traced in directories (postal, general and specialised); and their names also sought in indexes to local histories, biographies and published diaries or letters, all of these being plentiful within the immense topographical literature of Cornwall. An indication of the range of directories is given later, both under *Abbreviations* and *Bibliography*. Directories were issued for most counties and cities[6] − early town directories, copies of which were generally used to death, are extremely hard to find − and Cornwall and Devon were much less well served than, for example, a city like Bristol.

The date of any issue of a directory is the registered date of its publication for sale, not the date of its actual compilation by door-to-door agents, or postal trawls, or sheer piracy, and the gap may be anything from several months to several years.[7]

Local historians in Cornwall are lucky enough to have the invaluable three-volume *Bibliotheca Cornubiensis* of 1874−82 and its later companion of 1890, the thick equally useful one-volume *Collectanea Cornubiensia*.[8] These provide details of thousands of named persons, and tens of thousands of additional references. In the search, printed sources must be supplemented by all the official and local records, far too extensive to be described here, but today easily to be introduced to in record offices and public local-history libraries.[9] The historian of photography is concerned with the names, dates, trading careers or shop-locations of photographers, the life-dates of his human subjects, and the identification and dated changes of the scenes that were photographed. This narrows the field at the onset. In Cornwall, the early 19th century was a period when many learned, scientific and literary societies were founded − the same thing happened in other parts of the British Isles − and some of the societies have left us an abundant periodical literature. The use in this book of the *Annual Reports* of the Royal Cornwall Polytechnic Society at Falmouth[10] shows what a valuable fount of information these have been.

All these sources, and others, have been drawn upon. The work takes time, and those who cannot spare the time cannot expect to be able to compile more than simple pictorial albums. A great deal of attention is now being given to local histories of photography (and, at last, to photographers themselves), but in the final resort the national history can only be built up from the collation and comparison of local accounts. Given so intrinsically fascinating a topic, it would be hard to suggest a more rewarding and less exploited area of research.

Reproduction

In the few cases where the original glass plates in the Royal Institution of Cornwall's collection are in sufficiently good condition, new prints have been taken from them directly. For the most part, and in all cases where pre-1870 prints on paper have generously been lent for copying, new negatives were made and enlarged prints were taken from those negatives. Damaged originals have been used for illustration only when no cleaner print could be found and damage marks have not been erased. Where stereoscopic pairs (stereographs) were chosen, the clearer of any two images was copied.

Images from public and private collections, other than the Institution's, are reproduced by kind permission of their owners, and this is acknowledged in the captions. The question of photographic, as opposed to textual, copyright is left in abeyance. The Council of the Institution, which administers the Institution's holdings on behalf of the members, has decided not to make available any of its pre−1871 photographic items for commercial reproduction elsewhere while the Institution is engaged in publishing a projected series based largely on its own collection.

Format

The reproduced sizes of the illustrations bear no relation to the sizes of the originals, since printing layout would make that too difficult. Before 1870, a great many sizes and formats were used. The standard plate sizes were 6½ by 8½ inches (whole-plate), 4¾ by 6½ inches (half-plate) and 3¼ by 4¼ (quarter-plate). Prints from these could be enlarged, and other sizes were common; in 1856, William Jenkyns (visiting Tresco) was using hand-cut prepared plates 4 by 5 inches. Collodion 'positives' on glass or Ambrotypes, common in Cornwall from about 1855, were frequently quarter-plate size.

The carte de visite was a print of 2¼ by (just over or under) 3½ inches, mounted on a slightly larger piece of card, and 'carte format' is used here to mean a paper print of these dimensions. 'Cabinet' likenesses or portraits, similarly mounted, appear in Cornwall about 1869, generally a little later; and the usual print size was 4 by 6½ inches. Stereographs or stereoscopic pictures, as prints on paper made from 'wet' or 'dry' plates, were almost all about 3 inches square plus or minus a quarter-inch on either dimension, but again there are smaller formats less often seen.

1. Deacon, Bernard, 'How Many Went ? The Size of the Great Cornish Emigration of the 19th Century', *Devon and Cornwall Notes and Queries*, XXXVI.i (Spring, 1987), 5−8.

2. *A Hand-Book for Travellers in Devon and Cornwall* (John Murray, London, 1851 and later edns.); Collins, W. Wilkie, *Rambles Beyond Railways* (Bentley, London, 1851: 2nd, 1852: 3rd, 1861).

3. Blight, J.T., *A Week at the Land's End* (London, 1861); Halliwell, J.O., *Rambles in Western Cornwall . . . with notes on the Celtic Remains, etc.* (London, 1861).

4. See p. 56.

5. It has to be added that, more recently, Cornish children were taught the same about Devonshire folk.

6. See Norton 1984.

7. Useful discussion − Pritchard, 9−10, 20−22.

8. Cited here as BC and CC.

9. Cf. Tate, W.E., *The Parish Chest*, 3rd impr. (Cambridge, 1960); Bettey, J.H., *Church and Parish − A Guide for Local Historians* (Batsford, London, 1987).

10. Cited as RCPS, prefixed by number.

ARGALL, Frederick Ernest
Professional: Truro

In the last century hundreds of Cornish folk repaired to Argall's of Truro for their cabinet portraits. The Argalls were prominent in the city's life for over a century, and the family even produced a poetess, Annie S. Argall.[1] The Truro branch may have come immediately from St Agnes a few miles away,[2] though their more distant origin lay south of Truro.[3] Frederick Argall's first directory entry was in 1873 with his shop and studio at High Cross, Truro.[4] In subsequent advertisements, however, describing his premises as being opposite the Cathedral and next door to the General Post Office, Mr Argall invariably claimed to have been 'established 1866'.[5] High Cross was then, as now, a small area by the west door of the Cathedral, and the Argall establishment was at No. 9. An undated carte in the R.I.C's collection has an imprint with 'Fredk. Argall — From J.E. Palmer, Photographer, High Cross, Truro', confirming that Argall had taken over premises previously used as a branch studio by John E. Palmer of Plymouth. Mr Palmer used his Truro address up to 1866—67, but not demonstrably any later. A year of overlap during which Mr Argall worked himself in as Palmer's assistant, or local manager, would substantiate the claimed date of 1866, even if 1867 or 1868 was more accurate.

By November 1871 Frederick Argall was drawing attention to his 'new Cameo Vignette Portraits', a photographic novelty, with 'the studio comfortably heated'.[6] Argall's carte de visite imprints are many, and the earlier ones specify him as both artist and landscape photographer; we know that he was among the first to market souvenir views of Truro Cathedral. In 1881 he was exhibiting as a professional at the Falmouth Polytechnic,[7] and in 1882 his entry, entitled 'The Skipper', won him a First Class Bronze Medal.[8] Directory entries record the firm over a long period.[9] The business eventually passed to his son Ernest.

1. *The Inspiration of Song* (Netherton and Worth, Truro, 1894), etc.
2. S 1852, 49 — Joseph and Philip Argall, bootmakers, St Agnes.
3. Argall (or Argal) is a tenement in Budock parish.
4. K 1873.
5. K 1889, adverts. p. 83.
6. RCG 11 Nov 1871.
7. 49 RCPS, cat. p. 22.
8. 50 RCPS, 76.
9. P 1876, 103; H 1878, 1021; K 1897, 324 (but in K 1902, 335, under Ernest C. Argall, 'estab. nearly 40 years').

ASHTON, Edward
Professional: St Ives (Figs. 6—9)

Both Mr Ashton and his early work deserve to be better-known. He is believed to have been a native of St Ives; the surname certainly occurs in Cornwall (there

Fig.6 Downalong, St Ives
For this group of St Ives fisher-folk gathered in a sunny corner of the old harbour quarter ('Downalong') the artist must have wanted the top-hatted man, leaning on the gurry — a species of hand-barrow for carrying fish — and also his bearded friend. Others have, however, decided to join in, including the (blurred) infants whose patience was not equal to the exposure time. Edward Ashton is the most likely photographer; there is no evidence that the Penzance open-air artists (Brooks, Preston) visited St Ives much, if at all. The original would have been a plate view.
Unascr., probably Ashton, mid-1860s.   (R.I.C.)

is a hamlet called Ashton, near Breage). Less genteel than Penzance, less affluent than either Truro or Falmouth and lacking the learned societies that these other towns possessed, St Ives could not find the photographic custom that elsewhere supported men like J.C. Stephens and Robert Preston. Yet its picturesque warren of the fishermen's quarter, 'Downalong', cried out for cameramen, and a quarter-century later was very fully covered by the staff photographers of Frith's and Valentine's.

Edward Ashton is first recorded in 1873[1] with his main business as both greengrocer and photographer at West End, Hayle, and a studio at Tregenna Hill in St Ives. The gap in time between the 1856 and 1873 Kelly's *Directories* for Cornwall is misleading here, as in other cases; what may be Ashton's earliest dated view shows the wooden pier at St Ives under construction in July 1866.[2] His harbour and marine studies, and family scenes, imply someone intimately familiar with that town. Later mentions show Ashton only in St Ives, with no Hayle address, and the greengrocery presumably abandoned.[3] There must be some connection with the activities of Mr Burton, and it is suggested below[4] that Ashton began — after some private endeavours — as Burton's assistant, acquiring the St Ives studio between 1870 and 1873. Mr Ashton's career remains to be discovered in detail, but he appears to have ceased working around 1890 or so.[5]

1. K 1873, 765, 774.
2. Noall, *The Book of St Ives* (1977), 65.
3. K 1883, K 1889.
4. See p. 42.
5. Not in K 1893 (was Nicholas Ashton, Chemist, Market Place, his son?).

Fig.7 Billy Bray

William Bray, Cornish evangelist and the best-known of the early itinerant Methodist preachers, was born at Twelveheads near Truro in 1794. F.W. Bourne's biography, *The King's Son, or, A Memoir of Billy Bray,* went through numerous editions and is still quoted. Bray died on 25 May 1868 aged 74. Several photographs of him were widely reproduced and turned into woodcuts and, later, postcards; they all represent studio portraits of around 1860 or later.

Billy Bray visited St Ives in 1838 and was well received. No detailed itinerary of his preaching career survives but he must have re-visited the town on other occasions, and this particular print, from St Ives (W.J. Noall's collection), is annotated 'Probably taken at St Ives in Ashton's early days'. The preacher certainly looks like a man in his 60s.

Unascr., probably Ashton, c. 1865.   (R.I.C.)

Fig.8 Street Scene with figures

Ashton was producing a number of views of St Ives and area in the latter part of the 1860s, issued in carte format with his imprint. This particular scene is not located − expert knowledge might be able to fix it − but it makes a very pleasing vertical composition and suggests the work of an experienced hand, not a beginner.

Carte, paper print, Ashton, late 1860s.   (Private colln.)

Fig.9 St Ives, Before the Railway Came

This is a much-favoured view of St Ives − town, harbour and Island − both painted and photographed in the last century, and probably captured in whole-plate size by Edward Ashton among others (e.g., an unascribed print, R.I.C.'s collection). Here he presents it in his attractive carte series. The branch railway from St Erth was started late in 1873 and opened in June 1877; the St Ives station stood centre foreground of Ashton's pre-railway view. On Pedn-olva Point the curious tower is the 1860 engine-house of the North Wheal Providence mine (wound up in 1861, after which the engine-house was modified as a dwelling).

Carte, paper print, Ashton, late 1860s.   (Private colln.)

BARNETT, William
Professional: Falmouth (Fig.10)

Mr Barnett was certainly in business in Falmouth by 1862, in which year premises occupied by him in the High Street suffered in a fire, a disaster that also burnt out the shop of his photographic colleague J.C. Stephens.[1] The High Street address is confirmed in a directory entry shortly after this.[2] By 1864 William Barnett had a shop in Market Street, a separate studio 'in the Moor' and a private residence near the latter at No. 28 Killigrew Street.[3] There is no evidence that he was a local man − the surname Barnett is not found in Falmouth at earlier dates − though a Miss Barnett who kept lodgings at No. 8 Wodehouse Terrace in Falmouth[4] might have been a relative.

Fig.10 Unknown gentleman, Falmouth
The carte de visite portrait should be one of those shown in 1864 by Mr Barnett at the Polytechnic. The imprint of two diagonal lines is 'Barnett − Falmouth'. Our unknown leans cautiously against the wood-and-stucco, improbably Classical, pillar, and ignores the painted foliage behind him. The shiny object in his hand seems to be a telescope. The heavy jacket with black buttons is nautical; the expression is confident, firm, with a hint of authority. We guess that the portrait was destined for some admiring lady. Is he a pilot, a Customs Officer, or a Coastguard?

Carte, paper print, Barnett, early 1860s.   (Private colln.)

An advertisement of 1864 showed him as supplying card and vignette portaits and Ambrotypes; 'the high character which this Establishment has obtained for the unrivalled beauty and excellence of its products renders comment unnecessary'.[5] Possibly so; and in that year he exhibited some of his cartes de visite at the Polytechnic,[6] though a surviving example (*Fig. 10*) is nothing very special. Nor can we find out how long his Establishment flourished. William Barnett was not listed by 1873.[7]

1. RCG 18 Apr 1862, p. 3 col. 5.
2. H 1862, 843.
3. Wa 1864, 53.
4. *Ibidem.*
5. *Ibidem,* advert. p. 52.
6. 32 RCPS, xix.
7. Not in K 1873.

BERINGER, Fidelis
Amateur: Penzance

See under next entry.

BERINGER, John
Professional: Helston (Figs. 11−16)

In 1982 the house of Beringer celebrated its 150th anniversary as Cornwall's best known jewellery, watch-making and clock-making business; certainly the oldest continuing under its original name. Headed today by Fidelis Beringer's great-grandson, Mr Geoffrey L. Smith JP, the firm still has its shops in Redruth and Falmouth. Cornwall's debt to this talented family lies in the areas of mining education and practical technology. Over a century and a half of fine craftsmanship, laboratory skills, and chemical and optical expertise we could expect to find Beringers involving themselves in photography, and this is indeed the case.

Clock-making in 18th− (and early 19th−) century Cornwall, the hand-cutting or the assembly of mechanisms for 'long case' and other timepieces, was mainly a native industry.[1] It ran parallel to another, the production of all kinds of surveying and drawing instruments required − above and below ground − in mining.[2] As purchasing capacity extended through the social scale, new openings arose for those who combined the trades of watch-making, jewellery, and the silversmith's arts. This was partly met from outside. Starting perhaps with Moses Jacob, watch-maker and mineral dealer of Redruth in 1769,[3] we find by William IV's reign a small Jewish community in the main towns − Jacob and Charles Levy in Truro, Emmanuel Cohen in Redruth, Henry Levy, Aaron and Benjamin Selig and Samuel Shortman in Penzance. In Plymouth, a Jewish community led to a still surviving synagogue; Penzance, too, had its own synagogue, resident Rabbi and even a little Jewish cemetery.[4]

Fig.11 Freeman's Quarry, Rosemanewis, near Penryn

The granite quarries of Mabe parish, worked from at least 1820, supplied building-stone for public works all over the kingdom. That at Rosemanewis or Rosemanowas has been in the news again as scene of the deep-drilled geothermal or 'hot rocks' project conducted by Camborne School of Mines. Messrs Freeman, later the Penryn Granite Co., were leading quarry-masters. This fine view, highly suitable for stereoscopy, shows in the heat of summer the huge blocks, stepped mast of a jib crane, and the top-hatted manager among his men. The slide was issued in the W. Spreat, Exeter, series (see p. 22). The photographer is not named, but Beringer of Helston is bound to come to mind. Unascr. stereograph, probably Beringer, 1860s.   (Private colln.)

After 1825−30 a fresh element appears; Germans, but Lutheran Protestant or Catholic instead of Jewish, and with their emigration possibly connected with events in Germany (the rise of Prussia, popular uprisings, the 1832 curbs on the Press and universities, etc).

In Cornwall most of these incomers married, fairly quickly, into the local community. By 1861 the watchmaker Georg Kistler at No. 6 Causewayhead, Penzance, born in Germany in 1820, lived with his younger brother Matthias, and Matthias's wife Rosina,

Fig.12   Tram Way, Botallack Mine, Cornwall
The workings at Botallack Mine near St Just in Penwith included the famous incline shaft under the sea *(Figs. 96 to 98),* engine-houses perched on the cliff face, and this extraordinary piece of timberwork allowing the mineral trams to run along the precipitous rocks above the sea. Issued, like that in *Fig.11,* as a stereoscopic pair in W. Spreat's series of the early 1860s, this too has no ascription, but may be by one or other of the Beringer brothers.
Unascr. stereograph, possibly Beringer, 1860s.   (Private colln.)

a Wendron girl.[5] In Lemon Street, Truro, one could have found Joseph Schwerer, born in Germany in 1819, with his Cornish wife Mary and his young assistant Paul Zizpel.[6]

The Beringers formed part of this second wave of specialists. As far as can now be reconstructed, the family arrived headed by Fredric or Friedrich Beringer, who would have been born about 1800. Since the surname means, in German, 'a maker of rings', their calling must have begun a century or more, perhaps several centuries, before this period. The Beringers are known[7] to have come from somewhere described as Siedbach, near Neustadt, Freiburg.

Fig.13   Higher Town or Trevorder, Ruan Minor, 1865

Nineteenth-century Cornish views favoured granite mansions and whimsical cottages or curiosities. The large untidy secretive farms — often at the end of muddy lanes, with little enough welcome for nosey visitors — were far less often chosen. Trevorder, with the midden between door and duckpond and its occupants huddled shyly under the shadow of the thatch, represents an almost extinct style of residence. The serpentine block walls, high chimneys and first-storey barn up the outside steps, all make up a picture almost Breton in its archaic character.

On the back of the original carte in ink is 'A View of the Old Farm House' (and rest of title as above), and then 'Xmas 79 J.B.'. Ruan Minor is right down in The Lizard; in the 1860s the area must have seemed created, by God and man in partnership, especially for the benefit of photographers. This is one of John Beringer's 1865 'small Cornish views', shown the next year at the Polytechnic. The inscription suggests that, thirteen years later, he presented this copy to a friend.

Carte, paper print, Beringer, 1865.   (R.I.C.)

Unfortunately these place-names (the English equivalents would be 'Seethe-beck, New-town and Free-borough') are found widely throughout much of Germany, but the most likely provenances for the combination are in either Saxony or Baden. The family arrived in Redruth shortly before 1832.

Of Fredric's sons, Fidelis was born at Siedbach on 17 February 1823 and his brother Joseph (Josef) was noted in 1864 as 'not an Englishman by birth'.[8] Fredric Beringer formed a partnership of watchmakers and clock-makers in Redruth in 1844, under the title of Beringer, Schwerer and Co.[9] In 1847 the location was given as Fore Street[10] and in 1856 the partners' names were Fredric Beringer and Jacob Schwerer.[11] The latter was probably a younger brother, rather than son, of the Joseph Schwerer in Truro mentioned above. One could speculate that Beringers and Schwerers originated in the same German state or province.

There were at least four Beringer sons — Fidelis (who in 1853 married a Miss Jane Bawden), Jacob, Johann or John, and Joseph. A solitary shop in Redruth could not have supported all of them; by 1847, a branch had been started at Falmouth (No. 12 Market Street),

which included an outfitter's department.[12] Jacob was detached to run this Falmouth branch, where he could have been found in 1876.[13] John Beringer moved to Penzance, where by 1847 he became a watch-maker and clock-maker in St Clare Street.[14] He was joined by his brother Fidelis, who in 1864 was sharing premises with four other skilled craftsmen at No. 27 Market Place.[15]

It follows, therefore, that the Beringer noticed in Helston in 1847[16] as 'watch- and clock-maker, Meneage Street', was the fourth of the brothers, Joseph Beringer. The relative ages of the brothers are not known. Joseph must however have been one of the older sons, because by 1862 his own son 'John Beringer, junior' (i.e., junior to his Penzance uncle of the same name) was in business with him.[17]

In Redruth the original (1832) Beringer and Schwerer partnership continued for years. Some, if not all, of the branch concerns started in the 1840s by the four sons were apparently represented as aspects of the Redruth nucleus. The Penzance shop (John Beringer) was in the partnership name in 1864,[18] and by 1876 had moved to No. 16, The Terrace — the raised upper part of Market Jew Street, the town's best commercial location − as 'watch-makers, jewellers, opticians, etc'.[19] A decade or so later, Jacob Schwerer's name disappears from directory entries,[20] and he may have died, though his brother Joseph Schwerer was still a watch-maker and silversmith in Truro.

It is likely that quite a few of the Beringers took up photography but, for the era before 1870, two in particular must be mentioned. At Penzance, Fidelis Beringer was an amateur. He would have known William Brooks, Robert Preston and William Richards, and one or other (probably Brooks) may have encouraged him. In 1867, Fidelis entered at the Falmouth Polytechnic's competition 'thirty stereoscopic Cornish views', including one of Pengersick Castle.[21] There is no evidence that he marketed them himself, but examples could well have found their way into the commercial lists put out by others.

'Others' would include the principal photographer in the family, John Beringer junior at Helston, son of Joseph and nephew of Fidelis. If born in the early 1840s, his commercial output would have begun around 1860. John Beringer was specifically listed as 'photographer' in 1862.[22] A court case at Helston in 1864[23] featured a Mr Trethowan, who tried to obtain goods by credit from 'Mr Joseph Beringer, the watchmaker' and his son John, the photographer, said to be working at the same shop. The goods included jewellery and a photographic locket, and the fraudulent Trethowan got six months in prison. John Beringer's own first Polytechnic submission in 1866 was one of 'small Cornish views',[24] that is, scenic views in carte format. On the next occasion, 1871, the entry in the Professionals class was a scrap-book of Cornish photographs[25] from 'J. Beringer & Sons'. While John was the only photographer, his brother George − who eventually succeeded the father Joseph as the Meneage Street watch-maker and jeweller − had joined the firm; George Beringer became a councillor, borough magistrate and was Mayor of Helston in 1900, 1901 and 1908. There was also an unmarried sister, Lily, who ran the local British and Foreign Bible Society branch from the Meneage Street home. No evidence exists to let us suppose that George (or Lily) ever handled a camera, but the family firm was clearly a close-knit arrangement. Indeed, up to the end of the century all trade references to, or imprints upon, their photographs read 'Joseph Beringer & Sons', though as far as we know it was John Beringer who made all the images.

There is some evidence that a Beringer of the Falmouth branch, possibly a son of Jacob, was involved in photography later in the 19th century;[26] and we do not know how late Fidelis Beringer found time to take photographs (he is not mentioned in this light after 1867). Fidelis and Jane Beringer were otherwise occupied. They had eleven children, four of whom died as infants. Three surviving sons became more Cornish than the Cornish and made their names in the world of mining. Cornelius (1858−1903) was a brilliant chemist

Fig.14   Steeple Rock

Quite a few of Beringer's carte views show beach scenes, with or without people, around the coast of The Lizard. This is a stereograph, Steeple Rock being one such natural curiosity in the area. The slide has an ink stamp, Beringer & Son, Photographers &c., Helston. The addition of 'and Sons' (plural) to Mr Beringer's business title first appears in 1871 in an entry at the Polytechnic's competition; 'and Son' (singular) is a year or so earlier; and *(Figs.11 and 12)* Beringer's own un-numbered stereographs ought to belong to the latter half of the 1860s. We would think of 1867 or so.

Stereograph, Beringer, late 1860s.   (Private colln.)

and mineral assayer, working for a time in Spain with the Rio Tinto Copper Co. Heinrich Roland or 'H.R.' (1863−1937) taught at the Camborne School of Mines, and wrote a textbook on mineralogy.[27] Most famous was 'J.J.', John Jacob Beringer (1857−1915), who was trained initially as a chemist, graduated at the Royal School of Mines in London, became Cornwall's County Analyst, and produced a standard work of assaying. Teacher, champion of technical education, close friend of many of the leaders of the industry, and possessor of great determination as well as ability, J.J. served for 28 years as Principal of the Camborne School of Mines, where he is still regarded as the School's effective founder.[28]

Given this interesting background, it is hardly surprising that various Beringers took to the camera. More of their work should be sought; did no Beringer, for example, take early mining views? Whatever they set out to do, it was done properly. The family professional, John Beringer junior of Helston, has left a fair sample of his work (and the impression that he spent as much time as he could out of doors!), but Fidelis's stereographs have not yet been found. Meanwhile, it is pleasant to record that 'Beringer & Co.' can still be seen at No. 48 Church Street in Falmouth, and at the original home, No. 66 West End in Redruth.

Fig.15   The Tolmen, or Main Rock, Constantine

The Tolmen, a vast granite rock 33 feet long, 18 feet wide, over 14 feet thick and estimated to weigh 750 tons, was wantonly destroyed by quarrying on Tuesday 9 March 1869. Great indignation was aroused; angry letters, even a dirge, were published. This view of the Tolmen, a sepia-toned print 8¼ by 6 inches mounted on card, was put on sale, a label giving the date of the wanton destruction, and the dimensions, being pasted below. John Beringer favoured this style of outdoor view in good quality sepia finish — a very fine, though later, selection of such work was used for the plates in Coulthard, H.G., *The Story of An Ancient Parish; Breage with Germoe* (Camborne, 1913). 'The Tolmen' may have been among the views he showed at the Polytechnic in 1866.

Print from plate, mounted, Beringer, c. 1866−68.   (R.I.C.)

1. Brown, H. Miles, *Cornish Clocks and Clockmakers,* 2nd edn. (Newton Abbot, 1970).

2. E.g., William Wilton of St Day (H. Miles Brown 1970, 87).

3. *Ibidem,* 31, 82.

4. P 1830; P Devon 1830; CC 1653.

5. Census 1861.

6. *Ibidem.*

7. Beringer family tree, 1948 (info. Mr Geoffrey Smith, Redruth).

8. RCG 15 Jan 1864, p. 7.

9. P 1844.

10. W 1847, 148.

11. K 1856.

12. W 1847, 31.

13. P 1876, 47.

14. W 1847, 117.

15. C 1864, 41, 73.

16. W 1847, 64 (wrongly noted as 'John' Beringer).

17. H 1862, 861.

18. C 1864, 150.

19. P 1876, 82.

20. H 1878, 1028; but not in K 1889.

21. 35 RCPS, 16.

22. H 1862, 861.

23. RCG 15 Jan 1864, p. 7.

24. 34 RCPS, xxxii ('Mr Berringer of Helston').

25. 39 RCPS, cat. p. 18.

26. Material (plates) in store at Falmouth branch.

27. *Determinative Mineralogy* (Camborne Prtg. Co., 1912).

28. CC 1416, 1419; Piper, L.P.S., *A Short History of the Camborne School of Mines* (Trevithick Society, 1975): the book mentioned was by Cornelius and John Jacob Beringer, *A Text-Book of Assaying* (Chas. Griffin & Co., London, 1889).

Fig.16   Poltesco Mill
Neat, well-balanced and beautifully composed, this unsigned print in the Institution's collection shows the same little mill, footbridge and rocky valley that appear in William Brooks's slightly earlier view *(see Fig.24);* but now from the uphill side. Given the locale − Poltesco is in Ruan Minor, one of his favourite spots − and the sure touch, John Beringer is indicated. It is not one of his 1865 'Little views', but The Lizard landscape was his speciality, and we see a more mature piece, taken perhaps five years later.
Unascr. paper print, probably Beringer, c. 1870.   (R.I.C.)

BROAD, William Henry
Professional: Bodmin (Fig. 17)

The Broads form a large family spread over the eastern half of Cornwall. William Henry Broad, born in 1831,[1] was the son of John Broad, watch-maker of Honey Street, Bodmin, a well-established local craftsman,[2] and his wife Mary Ann from Pelynt.[3] A younger brother Joseph was baptised at Bodmin in July 1838.

By 1873 John Broad had apparently died and the business in Bodmin had passed to W.H. Broad as the elder son. He was now listed as a 'watch− and clock-maker, bell-hanger, etc'.[4] Since, at this period, other members of the Broad family were in similar businesses in other East Cornwall towns − Lostwithiel, Wadebridge and Liskeard − and since most of them also favoured the baptismal names of 'William' and 'John', it is not easy to sort them all out. However, it appears that by 1883 William Henry Broad had moved to Pound Street, Liskeard, and his younger brother

Joseph had taken over the Bodmin shop at Honey Street.[5]

From a rare surviving print *(Fig. 17)*, slightly smaller than a carte format, we have the imprint of 'W.H. Broad, Bodmin', around an ornate coat-of-arms and supporters, with the legend 'Negatives kept. Copies can always be had'. William Henry would have gone into partnership with his father in the 1850s; the father, John, probably died in the late 1860s, and by 1873 there is no evidence that W.H. Broad was still a photographer. His photographic career is thus most likely to have been confined to some such period as 1858 to 1870, and to have been only a sideline within the family business.

1. Baptised Bodmin 6 Apr 1831.
2. S 1852, 7; K 1856, 232; H 1862, 797.
3. Marriage at Pelynt, 18 Apr 1830.
4. K 1873, 714.
5. K 1883, 824, 1193.

Mr Brooks began with both ordinary and stereoscopic views of the Cornish coast, buildings, inhabitants and minor townscapes, in the Land's End and Lizard areas. In 1864 he had enough material to show two whole frames of stereoscopic coastal views at the Falmouth Polytechnic, where this — his first entry — won him a Second Bronze Medal.[2] Within the small circle of Penzance society he can hardly have avoided an early meeting with Robert Preston; all that we know of William Brooks suggests a sociable, attractive and enthusiastic person, and he and Preston apparently became friends and near-partners. At the same period Brooks would have met John Gibson, from Scilly, with whom he was to share at least one camera-outing (*Fig. 25*).

About 1864 Robert Preston, in the last phase of his somewhat uneven partnership with the Pooles,[3] issued a catalogue at Penzance of 'The Royal Series of Cabinet, Stereoscopic and Carte Views of the Scenery of West Cornwall and its Antiquities'.[4] It incorporated 'the series photographed by W. Brooks of London', and we know that within his own numbered series of stereographs Brooks had in fact labelled some of the earliest (1863 ?) as being by 'W. Brooks, Photographer, *London*' (*Fig. 18*), as if not yet wholly committed to a Penzance address.

Fig.17   St Thomas's Chapel, Bodmin

The tower is that of St Petroc's, Bodmin's large and handsome parish church; but in the same churchyard are the remains of the chantry chapel of St Thomas à Becket, of Canterbury, dating from 1377. The picturesque east window and ivy-clad walls attracted pen, pencil, brush and camera alike. Broad's little view would have sold readily to locals and visitors.

Small paper print, mounted, Broad, 1860s.   (R.I.C.)

BROOKS, William
Professional: Penzance (Figs.18–25)

William Brooks, an 'adopted' Cornishman, was after Robert Hunt one of the most influential people in early Cornish photography. His life merits considerably more than a passing notice. Born at Maidstone, Kent, on 31 December 1838, son of a father of the same names, Brooks was junior by a few months to his later Penzance friend Robert Preston. As a young man it seems that he was working in London. When half-a-century afterwards he was sending biographical details to G.C. Boase for *Collectanea Cornubiensia*,[1] he supplied (from memory) the date of 1863 for his first visit to Cornwall; this may be a year or so out, or have overlooked youthful trips. By his early twenties Brooks had become a competent *plein-air* photographer, we might guess with some independent means, and a visit to Penzance was extended into a period of residence. He stayed there until the end of 1870.

Fig.18   The Drawing Room, St Michael's Mount

Standing just north and east of the Church and traditionally the Lady Chapel of the pre-Reformation monastery, the room was restored and converted after 1740. Today, decorated in blue, it houses choice antiques and St Aubyn family portraits. In William Brooks's stereoscopic view it appears to be rather bare, with the chairs under dust covers. The slide is labelled 'No.10' with the words 'W. Brooks, Photographer, London'; this suggests that either he had not quite decided to settle in Penzance, or had only just done so and was not yet issuing such items in Preston's larger series.

Stereograph, Brooks, probably 1862–63.   (Private colln.)

In 1865 Mr Brooks showed further work, six large views and more stereographic frames, at the Polytechnic.[5] By now, the latter products were 'W. Brooks, Photographer, *Penzance*' (as in *Fig. 22*); the views, mostly in carte format, had an imprint showing a crowned wreath with a 'WB' monogram, and alternative legends. One, certainly used in late 1867 (*Fig. 24*) read 'W. Brooks, Photographer, Penzance'. The other, which was earlier, later, or just different — it is not possible to say — had 'W. Brooks's Mounts Bay Photographic Studio, Penzance'. There is no direct record of Brooks having his own trade premises[6] and it is likely that he started by using Robert Preston's studio before renting one of his own.

He left Penzance in 1870, after a visit to Scilly (*Fig. 25*); William Brooks was then 31, and possibly had married. From Cornwall he went to Reigate (Laurel Villa, Wray Park), where he lived for many years. In 1875 he became a vice-president of the South London Photographic Society, and a writer upon photography as well as being an inventor of photographic

Fig.20   The Village and Harbour, St Michael's Mount

From the 'Brooks album' again; the Mount was visited by most photographers who worked in Cornwall, residents or visitors, but this view (one of several similar) is unusual. It is low tide — note the causeway across to Marazion, high and exposed — and the masted vessels are tied up. We see, too, the Mount village at its largest extent; with between two and three times as many houses and buildings as can be seen today.

Paper print from album, Brooks, 1864–66.　　　(R.I.C.)

Fig.19   The Green Market, Penzance

The Institution owns a dismembered album, on whose cartridge-paper sheets had been pasted a series of 2 by 2 inches albumen prints, neatly ruled around and with brief titles in ink below each. Though not directly attributed, the close resemblances to many of Brooks's stereographs, the range of localities (Penzance and neighbourhood, Land's End and The Lizard), the evidence of date apparent in certain details and — to an indefinable extent — the style of the work, all point to Brooks in preference to anyone else. The album is thought to have come from Penzance and may have been made up by Brooks as a gift; the likely dates would be about 1864 to 1866.

Here is the old Green Market, the sun is south-east, hardly a soul is around and the shutters are still up at Dennis's shop and Cornish's grocery emporium. Is it a Sunday morning? The porch of the Three Tuns Hotel (right) bears the licensee's name, James. Thomas James took over the licence in April 1864. Compare Preston's slightly earlier view of the same part (*Fig. 96*).

Paper print from album, Brooks, 1864–66.　　　(R.I.C.)

processes.[7] This combination of the practical camera-man and the scientific innovator would, naturally, have been meat and drink to the fellow-enthusiasts at the Falmouth Polytechnic — Robert Hunt, still very much their champion, exemplified such a dual approach — and it is clear that William Brooks was a popular figure there. From Reigate, he frequently travelled down to Falmouth during the 1870s to act as a judge in the annual competitions. In 1878 he was precluded from judging because he himself was a competitor, in the Professionals class. His entry consisted of eight photographs of 'caves at Reigate' taken 60 feet underground by artificial light. Brooks's friends at Falmouth were more than impressed. The subterranean views, described as 'truly wonderful', won him the First Class Silver Medal, a considerable triumph.[8] The caves, the dene-holes or chalk-mines of the Reigate neighbourhood, were illuminated by 'yellow rays', only rather later explained to us[9] as having come from oil lamps. The official report commented that 'the discovery is capable of being applied in various ways, and in a mining county like Cornwall it may be invaluable, as it shows our deepest mines can now be photographed successfully. What next?' One might add, What indeed; as far as is known, the next venture of this kind, in Cornwall, was J.C. Burrow's, published in 1893.[10] Burrow in his preface referred to the underground photography by H.W. Hughes in Staffordshire, and by Arthur Sopwith in the coal-mines, but — very oddly — seems to have been unaware of the Reigate caves.

Fig.21 Botallack Mine − The Dressing Floors
One of a stereoscopic pair, this view is on a slide bearing the label 'No.87. W. Brooks, Photographer, Penzance', and it was therefore among the series that he published in conjunction with Robert Preston from 1864 onwards. It was a favoured view. Another version was produced by Archibald Coke *(Fig.27),* and there is a third − not ascribed; possibly Trembath's ? − taken from slightly further downhill in Noall, C., *Botallack* (Barton, Truro, 1972), 84.
Stereograph, Brooks, 1864.   (Author)

Fig. 22   Poltesco Mill and Valley

Though the recesses of The Lizard peninsula were less widely depicted than those of the Land's End, partly because of the effort of reaching them, they were made popular by writers like Rev. C.A. Johns *(Flowers of the Field* (1874) and *A Week at the Lizard* (1848), his best-known Cornish book). Brooks was an early visitor who appreciated the unspoiled rural scenery. Poltesco, an extremely remote little valley, seems to have been his favourite haunt. He made many Poltesco views, including some shown at the Polytechnic in 1869.

Paper print from albums, Brooks, 1864–66.   (R.I.C.)

Fig. 23   The Launch of the Lifeboat 'Daniel J. Draper', Penzance, 1867

The lifeboat was commissioned by the R.N.L.I. for the Mullion station in The Lizard. It was however launched at Penzance on 10 September 1867, as part of an inaugural day to mark the opening of the town's new public buildings. Before the launch, the *Daniel J. Draper* and three other lifeboats (Hayle, Penzance and St Ives) were drawn through the streets. Over ten thousand people assembled on the Esplanade to watch the Mayoress, Mrs Francis Boase, perform the ceremony.

William Brooks captured the crucial moment, issuing it as a carte with 'Christening of the Daniel J. Draper Lifeboat' added below. The imprint — crowned wreath around WB monogram, over 'W. Brooks, Photographer, Penzance' — may be earlier than that used for *Fig. 24.*

Carte, paper print, Brooks, 1867.   (R.I.C.)

Fig.24 The Mount, at High Wter

A carefully balanced composition, it shows the Chapel Rock (middle right) isolated at high tide on a very calm day, and the two little rocks at the water's edge acting as a counterpoint to the triangular mass of the Mount. This must have been among Brooks's entries at the 1869 Polytechnic competition, where it would rightly have been admired. The imprint is his second type, with 'W. Brooks's Mounts Bay Photographic Studio'.

Carte, paper print, Brooks, 1869;   (Private colln.)

In 1880 William Brooks was at Falmouth again, to lecture to the Polytechnic on recent improvements in photography and lantern-work.[11] Two years afterwards he was selected for the honour of participation in the 1882 Fifty-Years celebrations, where his talk was a major set-piece, 'The Rise and Progress of Photography'.[12] In the published version Brooks mentioned that another Falmouth pioneer, Thomas Brown Jordan, was still alive and living in Reigate where 'not many weeks ago I was in conversation with him'.[13] Throughout the 1870s, and later, there were quite a lot of Reigate entrants in the Polytechnic competitions, almost certainly encouraged by Brooks. It is interesting to notice that the, subsequently enormous, Francis Frith photographic coverage of Cornwall may have begun in the same fashion. Frith, already famous for his Middle East journeys and lavish books with real photographs, settled in Reigate in 1860, where he built up his photographic empire. It was in 1877, one of the years when Brooks was acting as a judge, that Frith & Co. of Reigate sent their first entries to the Polytechnic; four Cornish and four Devon views.[14]

Mr Brooks remained faithful to the Polytechnic long after 1882. For the years 1895 to 1897, he was elected a Vice-President, and was still ensured of a warm welcome as a speaker. We read of further lantern lectures on Haddon Hall, and on the Isle of Man, in 1892. In 1896 he gave a description of acetylene gas generators (useful for underground illumination ?), with a demonstration. In 1890, the Polytechnic decided to open a special 'Photographic Gallery' (its contents, alas, long since dispersed); on that occasion, the society's debt to William Brooks was expressed, for his interest and active co-operation and 'his personal influence with artists of the foremost rank'. This is a reminder that Brooks, who had been a photographer since the mid-1850s, must have known or met most of the leading London personalities during four decades; and that a great many of the national figures who had sent their work to Falmouth had been induced to support the Polytechnic's exhibitions through William Brooks's persuasions. All the evidence indicates that his help was genuinely appreciated. He became the Polytechnic's Photographic Expert, and his retirement

Fig.25 Building the 'David Auterson', Porthcressa, St Mary's

Issued as No.136 in his stereoscopic series, this image was made not long before William Brooks left Cornwall. It can be dated to late summer or autumn, 1870, during a visit to Scilly. The *David Auterson*, barque-rigged and 264 tons, was the last ship built at John Edward's yard on Porthcressa Bank. She was launched during 1871. Brooks's view is actually titled 'Hugh Town, from Buzza Hill, St Mary's, Scilly Isles'.

The main point of interest here is that Brooks must have been on a photographic outing with John Gibson at the time. Gibson's similar view (*Arlott, Cowan & Gibson, 1972*, Fig.27; see also in Jenkins, Alf, *The Scillonian and His Boat* (St Mary's, 1982), 129) implies that the two cameras were side by side, and very slight changes in detail (like persons having moved) imply that only a minute or so intervened between the two images being taken. Was this also the occasion when Gibson photographed, also from Buzza Hill, the German merchantmen at St Mary's (*Fig.35*), and did Brooks also photograph them? The ship itself was launched in late spring the following year, when Gibson alone was there to record the event (see Gibson, F.E., *Scilly and the Scillonians: A Pictorial History*, St Mary's, 1963 (two views), and (same author) *My Scillonian Home . . . Its Past, Its Present, Its Future*, St Mary's, 1980, pl. on p. 37).

Stereograph, Brooks, 1870.   (Private colln.)

from this, then discontinued, position in 1903 was marked by an address on vellum. In 1910, when he was 72, the Polytechnic elected him to Honorary Life Membership. Since 1833, very few people indeed outside Cornwall had been so consistently − and in this instance deservedly − honoured.[15]

By this time Mr Brooks had moved from Reigate to No. 10 Richmond Road, Ilford, in Essex. We are not informed how long he continued to take photographs; probably as long as he could move his fingers and hold his breath. He must have died in the closing years of the Great War. During that war, Falmouth became another place altogether and in the turmoil and confusion the Polytechnic lost contact with him, as with other of its once-prominent supporters. There is no formal obituary of the old lensman in any of the *Reports*. The memory of Mr Brooks has hardly been accorded justice. Here, a small sample of his pre-1870 work in

Cornwall may speak for itself. For this, and for a half-century of unobtrusive, willingly given, and profound, influences upon the development of popular photography in Cornwall, William Brooks deserves to be recalled with very particular gratitude and respect.

1. CC 110.
2. 32 RCPS, xxxix.
3. See p. 106.
4. BC 1015; Brooks himself (CC 110) implies a date of 1864.
5. 33 RCPS, xxiv.
6. Not in C 1864 (but, if a bachelor visitor in lodgings, he would not have been entered in directories).
7. CC 110.
8. 46 RCPS, 33 (see also, for 1869, 37 RCPS, 33).
9. In 50 RCPS (1882), 214.
10. Burrow and Thomas 1893.
11. 48 RCPS, 17.
12. 50 RCPS, 204−15.
13. *Ibidem*, 211.
14. 45 RCPS, cat. p. 19.
15. Details of Mr Brooks's involvement are given in W.L. Fox, 1915. He is among the platform party shown in *Fig. 2* (above) but, alas, there is no way of identifying him.

BURTON, J(ames?)
Professional: Hayle

A notice early in 1870 informed the world that 'Mr J. Burton of Hayle has opened a new photographic establishment on Tregenna Hill, St Ives. He has, at considerable expense, erected a good studio, which has plenty of light, and no doubt he will be able to turn out as good and faithful portraits here as he is celebrated for at his studio at Hayle. His terms are very moderate, as may be seen by his circular, and cannot fail to secure the support of the inhabitants'.[1] This implies that in 1869, if not earlier, J. Burton had a photographic business in Hayle. How much earlier we cannot say, since his name is not recorded in any appropriate directory.[2]

The imprint on a surviving carte de visite (the portrait is too faded for reproduction) has 'J. Burton, Photographer, Hayle and St Ives, Cornwall' and a further note that 'Mr Burton attends at St Ives on Monday, Wednesday and Friday, and at Hayle, on Tuesday, Thursday and Saturday, and an assistant on the alternate days.' As stated above[3] the assistant was almost certainly Edward Ashton, during the 1860s primarily a greengrocer in Hayle and an amateur (or semi-professional) photographer dividing his time between Hayle and his native(?) town of St Ives. After 1870, but before 1873, Mr Burton disappears and Edward Ashton, having re-deployed himself and his skills, emerges as a full-time photographer at Tregenna Hill.[4]

Burton's surname is not Cornish and, apart from the references just cited, he cannot be traced in Cornwall at all. The likelihood is that he came to Cornwall in 1868 or 1869 as a summer-months visiting professional, found adequate custom in Hayle, took a shop and became involved with Ashton. If his first name was James, he was probably from London.[5] What happened to him after the early 1870s is not known.

1. RCG, 9 Apr 1870.
2. Not in K 1856 nor H 1862.
3. See p. 28.
4. K 1873, 765, 774.
5. Cf. Pritchard, 32 (James Burton, 410 Euston Rd, NW, in 1867).

Fig.26 Gracey Briney
Grace Hichens was born about 1778. Known as 'Gracey Briney', she worked for years in the mines at the strenuous and exposed task of a kibble-lander (one who swung the heavy metal buckets, or kibbles, of ore onto the ground as the came up the shafts). From around 1830 she lived in Redruth, and always wore the same outfit; tall hat, blue claw-hammer coat with brass buttons, long frock and thick nailed boots. Gracey frequented miners' taverns, smoked a pipe, and was reputed to have been a fair hand at wrestling in her youth. Her long hair and grey moustache were appropriate accessories. A few weeks before her death in 1869, aged ninety-one, she walked over 50 miles to St Dominick for a load of cherries.
Carte, re-made from negative before 1869, Chenhall.   (R.I.C.)

CHENHALL, James
Professional: Redruth (Fig.26)

This Cornish surname under its various forms – Chenhall, Chenhalls, Chinnalls, Chynalls – is not very common, even in its home territory. Different forms represent different place-names and Chenhall in Wendron must have given rise to this particular family. James Chenhall was born at Redruth in 1845, son of James and Grace Chenhall.[1] His photographic career probably started with his acting as an assistant to one of the older Redruth photographers, and he first appears in 1866, when he was aged 21, as 'photographic artist, Buller's Row, Redruth'.[2]

A few years later, James Chenhall moved to No. 11 West End, a better address in the same town and an index of commercial success.[3] He continued there until 1910,[4] after which he is not mentioned, and had either retired or died.[5] It seems likely that, during the 1860s, he married, and at some stage in the 1880s he opened a branch of his business in Helston. At this period, the imprint on cabinet portraits was expanded to read 'Chenhall & Son'.[6] Mr Chenhall was not a particularly prominent photographer and virtually all of his work consists of portraits, early instances of which (*Fig 26*) are hard to locate. Presumably the Joseph Chenhall, professional photographer of East Street, Newton Abbot, Devon in 1873 was also a Cornishman, and even from this family;[7] but the connection, if any, is unknown.

1. Info. Mr Robin Fenner, Tavistock.
2. D 1866, 107.
3. K 1873.
4. K 1910, 300.
5. Not in K 1914, K 1919.
6. Imprints only; not in directories.
7. K Devon 1873.

CLINTON, Charles William
Amateur: Truro

During the 1850s a Mr William Clinton, born at Stonehouse (now part of Plymouth) in 1813, moved to No. 8 Vivian Terrace, Truro, and took up a post as a solicitor's accounts clerk.[1] His son, Charles William, born at Great Torrington in Devon in 1842, lived with his parents. About 1860 he had started work as a clerk assistant to the Registrar in the Court of the Vice-Warden of the Stannaries, the ancient and specialised legal centre for Cornwall's mining industry.[2]

In 1863 C.W. Clinton's photograph, titled 'The Missel Thrush', was among those featured in the Art Union of Cornwall prize draw for the year.[3] Unless the bird in question was dead, stuffed, or motionless with fright, this choice of subject argues a certain skill. As Andrew Lanyon has pointed out[4] in the case of Lewis Harding and the rooks, 'photographing wildlife was not really possible until the late 1880s or 1890s', because of the exposure-time required before this era.

The Botallick Mine.

Photographed by Archibald Coke.

Fig.27   The Botallick Mine

Mr Coke's view of the dressing floors at Botallack (which he spelled his own way) seems to be a little earlier than that by William Brooks, *Fig.21.* The stage above the lowest engine-house, extreme left, lacks a superstructure visible in the Brooks view, and the waste tip (right) is a little smaller.

New print from neg. of original carte, Coke, c. 1862.   (R.I.C.)

The Clintons stayed in Truro, but moved house (slightly); in 1889 C.W. Clinton was at No. 10 Vivian Terrace, and Mrs Elizabeth Clinton, his widowed mother, next door at No.9.[5] We have no other record of Mr Clinton's photography. As the first of the local amateurs to be discussed, his inclusion prompts the comment that − unless very clear evidence, with signatures and dates, is found − the chance of now identifying the work of any pre-1870 amateur photographer is extremely small.

COKE, Archibald L.
Visiting Professional (Figs. 27 and 28)

Very little can be said about Mr Coke, who does not figure in any of the usual sources for British photographers at the period; it is likely, from his name, that he was Scottish, and we know that this visitor to Cornwall produced both stereographs and plate views. The caption to *Fig. 27,* a single-image view, gives us his forename. Identified stereographs include *Fig. 28,* marked as '12' in his series on the printed label − which does not specify any town of origin − and another, of the entrance to the Drawing Room at St Michael's Mount, which has the number '22'.

The Botallack view, one that other photographers both resident and visiting also made, belongs to the early 1860s. On the reasonable assumption that Mr Coke made a single visit, and on the evidence of *Fig. 28,* this took place in late 1861 or in 1862.

1. Census 1861.
2. H 1878, 1020.
3. See p. 17 above.
4. Lanyon 1976.
5. K 1889, 1176, 1179.

Fig.28 Ostriches at Tresco
In the 1850s, one of the Tregarthens brought an ostrich back to Scilly from Rio de Janeiro; another was procured, and the birds began to lay. In 1861 two were actually reared from eggs and for many years the Tresco ostriches roamed the grounds. Archibald Coke's picture shows one of Augustus Smith's retainers looking rather warily at the flock (parents and children ?); the smaller birds are perhaps a year old, which effectively dates the view.
Albumen print, stereograph, Coke, 1861. (Author)

By 1857 J.H. Colliver had left the world of mining and was advertising the opening of his Temperance House and Coffee Room in Church Street, Liskeard.[4] It is possible that he had already become interested in photography, and we could dare hope that early views of Wheal Mary Ann might yet emerge. Earlier in 1857, before he started the Temperance House, he had made an arrangement (and inserted notices in the press to that effect) to act as host to Mr R.P. Yeo of Plymouth, a visiting photographer, who was prepared to take 'a correct and perfect likeness, mounted in a neat frame, for One Shilling'.[5] This is of interest in any case as the first reference to Richard Yeo as a commercial photographer,[6] and it also may explain why Colliver, observing the success of the venture, decided to follow suit. In February 1858 he put out yet another advertisement,[7] informing 'the Nobility, Gentry and Public Generally, that he has commenced Business as a PHOTOGRAPHER, and hopes by strict attention to share a part of Public Patronage'. Prices of the Colliver portraits, it was stated, would range from sixpence to One Pound.

We are not told what happened to the coffee house, but the new Church Street business is duly listed for 1862.[8] The first imprint was a simple one ('Colliver, Photographic Artist'), with the address. Mr Colliver did not participate, probably for reasons of distance, in

COLE, J.J.
Visiting Amateur

Mr Cole, described only as 'of Hornsey Rise, London', entered twelve views of cliff scenery from Dorset, Devon and Cornwall, all taken to show geological detail, in the 1865 Polytechnic competition at Falmouth.[1] Interest in practical geology, and its illustration by means of the camera, grew after the appearance of the 1853 one-volume edition of Lyell's *Principles of Geology,* and photographs of this kind were not uncommonly shown at the Polytechnic. A search through the usual bibliographies does not reveal Mr Cole as a practising geologist, and though there were various early photographers with this surname[2] none had the same initials.

1. 33 RCPS, xxiii.
2. See Gernsheim 1984, indexes.

COLLIVER, John Henry
Professional: Liskeard (Fig. 29)

Mr Colliver was born in 1826.[1] He began his career at Wheal Mary Ann, a well-known lead mine in the parish of Menheniot, opened in 1843 and named for the wife of the landowner, Reverend G.P. Norris.[2] Colliver, an engineer, is said to have done well, but the mining boom did not last and the mine closed in 1874 after a period of decline.[3]

Fig.29 Portrait of Richard Pryor
Mr Pryor, or Prior − his family used either spelling, as did others of the same surname in 19th-century Cornwall − was the son of a substantial farmer outside Liskeard. By early 1864 he was engaged to Julia Vivian Dunstan, elder sister of Joseph *(Fig.5)* and daughter of Mrs Julia Yewens *(Fig.86).* They were married on 17 August 1864, but poor Richard was killed in a riding accident not long afterwards (10 November). The carte portrait, from his mother-in-law's album, would have been made during the courtship or engagement.
Carte, paper print, Colliver, 18634−64. (Author)

Fig.30 Two Barges discharging salt in Cadgwith Cove

Among the most attractive of Henry Cox's uniformly attractive studies, this shows a couple of sailing barges pulled up on the beach at Cadgwith. The tide is out, the sea is calm, and the Cadgwith men are busy unloading. The salt was used in the process called 'bulking', that is, making alternative layers of pilchards and salt and then compressing them as a form of curing the fish.

Paper print, Cox, c. 1864.

(Levick album: Mr & Mrs Crumpler)

any of the Polytechnic's competitions at Falmouth. Apart from the part-time competition offered during the 1860s by Edwin Mayell,[9] adequate custom from Liskeard and district must have come his way. By 1873 he had moved his business to a new and larger shop in Market Street, the imprints on carte and cabinet portraits[10] from this period being notably more ornate, and referring to his 'Photographic Studio'.

Though, curiously, Mr Colliver is not listed in a directory of 1876[11] − as an established tradesman in the town, one would have expected to find his name included − he is thought to have continued as a photographer until the early 1880s. He retired, but remained in Liskeard at his home, Bay Tree Hill, where he died in January 1903, aged 77. It is also known that he was a staunch Wesleyan Methodist.[12] Despite the association with the east of the county, his family may originally have hailed from Penzance, where the surname Colliver is to be found a generation before his birth.

1. Info. Mr John L. Rapson, Liskeard.
2. Rector (from 1816) of East Anstey, Devon − CC 628.
3. Barton, D.B., *Mines and Mineral Railways of East Cornwall and West Devon* (Truro, 1964), 27−8.
4. *Liskeard Gazette* (LG), 8 Aug 1857.
5. LG, 25 Apr 1857.
6. See p. 139.
7. LG, 27 Feb 1858.
8. H 1862, 880.
9. See p. 89.
10. J.L. Rapson colln.
11. Not in P 1876.
12. See n.1 above.

COX, Henry
Amateur: Cadgwith (Fig. 30)

As an amateur, Mr Cox entered his photographs of Cadgwith in the Polytechnic's 1864 exhibition.[1] He was almost certainly the 'Henry Cocks' of Cadgwith Serpentine Works in 1856[2] and − more correctly − the Henry Cox, Serpentine Marble Quarry and Works Proprietor of Cadgwith, in 1873.[3] Still an amateur, he was awarded a Second Silver Medal in 1869 for his Polytechnic entry of 'charming artistic studies'.[4] Henry Cox's connection with the Polytechnic continued and at a later date[5] he was included, with Robert Fox and Thomas Hart, among the judges for the photographic entries.

Cadgwith has been extensively depicted, but the R.I.C. possesses no image as early as this, and it had been supposed that there was now little chance of finding Mr Cox's views. However, some have indeed been preserved − in Australia. James Levick (1815−1883), a Sheffield master-cutler and London merchant, had mining interests in Cornwall including the 1866 Lizard Serpentine Company. Mr Levick went to Australia and died there; his widow came to England, but in 1911 the two sons returned to Australia, and Guy Levick (d. 1965, aged 89), solicitor, farmer and classical scholar, preserved his father's unique album. This contains Australian views from 1857, a selection from Devon (some by R.P. Yeo), and many from the west of Cornwall (Preston; William Brooks; possibly Beringer as well).[6] At least six are of Cadgwith, one probably showing the Levick family on holiday there in the mid-1860s. Through the great kindness of Mr and Mrs Bernard Crumpler of Victoria (Mr Crumpler being James Levick's great-grandson) the R.I.C. has been provided with copies of the Cornish views. The wealth of local detail in the Cadgwith studies, and their style − fine, natural quarter-plate views choosing good weather and the right light − imply a man on the spot, and must point to Henry Cox, who no doubt gave prints to Mr Levick for the latter's collection. *Fig. 30* is thus presented here, with confidence, as a good example of Mr Cox's work.

1. 32 RCPS, xxxix.
2. K 1856, 32.
3. K 1873, 857 and 988.
4. 37 RCPS, 34.
5. 44 RCPS (1876), 38.
6. Info. Mrs Bernard Crumpler, Victoria.

COX, W.J.
Visiting Professional

Mr Cox's group of photographic images (not further described, unfortunately) won him a Second Bronze Medal in the Fine Arts section of the 1854 Polytechnic's competition at Falmouth.[1] He therefore shares with Mr Mitchell of St Austell[2] the distinction of being, after the rather earlier daguerreotypists, among the earliest of the photographic prizewinners in Cornwall. In 1855 he sent in a further, but possibly non-competitive, dislay − 'beautifully executed' − and the relevant report notes him, tantalisingly, as being 'of Devonport; photographer to the Admiralty'.[3] Mr Cox is included here because of the chance, perhaps the likelihood, that his views covered not just Devonport and Stonehouse, but the part of Cornwall just opposite, like Mount Edgcumbe. The surname Cox is not uncommon in Devon and Cornwall, and there is not necessarily any connection with the Edward Henry Cox who by 1873 was in business as a photographer at No. 6 Park Crescent, Torquay.

1. 22 RCPS, xxi; WB 8 Sept 1854 (list of prize-winners).
2. See p. 90.
3. 23 RCPS, xxxii.
4. K Devon 1873, 611.

DAWSON, James
Professional: Truro

As a family, the Dawsons tumble into sight from a very dimly glimpsed back-room, the prehistory of the English music halls and provincial theatre. We meet the first Dawson, an actor-manager of the 18th century, in Robert Dyer's amusing account of his early stage years.[1] The 'Exeter Comedians' were making a Cornish tour in their horse-drawn wagon. Among the props lay the inebriated body of one of their number, accompanied by 'the huge carcase of Triton, a mixed Newfoundland dog'. In the front sat the older Dawsons, 'Mrs D. with Phillis, a fat little goggle-eyed lap dog, in her lap', Mr and Mrs James Dawson junior and their infant son, then another couple, and finally Dyer himself − 'jolting along upon this load of sin and scenery'.

The date would have been about 1820. 'Mr James Dawson junior', father of the eventual Truro photographer, was born on 16 October 1799, according to one source at Scarborough,[2] or to another at Bath.[3] The location is hardly material; to begin with, the older Dawson was really called Cole, and had adopted 'Dawson' as a stage surname. The son (who from now on must be called James Dawson *senior*) married in 1817, when he was just eighteen, a Miss Louisa Angel from Falmouth two years his junior. He was later described, perhaps a little unkindly, as 'a low comedian of great ability'. All the Dawsons more or less settled in Cornwall. The eldest Dawsons, correctly Coles, disappear from life's stage. The middle Dawsons − James Theophilus Dawson and his wife Louisa − spent many muddled years barnstorming around the south-west. The fate of their 'infant son', noticed by Robert Dyer, remains unexplained, but in due season their union was blessed with further issue. James junior was born in 1837, Richard in 1839, and before them had come Henrietta in 1831 and Adolphus in 1833. Henrietta alone escaped; she married Henry Marsh, a song-writer from Sidmouth, and they emigrated to Australia.[4]

As time rolled on the life of an actor-manager became less certain, and the Dawsons decided to settle; originally in Falmouth, but then in Truro. The family had grown to eleven children, five (or six) of whom allegedly perished of scarlet fever contracted during a visit to Redruth. The survivors, as they reached adult state, were impressed into the family troupe. James Dawson had a second string to his bow − he was interested in The Dance, an art form about which he could write reams of pseudo-classical prose. There was money, as well as art, in dancing, and the Dawson family could now offer more of their talents to the unsophisticated Cornish public. A notice in 1843 proclaimed that, having refreshed his repertoire with a stay in London, Mr Dawson was about to re-open his 'Academies'.[5] These were simply peripatetic dancing-classes; Truro on Saturdays, Penzance on Mondays, Tuesdays in Helston, Falmouth on Wednesdays, and with Thursday and Friday split between Wadebridge,

Bodmin, Liskeard, St Blazey and St Austell. There were enough Dawsons to cope with this gruelling programme. They acquired a larger house at No. 15, River Street, Truro. Here in 1861[6] James Dawson senior, Louisa, Richard and the as-yet-unmarried Henrietta were all 'Professors of Dancing', Adolphus a Professor of Music, and the head of the family additionally represented himself as a Professor of Fencing.

One senses the Dawsons as being good fun in small doses; amusing company, but as a family wholly Dickensian and slightly raffish. In 1865 the elder Dawson published, privately, his autobiography.[7] It is the sort of book in which one has no idea how much to believe, short on hard facts, long on purple passages, and unintentionally a portrait of a man who was usually one step ahead of insolvency.

From this artistic but commercially unreal setting, James Dawson junior partly broke away, and in 1861 was described as 'photographic artist'.[8] The initiative displayed was only partial because he practised from the River Street home.[9] During the early 1870s however the Dawsons either sold, or gave up the lease of, No. 15 River Street. The parents moved around the corner into Castle Street, where the father died on 15 February 1878, aged 79.[10] We hear no more of Adolphus and his pianoforte; Henrietta had married, and gone to Australia; but James junior the photographer and his dancing-master brother Richard were in 1873 at No. 95 Pydar Street, Truro.[11] Ten years later, this address housed Mrs Brewer, a milliner, and James Dawson's studio was at No. 5 Boscawen Bridge Road.[12] This is the last trace of him.

Judging from the small range available, James Dawson was not a very good photographer and his *forte* was probably carte portraits at cut prices (the imprint is simply 'Photographed by J. DAWSON, Truro' below the Royal Arms). Nothing certainly earlier than the 1870s has been so far discovered. His principal claim to our interest resides in his picturesque background.

1. *Nine Years of an Actor's Life* (London and Plymouth, 1833); see also Crane, Harvey, *Playbill – A History of the Theatre in the West Country* (Macdonald and Evans, Plymouth, 1980).
2. BC 112.
3. Census 1861 (supplied by himself ?).
4. BC 336.
5. WB 28 July 1843.
6. Census 1861.
7. *The Autobiography of Mr James Dawson* (Netherton, Truro, 1865).
8. Census 1861.
9. H 1862, with this address.
10. BC 1153; CC 198; WB 21 Feb 1878, p. 6 col. 2.
11. K 1873.
12. Lake 1883, 30.

DOCTON, Edwin
Professional(?): Padstow

The Doctons originated at Docton, in Devon, but during the last century members of the family are to be found at several places in Cornwall. Thomas Docton, born about 1800, began as a pupil-teacher in Truro in 1819,[1] and a few years later became a tailor and bookbinder at Trewickett Street, Padstow.[2] The literary aspects of this odd combination triumphed; he moved to Broad Street in the same town[3] and set up as a printer, bookseller and stationer.[4] Edwin Docton, his son, began his working life in Padstow as a painter and gilder,[5] a not unusual background for Cornish photographers; gilders had to be most precise in handling chemicals. In 1856 he was living in Middle Street, Padstow, but as a painter only.[6]

During 1854 Edwin Docton lectured to the Wadebridge Literary and Scientific Institution, an eager body in the neighbouring town.[7] Describing himself (factually) as a painter, and also as a 'self-taught operator' (of photography), Mr Docton's discourse to his Wadebridge friends was on the subject of the Daguerreotype process. It was enlivened by a display of 'some beautiful examples of his own work'. Unhappily, he lived inconveniently too far from Falmouth to exhibit his prowess at the Polytechnic, and we thus lack what might have been another record. The newspaper report of his lecture adds that the speaker 'felt moved to rejoice in the evidence of intellectual movement among the class of which he with all modesty avowed himself to be a member'. For 1854, expressions of this kind (which read rather like a passage from Stephen Leacock's humorous tales) were not as priggish as they might seem today; but we are not told whether Mr Docton had in mind the middle class, the professional, or the artistic.

Of considerable interest as an early practitioner of of daguerreotype, Mr Docton may of course have taught himself how to make these particular images before 1850 (probably well before 1854); it can only be a guess that he was selling likenesses locally, and thus strictly moving from amateur to professional status. Whatever the facts, he was working very much in isolation. No further photographer from Padstow is listed until John Reynolds of Lanadwell Street, some years later.

1. Potts 1963, 313.
2. P 1823.
3. S 1852, 35.
4. K 1856, 75.
5. S 1852, 35.
6. K 1856, 75.
7. WB 24 Mar 1854.
8. K 1873.

DUNSTAN, William Henry
Professional: Falmouth (Fig. 31)

It is only a guess, but a reasonable one, that this man was also the William Henry Dunstan (born 1820) who, at the age of 18, showed at the Polytechnic an ingenious wind-powered device. This was to keep an alarm bell ringing on the Black Rock, a reef at the entrance to Falmouth harbour.[1] Dunstan is a common Cornish surname, and he may have been connected with the

Fig.31   Portrait of an Unknown Gentleman
Mr Dunstan's simple carte de visite is in a style favoured by many portraitists; the central bust, faded away below, on a slightly raised oval background set within a darker surround. The imprint is that of W.H. Dunstan, Photographer, 7 Berkeley Place, Falmouth, his address before his move to No. 9 Berkeley Vale in the early 1870s. This may be one of the cartes that he showed at the Polytechnic's 1868 competition.

Carte, paper print, Dunstan, c. 1868.   (Author)

Falmouth family of W.H. and J. Dunstan, builders, Smithick Hill.[2]

As a photographer, Mr Dunstan has left us a low profile; he possibly followed some other occupation altogether until he was in his forties. In 1868 he entered a frame of ten carte portraits at the Polytechnic,[3] his business address being given as No. 7 Berkeley Place, Falmouth. Since in 1864 this house was listed[4] as being in the occupation of Mr Walter Kastell, painter and carpenter, Mr Dunstan was perhaps renting a room for a studio. Eight years later, we find W.H. Dunstan in business at No. 9 Berkeley Vale.[5] The naming of adjoining streets (or parts of streets) in Falmouth at this period is somewhat confusing – Mr Dunstan's 1868 address at No. 7 Berkeley Place must be distinguished from Thomas Hart's photographic premises[6] at No. 7, *Upper* Berkeley Place – but No. 9, Berkeley Vale, we shall encounter again. This had previously belonged to yet another photographer, Charles Truscott,[7] and would have been acquired by W.H. Dunstan not long before 1876. The tangled affairs of the Truscott brothers

(Charles and Walter) are portrayed later. The imprint on Dunstan's cartes de visite in the 1870s read, however, 'W.H. Dunstan & Co., 9 Berkeley Vale' with the further legend 'Artists and Photographers'. Since Walter Truscott, who was primarily an artist (and could produce copy oils from enlarged photographs), had by now parted company with his brother Charles and was living very nearby at No. 13 Berkeley Place,[8] one suspects he had joined Dunstan in business.

No reference to Mr Dunstan can be found after 1876, though there are cabinet portraits that suggest he was in business until the 1880s.[9] *Fig. 130* shows the interior of Dunstan's studio some time after 1870. To avoid yet more confusion, Dunstan the photographer must be seen as quite distinct from another 'William H. Dunstan' (born 1821), who in 1852 was deputy clerk of the market at Truro[10] and by 1861 had also become licensee of the King's Head in Lemon Street.[11]

1. 6 RCPS, 151.
2. Wa 1864.
3. 36 RCPS, cat. p. 18.
4. Wa 1864, 87.
5. P 1876, 48; today (1988) the 'Vale Garden Centre'.
6. See p. 61.
7. See p. 135.
8. See p. 136.
9. Private colln. (Dunstan's daughter's album ?).
10. S 1852, 67.
11. Census 1861.

GENN, William James
Amateur: Falmouth

Mr Genn, one of the younger photographers recorded in this book, was the first son of William James Genn of Falmouth (b. 1811), a solicitor in partnership with a Mr Nalder and Town Clerk of the borough. W.J. Genn junior was himself born in 1846; in due course he qualified as a solicitor, but sadly died young (1870) while on a visit to Melbourne, Australia.[1] The Genns lived at No. 11, Woodlane Terrace, Falmouth.[2]

Like most of the town's professional class, they were closely associated with the Polytechnic. In 1864 W.J. Genn junior was praised for contributing a statistical analysis of the society's activities.[3] In the previous year, as part of the Art Union of Cornwall prize draw, his photographic entry had been titled 'The Faithful Shepherdess'. We can suppose that one of his five sisters was persuaded to dress up, and to stand still long enough, to effect this pretty conceit.

1. CC 271.
2. Wa 1864.
3. 32 RCPS, 20–23.

GEOFFROI, Henry Malcolm
Amateur(?): Penzance

Mr Geoffroi is included here only speculatively, but with the supposition that at some future date evidence of his engagement in photography may well be found. He was a British subject, born in France, and in 1861 lived at Regent House, Penzance, with his wife Elizabeth and their four children.[1] Earlier, in 1856, he was one of the five 'artists' listed for the whole of the county,[2] and he described himself as a Professor of Drawing and Painting. We know that Mr Geoffroi was also the first Master of the Penzance School of Art, founded in 1853, which began at Regent House and rather later moved to new premises at the top of Morrab Road. In 1866 the Geoffrois lived in Voundervoor Lane, Penzance next to the School[3] and for some years H.M. Geoffroi was, in addition, the master of Truro School of Art, which he visited weekly and which was also staffed by the Truro photographer-cum-artist R.P. Griffiths.[4] To this dual post was added that of (visiting) art master at 'Truro School' – i.e., Truro Grammar School, later Truro Cathedral School.[5]

There are two reasons to suspect that he may have had a practical interest in the camera. One is the association, at Truro School of Art, with Richard Price Griffiths (who was himself also an artist and certificated art master), and the fact that pupils of this school were encouraged to enter work in the Polytechnic's competitive sections for schoolchildren. The other is the unusually early appearance in 1854 of 'a fine collection of photographs' in the annual exhibition of work held at Penzance School of Art.[6] This date is too early for any of the known Penzance photographers, save possibly William Jenkyns, and in any case it was specifically the School's yearly show. If any pupils (or staff) were making images, who was teaching and encouraging them in this new Art?

1. Census 1861; he was probably married in 1843–44.
2. K 1856.
3. C 1866, 67, 89.
4. See p. 53.
5. P 1876, 102.
6. WB 18 Aug 1854.

GIBSON, John
Professional: Scilly (Figs. 32–35)

The outline of Mr Gibson's long life is well enough known.[1] Born in 1827 in another archipelago, the Aran Islands where his Scillonian father James happened to be stationed as a coastguard, he and his mother came back to St Mary's following the father's death in 1840. Times were not easy. They opened a general store in Hugh Town where among other commodities they sold meat, and John Gibson was burdened for life with the nickname of 'Johnny Prime'. From time to time he took a berth at sea, as he had done before his father's death, and did not marry (Sarah Gendall) until 1855. Their sons Alexander Gendall and

Fig.32   Neddy Betty's Lane, Penzance
The seaward side of Market Jew Street contained numerous old houses, even slums, in decrepit condition well into the last century. Gas lighting (note the bracket lamp) was introduced around 1830. The alley where the two men stand is now Albert Street, formerly 'Neddy Betty's Lane' after one Edward Betty, licensee of a public-house (the tumble-down thatched structure, centre) on the corner with Market Jew Street.

The photograph is undated and is a later print from, probably, a wet-plate original. The R.I.C. has several such prints, one with the ink stamp of Gibson & Sons, Penzance and Scilly Isles. The date could be in the 1860s, rather than in the 1850s (in which case the photographer would have been William Jenkyns, who would have made a much sharper image). One is inclined to suspect that this *is* by John Gibson, a trial run in his initial period when he was learning the business with Robert Preston.
Later print from plate, Gibson, early 1860s.   (R.I.C.)

Herbert John were born in 1857 and 1861. About 1860, like some other islanders drawn thither by the magnet of commerce, the Gibsons moved to Penzance.

At some stage in the period 1855–60, John Gibson acquired his first camera. Between voyages he taught himself to use it, and is thought to have built his experience on the taking of portraits. The Richards family, Penzance photographers over several generations, knew the Gibsons, and the present Mr Richards is certain that John Gibson, after he came to Penzance in 1860, was in some fashion apprenticed to Robert Preston.[2] This tradition must be credited. Despite a gap in their ages (Preston was younger by 11 years) the two men had much in common. They had come to Penzance about the same time; both had an innate sense of occasion when the timely view might be snatched; and both were masters of the set-piece composition, using a steady plate camera. One could add that both lived to a notable age – Gibson to 93, Preston to 94.

Supposedly around 1865, John and Sarah Gibson returned to Scilly. Though they opened a general shop, by 1870 Mr Gibson was firmly in business as a photographer. Their establishment in Church Street had a large shed at the rear, acting as studio and processing-area. The two sons joined their father. The combined family repertoire with its unusually strong emphasis on dramatic shipwrecks,[3] natural phenomena and the antiquities both of Scilly and of west Cornwall attracted custom far beyond the Isles. Standards were high, the results striking (even when clouds were brushed into the negatives, and unwanted humans or cattle brushed out!), and the large prints were available singly or in extensive sets. The Gibsons had a keen notion of marketing. As the sons grew, and contemplated families of their own, the capacity of the one shop in Hugh Town was pushed to its limit and about 1877 John Gibson bought another premises on the promenade at Penzance. In 1879 this was exchanged for a branch in the centre of the town, at No. 10 Market Jew Street; not far from Preston's own establishment at No. 23, it became a great attraction for visitors.

Fig.33 Augustus Smith among the Ferns

The great man was born in 1804, and died in 1872. As the 1856 Jenkyns portrait *(Frontispiece)* shows, he retained his dark hair and somewhat aquiline features certainly into his fifties. Views taken in 1871 — with the pilots from Agnes, for instance *(Arlott, Cowan & Gibson, 1972,* Fig.5) — indicate the face fleshing out, and the hair and sideburns quite grey. On these grounds alone the portrait here cannot possibly be from his final years. It depicts a man older than that shown in 1856 by Jenkyns and anyhow does not come from the Jenkyns plates. If, as is claimed, this is by John Gibson — and there is no strong reason to doubt the claim — it can hardly be after 1865−66, and must have been made about the time that Gibson went back to Scilly.

Later print (original plate), Gibson, 1865−66.   (F.E. Gibson)

Fig.34 A View of Dolphin Town, Tresco

This splendid image, clearly a Gibson, is known only from an early (commercial) print that came to light a few years ago. The viewpoint (hill behind the vicarage) is one that all the Gibsons favoured. The interest lies in the long building with arched door and two dormer windows, the post-Civil War church of Tresco which was demolished around 1877, when the present St Nicholas Church was completed. An even earlier version of this view, probably a John Gibson of the mid-1860s, was noted at Tresco Abbey by Michael Tangye *(Scillonian, No.207, 1978, 80−85,* sketch at p. 81). The photograph here may be around 1869−70.

Later print (original plate), Gibson, 1869−70.   (F.E. Gibson)

Fig. 35   German Merchantmen in the Road, St Mary's

On July 19 of 1870, France declared war on Prussia and the German states. A small fleet of German merchant ships happened to be at Scilly and anchored in The Road, the sheltered area beyond St Mary's harbour (the two hills in the background, centre and left, are the island of Samson). John Gibson photographed them from a vantage point at the end of Hugh Town, incidentally giving us a very detailed, back-garden look at the little town. This photograph is often supposed to be the earliest dated Gibson view — it is, if one looks for external independent verification, but it cannot by any means be Gibson's first photograph taken in the Isles.

Later print (original, plate), Gibson, 1870.   (F.E. Gibson)

The later part of the story, in detail, lies beyond the scope of this book and can only be summarised. John Gibson remained in Scilly. Alexander — with his archaeological and literary tastes, and the eccentricities that became so prominent in latter years — and Herbert John divided their working life. One or other might spend summer in the Isles, where tourism was beginning to offer rewards (though, curiously, it was not until 1925 until the famous Gibson guide-book was produced).[4] Winters — the shipwreck seasons — were spent in Penzance, and beyond; for example, a set of Stonehenge views was made about 1900.

In 1910 John Gibson, aged 83, finally retired. He moved back to Cornwall, dying in 1920 at St Buryan, where Augustus Smith (*Fig. 33*) had also been laid to rest. Five years later the brothers dissolved their partnership. Herbert John remained in Penzance; Alexander took over the business in Scilly. Here 'Gibsons' came to mean both Alexander and his son James, born in 1901. During the 1930s Herbert John re-joined his elder brother and his nephew James — now a married man and a father, in Hugh Town. By the time that

Herbert John died (1937), Alexander, whose erratic ways and constant absences made relationships impossible in this now ill-assorted family firm, had quarrelled with James. In 1940, having agreed to sell out, Alexander departed from Scilly and went to Oswestry in Shropshire, where he died in 1944. *En route,* he cleared the Penzance shop, sending the (purchased) shipwreck plates, bundled up any-old-how, back to his son James in Scilly, and then flinging the rest down a mineshaft. James Gibson in due course sold out his interest (1958) to his son Frank and retired to Falmouth, where he died recently.

Those who study closely the Gibsons' work, the huge unquantified record made by four generations during a century and a quarter, will end up with very little doubt that John Gibson must have been making plate photographs well before 1870. With rare exceptions, because of Alexander's final outburst, the present range of Gibson prints (other than the famous shipwreck series) have to come from new negatives made from surviving prints, many a century or so old. Any key to a system of numbering has long been lost.

In print, it has tended to become a repeated axiom that the earliest, dated, John Gibson picture is that of German vessels sheltering at St Mary's in 1870, when the Franco-Prussian War broke out (*Fig. 35*). More careful scrutiny upsets this idea. The well-known study[5] of the barque *David Auterson* being built on Porthcressa, St Mary's, was certainly made in the latter part of 1870, proof of this coming from the discovery that Gibson was at the time entertaining William Brooks from Penzance, who took a near-identical plate[6] and who was not in Cornwall after the end of that year. The portrait of Augustus Smith among the tree-ferns (*Fig. 33*) was made well before 1870, probably about 1866. There should be other images, still to be recovered from old prints, representing John Gibson's camerawork of these initial years. He himself must have returned to St Mary's with every intention of becoming the Isles of Scilly's resident photographer; and with the ability and equipment to realise that intention. We know almost nothing about a rare series of early stereographs. One, of the Ballowal cairn at St Just, is blind-stamped 'J. Gibson − Photographer − Scilly Isles'.[7] It could well have been taken *before* John Gibson's return in 1865, on an outing with Preston or Brooks, and then issued from Scilly in 1866−70; in fact, this is by far the most likely explanation.

1. Arlott, Cowan and Gibson 1972; further information here is from Mr Francis E. Gibson, Scilly.
2. Info. Mr Edward Richards, Penzance, 1987.
3. Cf. *On The Rocks: Photographs of West County shipwrecks, by the Gibson family* (catalogue − National Maritime Museum, 1984).
4. *The Isles of Scilly . . . The Visitor's Companion in Sunny Lyonnesse* (Gibson & Sons, Scilly Isles and Penzance, n.d. = 1925); this, with a subsequent, edition was written by Alexander Gibson.
5. Arlott, Cowan and Gibson 1972, Fig. 22.
6. See p. 42 and Fig. 25, above.
7. Author's colln.

GILL, John
Amateur: Truro

Though the entry in question was not specified in the Annual Report's description of the 1856 Polytechnic exhibition at Falmouth, a parallel newspaper account[1] stated that 'Mr Gill, master of the School of Design at Truro, exhibited three good coloured photographs'. These would have been prints on paper with colour added by hand. It remains an assumption, but Mr Gill was entering a competition and is thus likely to have taken the photographs himself.

The Schools of Design differed from the (private) schools of art discussed earlier,[2] being held on various premises as science and art classes conducted by visiting teachers, in connection with the so-called 'South Kensington' examinations arranged by the 1853 Department of Science and Art. A Science School of this sort was started at Falmouth in 1864 under the auspices of the Polytechnic, and was later merged into other Falmouth provisions for the South Kensington scheme.[3] Early newspaper reports are not of course precise and it is not always clear today, reading generalised and brief accounts, whether all the 'Schools of (Art and) Design' were wholly separated from the Penzance and Truro Schools of Art, or formed an aspect of the latter on certain days and for certain age-groups.[4] At Truro there does seem to have been a distinction. In 1856 Mr Gill must have been fairly young. He was however remembered as late as 1927, as having been responsible for teaching 'South Kensington' science and art classes at Truro, and subsequently also at Helston and at St Just.[5] His name does not figure in membership lists of any of the Cornish scientific societies with whose work he would, educationally, have been associated. John Gill was presumably a Cornishman, and one would suspect him to be connected with the Gills of Penryn. This family included John Gill the printer and well-known peace reformer, a Quaker, like the Foxes.[6]

1. WB 19 Sept 1856.
2. See p. 17 above.
3. 32 RCPS, xiii.
4. Cf. the remarks in 27 RCPS, xxxv.
5. *Cornwall Education Week Handbook, Truro 1927* (Cornwall County Council), at p. 26, 'Early Educational Facilities in Cornwall'.
6. Monk, Wendy, *John Gill of Penryn 1811−1905* (1971).

GREGORY, (Henry?)
Amateur: Falmouth

In respect of his photographic prize drawn in the 1863 Art Union of Cornwall event,[1] the report described Mr Gregory, not very informatively, as 'C.E., Falmouth' (i.e., a chartered engineer, suggesting perhaps the dockyard, certainly not the mining world). It has not proved possible to find any independent reference to him in this capacity. The photograph was called 'Egeria', the Roman nymph or muse who offered wise counsel to a statesman, and a young lady must have been engaged as a model. Assuming that Mr Gregory, like W.J. Genn junior and Francis Luke junior, was another youthful camera enthusiast, not long professionally qualified, he may well have spent his life at Falmouth and retired there. In such a case, was he the 'Henry Gregory, engineer', listed in 1902 as living at No. 9 New Budock Terrace, Falmouth?[2]

1. See p.17 above.
2. L 1902, 69.

GRIFFITHS, Richard Price
Professional: Truro (Figs. 36−38)

Richard Griffiths was Welsh. He was born at Holyhead, Anglesey, in 1819; his wife Ellen was also Welsh and their three children − Evan, Boadicea and Richard Price junior − were born at Caernarvon between 1848 and 1857.[1] About 1860 the family came to Truro. At first they had a house in Ferris Town, a planned development at the west end of River Street and Frances Street, and Mr Griffiths was entered in the 1861 census as 'Master of a school of art'.

Fig.36 John Garby, Mineralogist, 1812–1864

Mr Garby, from a well-known Redruth mining family, was born on 20 October 1812, contributed various papers to journals and died on 8 March 1864 while on a visit to Brazil (*see BC,* 168; *CC,* 267). In this portrait, perhaps on the eve of departure to South America, he is about 51, and doing his best not to smile as he pretends to examine some mineral specimen. Cornish people will recognise that, in a wholly undefinable way, Mr Garby's features and build are both quintessentially Cornish.

The print was made by E.I. Ellery, who did not start in Truro before the 1880s and cannot possibly have taken the original. Since it was Ellery who bought both the Griffiths premises in Truro, River Street and Pydar Street, he probably acquired the stock of Griffiths portrait plates and negatives; and R.P. Griffiths is therefore indicated as the artist.

Plate-size paper print, Griffiths, 1862–63.   (R.I.C.)

This was his original calling, and well into the 1880s he was still available to paint portraits, using the letters 'C.A.M.' after his name.[2] They presumably stood for 'Certificated Art Master' and the imprint on his cartes de visite described him, below the Royal Arms, as 'Artist under Government'. What this tells us is that he may have acquired an art teacher's certificate somewhere in Wales and that he was employed in art schools where pupils took examinations under the South Kensington scheme.[3] Some confirmation is provided by a notice in the Polytechnic's annual report for 1864, where we read[4] that 'Mr Griffiths, of the Truro School of Art, exhibited an excellent lithograph of Dr George Smith'. From other sources it is known that Mr H.M. Geoffroi, of Penzance, was the (visiting) head of this school.[5] Griffiths's position may have been permanent but it must also have been subsidiary.

After 1861 the Griffiths family moved to No. 32 River Street, Truro, a home they were to occupy for many years. Meanwhile, Richard Griffiths had expanded into commercial photography. If, as seems very likely, the portrait of John Garby (*Fig. 36*) is his work, the expansion had taken place by 1863. In 1867 he entered views of various Truro and district churches at the Polytechnic.[6] Further material was submitted,

all in the class for 'Professionals', in 1874, 1876 and 1878.[7]

Slightly before 1880, Mr Griffiths was joined in business by one or both of his sons. In 1875, Evan was 27 and Richard Price junior was 18. A second studio was acquired by 1873, when Griffiths was listed[8] both at the River Street home and at No. 97 Pydar Street (almost certainly a mistake for 'No. 96'). By 1878 however the latter had been given up in favour of a more central shop at No. 30 Boscawen Street, in the middle of Truro.[9] Here, Richard Price Griffiths was 'bookseller, stationer, fancy depot, portrait painter and photographer'; a fair spread for one man.

About 1880, too, the Griffiths family opened a completely new branch in Commercial Square, Newquay.[10] That town was now an up-and-coming resort, attracting large numbers of summer visitors and acting as the centre of a still unspoiled stretch of the Cornish coast. The only competition in Newquay would have come from the local stationer Frederick Waren, a photographer as early as 1881.[11]

In 1889, when Mr Griffiths senior was 70, the River Street home was no longer theirs. The shop in Boscawen Street had become only a stationer's and

Fig.37   Interior of St Mary's, Truro

Richard Griffiths's carte view, its ornate imprint being the same as that for the portrait of Frances Hunkin *(Fig.38)*, shows the interior east end of 'Old St Mary's', the medieval parish church largely demolished for its incorporation within John Loughborough Pearson's cathedral. This was one of Mr Griffiths's entries in the 1867 Polytechnic competition, for which he was awarded a 10s. prize *(35 RCPS, cat. p. 16)*. It appears to be entry No.567, entitled 'The Monument and St George's Window'.

Carte, paper print, Griffiths, before 1867.

(R.I.C.)

Fig.38 Portrait of Miss Frances Hunkin
The many who remember Joseph Wellington Hunkin, the greatly loved Cornishman who became Bishop of Truro in 1935 and died in that office in 1950, will recognise the young lady at once as a member of the same family. How nice this would have been in colour, doing justice to Mr Griffiths's rather arty composition! In the last century the Hunkins, who came from Mevagissey, lived in The Parade, Truro; Captain Thomas Hunkin at No.3, and further along J.W. Hunkin senior — coal merchant, shipowner, fervent Methodist and impromptu pavement evangelist. The future Bishop, 'Coalie' Hunkin's eldest child, was born there in 1885. Frances Hunkin belongs to the previous generation, and shows clearly the dark hair, distinctive features and short stature of her family. Carte, paper print, Griffiths, mid-late 1860s.   (Private colln.)

bookseller's establishment, and would have been run by one or both of the sons.[12] Photography, however, was continued at Newquay, and it is likely that the Griffiths parents had retired there, the better to enjoy the Atlantic waves that also lapped the shores of their native Wales. R.P. Griffiths was at the Newquay address in 1893, and probably died early in the present century.[13]

Mr Griffiths's story suggests that, having applied his art to commerce, he was fairly successful. If one takes into account the coincidence of the addresses,[14] the main photographic business was passed (by sale) to a younger Truro man, Edward Iddol Ellery, during the decade 1880–1890; and thus (*Fig. 36*) we can deduce that Ellery most probably took over the stock of Truro portrait negatives.

1. Census 1861; he is found as 'Griffith', but he spelled his name himself with a final -s-.
2. Lake 1883, 98, 132.
3. See p. 17 above.
4. 32 RCPS, xix.
5. See p. 50 above.
6. 35 RCPS, xx, xxi, xxxv, cat. p. 16.
7. 42 RCPS, cat. p. 17; 44 RCPS, cat. p. 21; 46 RCPS, cat. p. 23.
8. K 1873; the River Street number is also wrongly given as '33'.
9. H 1878, 1024; also Lake 1883.
10. K 1883.
11. Oliver, *Guide to Newquay* (4th edn., Truro, 1881), with Waren's full-page advertisement.
12. Presumably Richard — Evan became a chemist at Padstow (K 1889, 1101; K 1906, 248, 426); see K 1889, 1183; by 1897 'Miss B.A. Griffiths' (Boadicea) was proprietor or manager at Truro (so K 1897, 326).
13. Listed in K 1906 (unless this was Richard jnr.); not in K 1910.
14. Ellery was at 96 Pydar Street in K 1883, and at the Griffiths's old home, 32 River Street, in K 1889, 1182; the latter was the Ellery premises until the 1930s, and is now the eastern half of Messrs Trevail's, outfitters.

GUTCH, John Wheeley Gough
Visiting Professional: Penzance (Figs. 39–42)

The Gutch family was at Tisbury in Wiltshire during the 16th century.[1] John Gutch's great-great-grandfather and great-grandfather were successive Town Clerks of the city of Wells. His grandfather the Reverend John Gutch, F.S.A. (1746–1831), was an Oxford divine and well known as an antiquary and author;[2] and his father John Matthew Gutch, F.S.A. (1776–1861), once schoolfellow of Charles Lamb and S.T. Coleridge, became a Bristol printer and publisher.[3]

J.W.G. Gutch was born at Bristol in 1809, and duly qualified as a surgeon (M.R.C.S.L.) before travelling to Italy. He spent some time in Florence where, in 1832, he married Miss Elizabeth Frances Nicholson. Gutch may have returned to England on occasions, and was appointed a Queen's Messenger, a post he held for many years. An only child, John, was born at Florence in 1833, but died in 1838 at Swansea. The Gutches came back to Bristol during the 1830s, and from 1842 to 1856 John Gutch edited a cumulative encyclopaedia, *The Literary and Scientific Register*.[4] He travelled in parts of Britain — Wales in 1857, Cornwall in 1858 — and died at Bloomsbury Square, London, in April 1862. His widow died at Weston-super-Mare in 1869.

These general scientific interests led John Gutch at an early date into photography, an art where his competence was obvious. A book of seven photographs of Bristol churches, inscribed to a Miss Zoe King and titled 'Photographic Illustrations by J.W.G. Gutch, M.R.C.S.L.', bears a date of 1850.[5] Scenic and architectural studies of North Wales (the Gutches were probably staying at Llandudno) are known from 1857.[6] A collection of views of Bristol churches and buildings, and other individual Bristol views, belong to 1858.[7] In 1856 John Gutch supplied runs of six albumen prints to illustrate *The Sketcher*, by the

Fig.39 Lanyon Quoit

John Gutch's view was probably taken in the summer, 1858, from the shadows in the fairly late afternoon. The closeness of the grass reflects the position of this famous (but also restored) monument in a field used for cattle. The small child also appears in *Fig.42*.

Print from original plate, Gutch, 1858.

(R.I.C.)

Reverend John Eagles.[8] Major albums of his work passed, after his death, to members of his wife's Nicholson family.[9]

In 1858 John Gutch visited west Cornwall; his most likely place of stay would have been Penzance. During the August he made one hundred (or more) views of Cornish scenery and antiquities. Most are from the Land's End peninsula showing coasts, ancient houses and prehistoric stone monuments (and also Botallack and Levant mines). A few of them relate to a trip to Mullion, Kynance and The Lizard. The series of one hundred was published. Single views, 6½ by 8½ inches (whole-plate albumen prints), mounted on card, were sold for 2s. A drawing-book containing eleven views 'and a Floral Title' could be had for one guinea. Mr Gutch's outlet was the Penzance bookseller Edward Rowe,[10] but the series — together with a smaller one comprising 'Photographs of Geological Phenomena'[11] — could also be obtained from a Bristol bookseller, Mr Weston of Corn Street. A highly detailed printed label (*see illustration*) was pasted on the back of each mount.

PUBLISHED BY E. ROWE, BOOKSELLER, ETC., PENZANCE,

A SERIES OF 100 PHOTOGRAPHIC VIEWS,

Illustrating the Scenery, Antiquities, and Geological Phenomena of Penzance—The Land's End—The Lizard—St. Ives—and the localities adjoining.

Single Views, price 2s., mounted on Card Board; or in a Drawing Book, containing 11, and a Floral Title, £1:1:0.

SIZE, 6½ BY 8½.

By J. W. G. GUTCH, M. R. C. S. L. (Late Foreign Service Queen's Messenger)

Taken during the Summer of 1858.

View of Penzance from the harbour—Harbour and Shipping—The Esplanade from opposite Marine Terrace—Gulval Church—Ditto from the Village—The Rectory, Gulval—Porphyritic Rocks opposite the Esplanade, "The Chimney Rock"—Pilchard Boats—Group of Fishermen with Pilchard Nets—Newlyn from the Bridge—Tolcarne, near Penzance—Group at Tolcarne—Trereiffe, the Rev. C. V. Le Grice, near Penzance—Lanyon Cromlech—Ditto from the road—Chun Cromlech—The four Cromlechs on one sheet, viz., Lanyon, Chun, Mulfra, and Zennor—Sancreed Church—Old Cross in Sancreed Churchyard—St. Michael's Mount—Ditto from the harbour—Rocks on St. Michael's Mount—Ditto on the East side, the "Giant's Chair and Footstool"—View of Marazion from ditto—The Castle, St. Michael's Mount—Ditto from the East—Group of Boatmen, St. Michael's Mount—The Land's End—Ditto from near the Inn—Columnar Granite Rocks at ditto—Pardennick Point, ditto—Green Island and armed Knight, ditto—"First and Last Inn," Sennen—The Logan Rock, Castle Treereen—The Logan Stone—The Logan Rock, from a Drawing of Mr. Pentreath—The Logan Village—Galva Tin Mine—Group of Miners at ditto—Botallack Mine—Ditto—Huel Cock Mine—Carn Vellan Headland near ditto—Group of Miners at ditto—Levant Mine—Group of Miners at ditto—Group of Greenstone Rocks near ditto—St. Just Market Place and Church—Balleswidden Tin Mine—Old Cottage at Castallack—Ditto—Jetty and Granite Quarry, Lamorna Cove—The Merry Maidens, Druidical Circle—St. Buryan's Church and old Cross—Porthgwarrah Cove and subterraneous passage in rocks at ditto—Porthgwarrah Cove—Group of Pilchard Fishermen at ditto—Granite Rocks at Perloe Bay—Group of Rocks near ditto—Cheese Ring and Cup Rocks near Zennor, from a Drawing of Mr. Pentreath—Rogers's Tower, Castle-an-Dinas—Zennor Church Town—Logan Stone, Zennor—Zennor Quoit or Cromlech—Mulfra Quoit or Cromlech—The holed or crick Stone, Morvah—Granite Quarry, New Mill—Pengersick Castle—Village of Pengersick—Kenegie, W. Coulson, Esq.—Pendrea, R. F. Bolitho, Esq.—Trewidden, E. Bolitho, Esq.—Acton Castle, J. Lanyon, Esq.—Alverton Cottage, A. Bennett, Esq.—St. Ives, from Porthminster Point—Ditto from Penolva—Gurnard's Head—Ditto—The Lizard—Natural arch of Serpentine Rock in Kynance Cove—The Vroe Rock, Mullion Cove—The Light Houses, Lizard—The Bumbles Rock, Lizard Point.

Also, by the same Author, a SERIES OF PHOTOGRAPHS OF GEOLOGICAL PHENOMENA, illustrative of the following formations—Oolite—New Red Sandstone—Coal Measures, Pennant—Limestones below the coal—Old Red Sandstone—Slate—Quartoze Slate—Serpentine—Elvin—Granite—Hornblende—Porphory—in nearly fifty views, taken expressly to show the above named strata.

Any of the above are constantly on Sale at Mr. ROWE'S, Penzance; and Mr. WESTON'S, Bookseller, Corn St., Bristol.

Fig.40   Lanyon Quoit, again
A picture of the 'quoit' − the huge granite remnants of a late Neolithic chambered tomb, formerly encased in a long cairn of earth and boulders − taken from the other side. The gentleman reposing beneath the capstone, and the child, may be from Gutch's hosts on his visit to Cornwall.
Print from original plate, Gutch, 1858.   (R.I.C.)

In the last few years, specimens of Gutch's prints have fetched consistently high prices at auction[12] and a full collection of the one hundred Cornish photographs would (apart from present sale value) be of enormous interest as an accurate and dated record; many of the individual monuments have since 1858 been eroded, altered, and even obliterated. The Royal Institution of Cornwall possesses only one mounted print, but it has five of the original glass plates, acquired under curious circumstances. John Gutch's nephew Wilfrid Gutch (b. 1871), educated at Harrow and Cambridge, was a barrister and used at one period to take holidays in the Isle of Wight.[13] We can only guess, in the absence of better evidence, that Wilfrid Gutch inherited, along with his Nicholson cousins, some of his uncle's plates and prints; and that (while in the Isle of Wight) these passed to, or were given to, another person. In June 1940 a Mr William Dotesio, writing from the 'Isle of Wight War Service Committee' at Shanklin, offered the Institution at Truro 'a set of five negatives taken in 1858 of Cornish Cromlechs' which had come into his possession.[14] Mr Dotesio stated that these were documented − and indeed to a limited extent they must have been, since the date and subjects would not otherwise have been apparent − and that he had also sent details to (Sir) Thomas Kendrick at the British Museum.[15] The plates arrived safely at Truro in July of 1940 but, in the absence of further detail, were stored in a 'Miscellaneous Antiquities' section. Only during 1987, in the course of re-examination, were they recognised as John Gutch's work. 'I wish there were more of these early negatives' wrote George Penrose,

Fig.41 Chun Quoit
This lies a short walk from Chun Castle, an Iron Age fortress dominating a rounded hill in the Land's End peninsula. Gutch's view shows some remains of the surrounding cairn or mound; very little of it remains today. Casual robbing, for nearby field walls, must have been taking place — note the many exposed stones.
Print, from original plate, Gutch, 1858.

(R.I.C.)

then the R.I.C.'s curator, in thanking Mr Dotesio. Echoing that wish, one wonders if a further 95 miraculously remain, unbroken, in a Shanklin attic.

1. Gutch family pedigree (College of Arms, c. 1928), and info. from Mr Christopher Gutch, Maidenhead, and Mr Richard Gutch, London.

2. *Dictionary of National Biography,* and records of the Society of Antiquaries of London.

3. *Ibidem.*

4. *D.N.B.* (under J.M. Gutch).

5. Bristol Record Office, acc. no. 17563(4).

6. Sotheby's Belgravia sale catalogues; 29 Jun 1979, lots 187−194, 24 Oct 1979, lots 266−274, 29 Oct 1982, lot 117 (37 views of North Wales, sold for £3300).

7. Bristol Record Office, acc. no. 17567(3).

8. Gernsheim 1984, 23 (no. 52).

9. Info. Reverend Nigel Nicholson, Guildford.

10. C 1864, 41 and 114; CC 843. Rowe (1798−1878) was a Penzance man, and had the lion's share of that town's bookselling.

11. Fifty or so, but mostly non-Cornish.

12. Cf. Sotheby's Belgravia, 27 Oct 1978, lot 163 (album of 45 photos given to A.J. Nicholson, £2000); 12 Mar 1982, lot 410 (album of 50 photos, ditto, £2420).

13. Info. Mr Christopher Gutch, Maidenhead.

14. R.I.C., Accessions file, 1940.

15. Search of the relevant Departmental correspondence, British Museum (kindly conducted by Dr Ian Kinnes), fails to reveal precisely what information Mr Dotesio was able to supply.

Fig.42 Zennor Quoit
The fourth of John Gutch's views of antiquities included here is of Zennor Quoit, with its enormous slipped capstone (left). The child from *Fig.39* appears again, besides an older sister (?); the man on the left looks like a local who has been acting as guide.
Print, from original plate, Gutch, 1858.   (R.I.C.)

GUTTERES, Frederic E.
Amateur: Falmouth

The Reverend Mr Gutteres spent four or five years at Falmouth as the Chaplain of H.M.S. *Russell.* She was a vessel of 1751 tons, 60 guns and 200 horse-power, stationed along with her tender H.M. Screw Gunboat *Hind* as headquarters of the Falmouth District, Coastguard Service.[1] There was plenty of opportunity for officers of this service to attend Polytechnic events and to socialise in and around the town. Mr Gutteres was a champion of the Royal Cornwall Sailors' Home at Falmouth, on behalf of which he preached and published a sermon delivered on 20 March 1859.[2]

He was also a keen photographer. The first indication comes in 1858 when his name is in the list of those who 'kindly lent pictures for exhibition' at the Polytechnic's autumn gathering.[3] The loan is specified as 'Photographs of Sebastopol, &c.' and, since it transpires that he himself used a camera, these Crimean views are more likely to have been his own than commercially-purchased ones made by, say, Roger Fenton. Indeed Mr Gutteres may well have been a Royal Navy chaplain during the Crimean War.

In 1859 he submitted, this time within the competition, 'a book of very good photographs'; good enough to win First Bronze Medal.[4] A further series was entered in the following year.[5] In 1861, which was possibly the last year of his stay at Falmouth, a set of eleven stereoscopic views aroused admiration.[6] It is a pity that none can be traced. Falmouth was a busy port, naval and mercantile, and there are surprisingly few early studies of its shipping.

1. Wa 1864, 40.
2. Barclay Fox, 169; the sermon, BC 200.
3. 26 RCPS, xxi.
4. 27 RCPS, xxxviii; RCG 30 Sept 1859.
5. 28 RCPS, xxxix.
6. 29 RCPS, xlix −1.

HAMBLY, Samuel Symons
Amateur: Wadebridge

Mr Hambly was a member of a very old North Cornwall family, who lived at West Park House, Sladesbridge[1] − in the neighbourhood of Egloshayle, the older settlement on the east bank of the river Camel, now eclipsed by its offshoot Wadebridge on the opposite side. In 1868 he entered a number of photographic views in the Polytechnic's competition; they were listed[2] as being of 'Wadebridge, Trevose Head, St Endellion and St Kew', all within an easy ride of his home. A search among albums now in the possession of his collateral descendants[3] reveals some photographs of a later date, unascribed, but so far nothing corresponding to this 1868 series.

1. CC 312.
2. 36 RCPS, cat. p. 19.
3. Info. Dr Francis Hambly, Camborne.

HAMBLY, W.J.
Amateur: Camborne

All we know of this gentleman as a photographer is that one of his views, 'Durham Cathedral', formed one of the ten-shilling prizes in the Polytechnic's 1863 Art Union of Cornwall draw.[1] His address was given as Camborne; he was not a subscriber, or member, at the Polytechnic; and his surname is too widespread for him to be identified, in the absence of further detail. Given the subject of his photograph, the likelihood that he had visited the North of England in an amateur outing with John Rule of Camborne and Francis Luke of Scorrier is discussed under the entry for the latter.[2]

1. See p. 17 above.
2. See p. 87 below.

HAMPTON, T.A.
Visiting Professional: Liskeard

In autumn, 1856, Mr Hampton issued an advertisement[1] addressed to the inhabitants of Liskeard and neighbourhood, announcing that he had fitted up 'a Most Commodious suite of apartments' at Mr Dingle's Union Hotel in the town, for the purpose of making photographic portraits. Ambrotypes, or small cased collodion positives, would be indicated at this date. The investment suggests a visit of several weeks or even a few months. Mr Hampton further stated that he was 'just from Messrs Blake and Smith'. The grandeur of the claim lessens when we find that neither he nor his principals were known in London at this period.[2] In fact, he was referring to some now-forgotten Plymouth partnership, probably known to those Liskeard people who ever went to Plymouth. Mr Robert Smith of No. 9 The Octagon, was later advertising portraits from his Photographic Depot;[3] Mr John Blake was at the same time at No. 2 Cecil Street, Devonport, and may later have been part of the firm of Blake Brothers, No. 99 Fore Street.[4] Mr Hampton himself was presumably also a Plymouth man.

1. Info. Mr John L. Rapson, Liskeard; LG 13 September 1856.
2. Not in Pritchard.
3. H 1862, 685 and separate advert.
4. H 1862, 685 and 749.

HARDING, Lewis
Amateur: Polperro (Fig. 43)

Mr Harding, born in 1806, was the son of John Cooke Harding and of Mary, the sixth child and youngest daughter of the Reverend Sir Harry Trelawny (sixth baronet: 1756−1834) of Trelawne, Pelynt. Lewis Harding returned from Australia in 1846 with some unspecified nervous complaint, settled at Trelawne − home of his mother's ancient kin − and spent the year 1847 in compiling a diary of observations about a large colony of rooks. Some time after 1850 he moved to a cottage, owned by the Trelawny family, in Polperro; Osprey Cottage. By the middle of the 1850s he had become interested in photography. Until well into the 1870s he practised this art, and nearly all the surviving prints of his work were pasted, by another hand, into the MS of Dr Jonathan Couch's *History of Polperro,* the village where Couch practised as a doctor and spent much time as a naturalist. This work, completed in 1856, was edited after Dr Couch's death by his son Thomas and published in 1871.[1] Harding died in 1893.

The identification of Mr Harding as the un-named photographer, and moreover as an early amateur of outstanding interest, followed the brilliant investigations of Mr Andrew Lanyon and Dr Frank Turk.[2] Lewis Harding's output may have started as early as 1854; he was certainly photographing by 1858. It constitutes an extraordinary, if isolated, facet of Cornish photography (there is no evidence that Harding was ever in contact with any other photographers locally). Since it is desirable that his images should be separately published, a single example only is shown here.

1. The R.I.C. owns this, as well as other Couch MSS.
2. Lanyon 1976; Lanyon 1984a.

HART, Thomas
Professional: Falmouth (Fig. 44)

Thomas Hart the artist was an interesting man. He would be even more so, if connected with the Cornish-Jewish family of Lazarus Hart of Marazion (d. 1803) whose son Lemon − so named in honour of the Lemon family of Carclew (cf. *Fig. 129*) − became a wine and spirit merchant in Penzance and, as a contractor to the Royal Navy, gave his name to that famous restorative, 'Lemon Hart Rum'.[1] The connection, if any, is obscure; more immediately, Thomas was the son of a senior foreman at William Broad's, the large firm of general traders in Falmouth.

Mr Hart would have been born between 1820 and 1830. He began to paint professionally, and built up a considerable reputation. By 1854 he was exhibiting his

Polperro Fishermen in Fishing Costume (Mr. Harding).

Fig.43 *Polperro Fishermen in Fishing Costume*
Typical of Lewis Harding's style, this shows three of the Polperro men carefully posed near the harbour (note the artistic touch of the trailing rope). The handwriting below is Thomas Couch's, and this image was inserted into one of his father's manuscripts.
Albumen print, Harding, late 1850s.   (R.I.C.)

paintings at the Polytechnic and still living in Falmouth.[2] The next year, he started to act as a judge in the 'Fine Arts' section of the Polytechnic's annual competitions.[3] Frequent reference is made in the Society's Reports to his 'effective marine pictures' and similar productions. He either took private pupils, or instructed in some early and private art-school in the town; in 1857 no less than eleven pupils of 'Mr T. Hart, F.S.A.' won prizes in the Schools Productions section of the competition.[4] Between 1865 and 1880, Thomas Hart exhibited work in London, in 1872−73 at the Royal Academy. He was elected a Fellow of the Society of Artists during the late 1850s − hence the 'F.S.A.' suffix. This usage was frowned upon by the Society of Antiquaries of London, whose own Fellows had a much older, and pre-emptive, claim to the same letters.

Fig.44 *Portrait of an Unknown Artist*
The carte de visite bears Thomas Hart's Plymouth imprint, of '10 Flora Place', the address from which he seems to have worked about 1859−60. The sitter appears to be an artist. His features give rise to the feeling that one ought to be able to recognise so distinctive a face, but there is no clue as to his identity, and he may have been a colleague from Plymouth's circle of marine artists and teachers of painting.
Carte, paper print, Hart, c. 1860.   (Author)

Though Thomas Hart, until the 1870s, usually gave Falmouth as his address, and made his living both from sales of his work and from teaching painting, there was a period in his life when he practised as a commercial photographer. This he undertook, not in Falmouth, but in Plymouth. One possible explanation is that he had become involved with the much larger circle of marine painters and art-classes then flourishing in Plymouth and that − reversing the custom of the few Plymouth photographers like J.E. Palmer[5] who had branch studios in Cornwall − Mr Hart travelled to Plymouth one or two days a week. After 1859, railway travel would have made this easy. A carte de visite has an imprint of a crowned circular device with 'T. HART FSA' and the address of 10, Flora Place, a small road off Union Street. We know that by 1861−62 his studio had moved to No.16, George Street, Plymouth.[6] In 1862, he married a Miss Louisa Hallamore of Penzance[7] and no doubt abandoned the Plymouth visits at the same time. The same year, he entered some photographs at the Polytechnic;[8] the fact that a further entry,[9] in 1863, consisted of 'a large number of cartes de visite', looks as if portraiture was too useful a side-line to give up at once.

By 1864 he and Mrs Hart, with the first of their (seven) children, were living at No. 7 Upper Berkeley Place, Falmouth.[10] Here, Hart was now listed solely as 'artist'; however, in subsequent years he was often a judge for the Polytechnic's photography section in the annual competitions,[11] and we can suspect that commercial photography was maintained alongside higher forms of art.

Many of Thomas Hart's known paintings featured The Lizard. While the family was still at Falmouth, he probably bought a second house there − Polbrean, at Landewednack. By 1872 the Harts had decided to move to Polbrean, and Mr Hart became Secretary to Landewednack School. In 1889 he was still there, as a private resident and artist,[12] and is thought to have died about 1910. His third son Sydney Ernest Hart also became a successful artist, working from The Lizard, as did a third member of the family, Thomas Dyke Hart, perhaps a grandson.

1. CC 325.
2. 22 RCPS, xiii.
3. 23 RCPS, xxi.
4. 25 RCPS, xxx−xxxi.

Fig. 45 Redruth − the old railway station
The broader date bracket for this view of the former railway station is approximately between the mid-1850s and the early 1880s; local historians and railway enthusiasts favour a date before 1865, and if by Hawke this would be correct. Carn Brea, crowned by its castle and the Basset Monument, dominates the background.
Print (from plate), Hawke, c. 1863.

(R.I.C.)

5. See p. 97 below.
6. H 1862, 685.
7. CC 325.
8. 30 RCPS, xxv, xxxvi.
9. 31 RCPS, xxiv.
10. Wa 1864, 63, 87.
11. 1870–72, 1875–76, 1880.
12. K 1889, 1036.

HAWKE, Edward. jnr.
Amateur: Gwennap (Fig. 45)

This entry is inferential. Among the 1863 entrants at the Polytechnic's annual competition was a certain Mr Hawke ('Mr Hawke and Mr Trull likewise exhibited very fine collections . . .').[1] Elsewhere in the same Annual Report we have the comment[2] that 'strangers about to visit Cornwall at our next exhibition may see in Mr Hawke's series the features of the railway along which they will have to travel'.

It is a pity that we are not given Mr Hawke's initials. There have long been indications that some person, other than R.P. Yeo,[3] was making images of scenes along the Cornwall Railway, and unascribed views of stations and broad-gauge trains appear from time to time. One, well-known, portrait photographer at this period was Mr John Hawke of Union Street, Stonehouse (now part of Plymouth)[4] but, as far as is known, he confined himself to cartes de visite made at his studio. There is no record of his having worked in Cornwall nor, unlike his Plymouth and Devonport colleagues (Cox, May and Yeo), did he ever exhibit at the Polytechnic.

We can therefore consider the idea that the railway photographer was a Cornish amateur. One member of the Polytechnic in the 1860s was 'E. Hawke, jnr.', in a group of nine members from Gwennap and area, others being the Misses C. and J. Hawke, presumably his sisters. This is an identifiable family. Edward Henry Hawke was the proprietor of a Rope Manufactory at Tolgullow, Gwennap, and by 1866 his son Edward junior was his partner.[5] In the preceding generation a Miss M. Hawke, who would have been Edward junior's aunt, married a Mr Hugh Sims (1799–1877) of Whitehall, a large isolated house in Scorrier.[6] The relevance of this is that by 1863 the Sims had sold, leased or otherwise conveyed Whitehall to another local family, the Lukes; and Francis Luke junior happens to be known to us, also in 1863, as an amateur photographer.[7] Lukes and Hawkes were in some way connected. There is at least a hint of an amateur photographic circle.

The main railway line passes very close to Whitehall, on its northern side. If Edward Hawke junior was the railway photographer, he is probably responsible for one well-known view; that of the old Redruth railway station. It has been published before,[8] but in this context it can stand re-issue. The date must be between 1852 and 1880, and the view is not otherwise attributed. This station is only a few miles from

Tolgullow. Edward Hawke junior, the rope-maker, is on balance a little more likely than John Hawke of Plymouth, the portrait photographer. It would be pleasing to think there are, somewhere, others of the 1863 'features of the railway' awaiting discovery.

1. 31 RCPS, xxiv.
2. *Ibidem*, xxxiii.
3. See p. 139 below.
4. Later at No. 8 George Street, Plymouth.
5. H 1862, 926; D 1866, Gwennap p. 14.
6. H 1862, 926; BC 653; CC 901.
7. See p. 87 below.
8. Michell, Frank, *Annals of an Ancient Cornish Town – Redruth* (Redruth, 1978), 139.

HAWKEN, Thomas Edward
Professional: Lostwithiel (Fig. 46)

There were several Lostwithiel families of this name. In 1830, John Hawken was a tailor in the town,[1] with William Hawken (his son?) listed in the

Fig.46 St Bartholomew's, Lostwithiel
The 12th-century Borough of Lostwithiel boasts the fine old church of St Bartholomew (actually as a chapelry to Lanlivery, a nearby and older parish, until the 15th century). The spire, an unusual feature in Cornwall with its many solid granite church towers, is possibly 14th century, and has been claimed to show Breton influence. Mr Hawken's interesting view is probably the earliest photographic depiction of the church.
Carte, paper print, Hawken, late 1850s(?)   (Private colln.)

same trade in 1847.[2] Five years later, we can also find[3] Richard Hawken the stone-mason and Thomas Hawken, maltster. By 1856, the Hawkens were represented by Thomas, the maltster, in North Street, and William, the tailor and woollen draper, in Fore Street.[4] It is a safe bet that all these men were cousins in some degree.

Thomas Edward Hawken, baptised at Lostwithiel on 8 January 1837, was the son of the stone-mason Richard and his wife Ann. His career broke new ground, and by 1873 he was listed[5] as 'watchmaker and photographer, Queen Street'. In the latter capacity his work is rare. Two cartes are known[6] both with an imprint in green, showing a displayed eagle above the wording 'T.E. Hawken, Photographer, Lostwithiel'. Because of the gap (between 1856 and 1873) in Kelly's Directories, we are entitled only to infer that Mr Hawken opened his business after 1856 — he would have been 21 the year after — and that the photographic side-line is inherently likely to have begun earlier than 1873. The style of the surviving carte views does indeed suggest a decade earlier. It would be interesting to know whether T.E. Hawken was in any way associated with W.H. Broad,[7] his Bodmin contemporary in the watch-making and part-time photographic line, who had Lostwithiel connections.

T.E. Hawken is not found after 1873; by 1883, the business at the same Lostwithiel shop (No. 14, Queen Street) was conducted by *William* Edward Hawken, who was also a photographer in addition to watch-making and jewellery, is listed here in *Appendix II* below, and continued until at least 1902.[8] The most likely explanation is that he was T.E. Hawken's younger brother, who succeeded him in the period 1873−83.[9]

1. P 1830, 151.
2. W 1847, 97.
3. S 1852, 32.
4. K 1856, 61.
5. K 1873, 805.
6. Private colln.
7. See p. 36 above.
8. K 1883, 943; K 1902, 198 (last entry).
9. H 1878, 863, lists confusingly ' Hawken, Edwin', w/maker, photogr.

HAYMAN, Henry
Professional: Launceston (Figs. 47 to 49)

The Haymans were specialised merchants in Launceston. The main concentration of their name occurs around Plymouth and they may have come in from Devon. In 1856, Henry Hayman was offering his Launceston customers[1] the services of 'a fancy repository, jeweller, berlin wool warehouse and haberdasher' (Berlin wool, now forgotten, was fine dyed wool used in tapestry or embroidering). To this mixture he added photography; how soon after 1856 is uncertain, but probably before 1860. Hayman's work — cartes de

visite, but also plate views of Launceston, its surrounds, and the adjoining areas of Devon — is of high quality. In 1866, despite the considerable distance, he entered a selection of his scenic images at the Polytechnic,[2] and not many years later the shop in Church Street, Launceston, was listed as a photographic business.[3] At this time, the Haymans further enlarged their commercial scope, and part of the shop became a Pianoforte, Harmonium and Music Warehouse.[4]

Around 1870, Henry Hayman was joined in his multiple venture by his son. Carte imprints now proclaimed H. Hayman & Son, of Church Street, Portrait, Group and Architectural Photographers. From then onward photography and music were promoted in a happy artistic balance, berlin wool and other fripperies being relegated to the past.

By 1889 the Haymans' 'artistic photographs of North Cornwall',[5] usually sold as sepia-toned half-plate prints, covered Bude, Boscastle, Tintagel, Crackington (Haven), Trebarwith and Bossiney, encroaching deeply into what, photographically, had been Thorn territory.[6] It is not easy, unless one looks for the tiny marginal blind-stamping, to distinguish between certain Thorn and Hayman products (though the Thorn brothers do not seem to have made views in Launceston). Henry Hayman's business is not found after 1893.[7]

1. K 1856, 42.
2. 34 RCPS, xxxii.
3. K 1873.
4. P 1876, 65.
5. Weighell's *North Cornwall Guide* (Launceston, 1889).
6. See p. 125 below.
7. K 1893, last entry.

HEATH, William
Visiting Professional: S.E. Cornwall (Fig. 50)

Mr Heath was a Plymouth man, baptised on 12 October 1823 at 'Granby or Mount Street Independent Chapel', son of William Heath and his wife Alice Cornish. He became one of the best-known Plymouth photographers. By 1873, he was in business at No. 24 George Street, a central address,[1] and a slightly later extended entry[2] described him as 'optician and mathematical instrument maker, photographer and optician to the Royal Eye Infirmary, Plymouth'. During the 1880s he formed a partnership with Henry Bullingham — carte and cabinet portrait imprints[3] are of 'Heath & Bullingham, Photographers, 24 George Street' — though Mr Bullingham later departed for his own business in London[4] and, by 1897, William Heath (as 'William Heath & Co.') was trading, still at the same address, under his own name.[5]

In most Cornish family albums, Mr Heath's portraits are amply represented; he was much patronised by Cornish people visiting Plymouth. However, earlier in his career he was marketing stereoscopic views. Four

Fig.47   A Scene at The Target May 17th 1861 — 'Commence Firing!'

The ivy-clad tower of Launceston Castle features in numerous Hayman views, and the attribution here is virtually certain. The 6th Cornwall Rifle Volunteer Corps was formed at Launceston on 10 January 1860, through the efforts of the Archer family of Trelaske. Edward Archer (b. 1816) received his Volunteer commission as a Major in 1861, and by 1874 was honorary colonel of the 2nd (East Cornwall) Battalion of the Rifle Volunteers. In this scene, an officer and bugler pose in front of five privates, with a sergeant and corporal at the back. The men hold long, scoop-action, Martini Henry rifles. The officer is either Edward Archer himself, or else John Dingley, a Launceston solicitor, who was elected Ensign at the November 1859 inaugural meeting and became captain commanding the corps in late 1861.

Albumen print, mounted in album, Hayman, 1861.   (Cornwall C.R.O., D.D.A. 100)

Fig.48 6th Cornwall Rifles Volunteers − A Scene After The Target

It seems unlikely that there was ever a range inside the precincts of Launceston Castle (then, as now, a public park) and the clay pipes, beer and general air of relaxation all suggest a pose. The uniform is grey cloth, with black or dark blue braid sleeve-knots; the caps are grey 'kepis' with dark cloth band and patent-leather peaks. On his fore-arm the bugler has an embroidered double-bugle device, and the sergeant and corporal have silver lace chevrons. For the men the cap ornament is a plain stringed bugle horn in white metal; the officer's (see *Fig.47*) is a French horn with '6' in the centre, surmounted by a crown or possibly Plume of Feathers, all in silver. Waistbelts are black leather with oxidised snake buckles. Shoulder-belts and cartridge pouches are black, or dark brown, leather. The sergeant (seated, right) has a silvered lion-head boss, whistle and chain on his shoulder-belt.

Albumen print, mounted, Hayman, 1861.   (Cornwall C.R.O., D.A.A. 100)

Fig.49 Southgate, Launceston
The handsome old Southgate still stands. It marks the exit, in the direction of England, from the medieval walled town. In the 15th century the lower room over the arch served as a prison, with caged cells, the upper room being kept for debtors. Hayman's carte view, with his first imprint, is not long after 1860; it shows the building before certain alterations were carried out by the Launceston Historical Society, which for many years used part of it as a town museum.
Carte, paper print, Hayman, early 1860s.   (R.I.C.)

surviving examples,[6] which must be part of a wider series, were made in the Rame peninsula, the five small parishes of south-east Cornwall directly opposite Plymouth (and containing the park at Mount Edgcumbe). Identical in style, they have no printed labels and are labelled in ink by the same hand — in itself an indication of an early date — but one of them is also blind-stamped 'Wm. Heath'. The compositions are attractive and the stereographs are probably early within the period 1860−70.

William Heath, unlike his fellow-Plymothians May and Yeo, did not work in west Cornwall; nor did he send any work to the Polytechnic. This early foray into the Rame area was possibly his only Cornish field-venture.

1. K Devon 1873, 616.
2. White Devon 1878−79, 636.
3. Examples, R.I.C. collection.
4. Pritchard, 32; at 25 Harrington Road, S.W., in 1891.
5. K Devon 1897, 1053; see also Fenner 1986, 121.
6. Author's colln.

HENDERSON, James
Visiting Professional: Launceston

James Henderson was an early, and subsequently widely known, London portrait photographer.[1] In 1855 he made a visit to Launceston, during that autumn. A press notice went as follows:[2] 'For A Short Time Only. Photographic Portraits in the highest style of the Art. Mr James Henderson (from 204 Regent Street, London) begs to inform the Nobility, Gentry and Inhabitants of Launceston and its vicinity that he had opened Rooms in Westgate Street, Launceston, for the purpose of taking Portraits by this interesting and truthful art.'

What the inhabitants of Launceston probably did not know was that James Henderson was in the middle of a significant episode in early photographic history. In 1854, W.H. Fox Talbot had moved to obtain an injunction against Henderson in the Court of Chancery, on the grounds that Henderson was using a certain process to make paper prints for sale and thus infringing Fox Talbot's patent.[3] The case caused a great deal of interest in photographic circles; feeling ran against Fox Talbot for what was seen as an unreasonable restriction; and many other photographers had a personal concern as to the outcome. Eventually, in 1856, Fox Talbot was defeated in the court, with damages of £150, and taxed costs for Henderson of £210.3s.6d. The records of the engagement[4] include the information that, as late as April 1856, James Henderson was still in Launceston — a stay of some eighteen months. Presumably he returned to London after the judgement.

1. Pritchard 55 − at 204 Regent Street, W., in 1854−55.
2. WB 12 Oct 1855.
3. Arnold 1977, 198 ff.
4. *Op.cit.,* 209 (Ladock Abbey letters, LA 56−18).

HIGGS, William Henry
Professional: Bodmin

Mr Higgs is another instance of a local photographer whose participation in the art we know only from scattered allusions. In 1872, a newspaper notice[1] advertising the services of a visiting surgeon-dentist stated that he might be consulted in Bodmin 'at Mr W.H. Higgs's, Photographic Artist, China, Glass and Fancy Repository, next the Post Office'. Without this, one would hardly have known that the fancy repository offered portrait-taking. Not until the following year is Mr Higgs even mentioned in a directory,[2] and then only as a stationer and fancy warehouse proprietor, Fore Street, Bodmin.

He was baptised at Lanlivery, a village some way south of Bodmin, on 11 July 1827, son of Samuel Nicholas Higgs and his wife Maria. A connection with Bodmin may be indicated by an earlier mention of a Mr Henry Higgs (an uncle ?), hairdresser of Fore Street.[3] A degree of commercial versatility was present; a decade later, Henry Higgs was mentioned[4] as an 'ironmonger and toy dealer'. It may have been his shop that W.H. Higgs eventually acquired for his Fancy

Fig.50 Empacombe, Mount Edgcumbe, Cornwall
The title is William Heath's. Empacombe in the parish of Maker was a demesne farm adjoining the Mount Edgcumbe estate. It stands in a sheltered valley near the coast. The house itself is a modified late 17th-century dwelling, and the 18th-century folly (right) concealed the Mount Edgcumbe kitchen garden. Early views of individual houses in the Rame Peninsula parishes are rare indeed, and Mr Heath's nice composition does justice to an unusual subject.
Stereograph, Heath, early-mid-1860s. (Author)

Repository. Given such greater security, Mr Higgs was able to contemplate marriage, and on 14 June 1865 he was wedded to Ann Badgery, at Bodmin. Their shop, as we know, was in existence in 1873; but by 1883 the business, at that address, is listed as belonging to Mrs Annie Higgs[5] with the implication that she was by then his widow.

On 13 November 1860, John Tremayne of Heligan, St Ewe, son and heir of John Hearle Tremayne (1780−1851 and an M.P. for the county, 1806−1825), married Mary Charlotte Martha, eldest daughter of Baron Vivian of Glynn, at Bodmin.[6] The newspaper report of this grand social occasion tells us that 'Messrs

Oke and Higgs of Bodmin were successful in photographing groups of the wedding party'. Mr Oke's part is discussed further[7] along with the bridegroom's own interest in photography; the report is evidence that W.H. Higgs was taking images, for money, as early as 1860.

1. RCG 18 May 1872.

2. K 1873, 714.

3. W 1847, 13; S 1852, 6.

4. H 1862, 796.

5. K 1883, 825.

6. RCG 16 November 1860, p. 4 col. 4.

7. See p. 96 below.

HOCKING, Samuel
Amateur: Camborne

The occasion of Robert Hunt's lecture and photographic show in 1859 at the Camborne Literary Institution has already been mentioned.[1] Another, rare, glimpse of this body's proceedings comes from a report in 1870.[2] 'The photographic collection was particularly rich, the principal contribution being by Mr S. Hocking, whose contributions numbered no fewer than 45 subjects, all of great excellence'. Others showing their work at what seems to have been a New Year conversazione were Captain F. Townley Parker, Mr White, and the local professional William Piper.[3]

In Camborne at this date, the name 'S. Hocking' immediately conjures up a vision of the novelist Silas K. Hocking (1850–1935); but in 1870 he was elsewhere, training for the United Methodist Free Church ministry to which he belonged for some years. The photographer, whose camera-work must have started well before 1870, would have been Samuel Hocking, a prominent member of the Institution and a Camborne watch- and clock-maker.[4] As with other photographers in Cornwall, this particular business seems frequently to have been combined with a photographic subsidiary. It is assumed that Mr Hocking's interest was entirely that of an amateur enthusiast.

1. See p. 16 above.
2. RCG 8 Jan 1870.
3. See pp. 98 and 99 below.
4. S 1852, 11; H 1862, 807 (Market Place, Camborne).

HUNT, Robert, F.R.S.
Professional: Falmouth (Fig. 51)

Since any mention of Robert Hunt's life and achievements, other than a full-length biography,[1] can be no more than an apology for appropriate treatment only the barest outline is given here. He was born at Devonport (Stoke Damerel parish) on 6 September 1807, son of Robert Hunt, ship's carpenter – drowned before his son's birth – and Honour Thomas of St Levan. Half-Cornish only, he more than contributed to a dozen aspects of Cornwall's cultural and scientific progress. In his early schooling he showed remarkable memory and aptitude. His mother's tiny Navy pension proving insufficient, Robert Hunt's career as a chemist started when he was 12, in the dispensary side of pupillage with London medical men, and then the management of a small dispensary. In 1827 he inherited some money from his paternal grandfather, and in 1831 joined his mother, who had re-married, at Penzance; here Hunt and his uncle James Thomas opened a chemist's shop. In 1834 Robert Hunt was able to marry Harriet Swanson from Stoke Damerel, probably a childhood sweetheart, their first son (Robert) being born at Christmas.

It was during this Penzance period – interspersed with periods in London – that Hunt first involved himself in adult education, at the new Penzance Mechanics' Institution. He progressed to analytical chemistry and published his first paper in 1838. By 1839 he had become interested, as a chemist, in the first attempt to evolve a method of making direct-positive photographic images on paper. He was successful, published his discovery, and during 1840 tried to market it. During all this he was in touch with Sir John Herschel and through him the Royal Society. In Cornwall, Robert Hunt's reputation was already such that in 1840, on T.B. Jordan's resignation,[2] the Polytechnic at Falmouth looked no further for a replacement. Here, Hunt was inspired by the President, Sir Charles Lemon, to establish classes for young miners and to provide the chemistry lectures; and, looking onwards, past the 1859 creation of the Miners' Association of Cornwall and Devon in which Hunt was also influential, one can say that Hunt and Lemon laid the foundations for the eventual Camborne School of Mines.

This practical interest in mining, a subject he rapidly mastered, led to Hunt being offered the post of Keeper of Mining Records in London in 1845 (again following T.B. Jordan). Once in London, though he never neglected either the Polytechnic or his myriad other contacts in Cornwall, Hunt was an established figure. From 1840 he was active in the British Association for the Advancement of Science. Involved in the 1851 Great Exhibition, he joined the Society of Arts[3] in 1852, and in 1851 was appointed Professor of Mechanical Science at the new School of Mines attached to the Geological Museum (now the Royal School of Mines). In June 1854 he was elected Fellow of the Royal Society. Schemes, surveys, publications, editorial posts and more fellowships and memberships filled his working days. He returned to the fray as a champion of mining education, when the Miners' Association was founded, and continued to publish, principally upon the subject of mining in Britain. A fuller account could include details of Hunt the poet, Hunt the would-be mystic novelist, Hunt the pioneer collector of Cornish folklore, Hunt a mainstay of the South Kensington scheme and every form of Art and Science education. Life was simply not long enough.

Robert Hunt suffered illnesses in early life. His health was never good and like Charles Darwin he may have suffered from migraine and nervous indispositions. He died in 1887, his memory honoured by numerous tributes[4] and the creation of a Hunt Memorial Museum at Redruth.

He probably never thought of himself as a photographer. Yet, in James Y. Tong's words, 'Robert Hunt, Sir John Herschel, and William Henry Fox Talbot are probably the three most important English pioneers in photography'.[5] He invented processes; his book, *A Popular Treatise on the Art of Photography*[6] was the first general manual on the subject ever published in English, and was the stepping-stone to his later books on his own broader interest − photography, optics and light. From all accounts Hunt was in the first rank as a popular lecturer, sparing no effort to inform, elucidate, and even to expound unpublished results. Audiences at the Falmouth Polytechnic, in this respect, were photographically speaking privileged indeed, and the amateur following so inspired must of course have been much larger than the, fortuitously recorded, sample of names given in the present book. Mercurial, brilliant, always as helpful as he was enthusiastic, Hunt must have been a most stimulating companion and talker. The present writer − whose great-great-grandfather knew and much admired Robert Hunt[7] − regrets, not for the first time, that he himself was born in 1928 instead of 1828.

Soon after his Polytechnic appointment, and move to Falmouth, Robert Hunt wrote (17 January 1841) to Sir John Herschel, airing the idea of writing a popular treatise on photography. Compilation of this book continued alongside his duties as Secretary, as did the correspondence with Herschel and Hunt's attempt to discover precisely the scientific details of the Fox Talbot process (named by him 'Calotype' in February 1841). Eventually the two were in a wary correspondence. In the autumn of 1841 Robert Hunt sent to Talbot some of his 'camera views', as an indication of what might be done using Hunt's system of developing and fixing images. We know that, in correspondence with Herschel on May 16, 1840, Hunt − having received specimens of Talbot's photographs − replied 'I have produced somewhat similar pictures − by acting on the bromide of silver by hydrochloric acid'.[8] At some unknown date, either in 1840 or more probably when sending examples of his work to Fox Talbot in 1841, Robert Hunt submitted to Sir John Herschel five views, today preserved in the Herschel Collection at the Science Museum, London. Four have now deteriorated to the point of near-invisibility; one is still visible. It could be argued (as Fox Talbot did indeed argue in Hunt's presence in 1844[9]) that these independent variations on the 'Calotype' process should not be given confusingly novel titles. Hunt's particular system was given, by him, the name of 'Energiatype' − this name was announced in 1844 in a communication to the *Athenaeum*.[10]

The Energiatype, by courtesy of the Science Museum, is illustrated here *(Fig. 51)*. It was recently brought to light by Andrew Lanyon[11] who realised that it should show '. . . houses, probably in Falmouth'. Another print of the same image doubtless went to Fox Talbot, and it should certainly be dated no later than 1841, probably made on a summer's late afternoon. As Mr John Ward, Curator of Photography and Cinematography at the Science Museum, acutely guessed might be the case, it was made in Robert Hunt's front garden. From 1840 to 1845, Robert and Harriet Hunt were living in Berkeley Vale, Falmouth. The number of their house (in the manner of the period, usually omitted from correspondence) was No. 20. Early in 1987 the present writer, armed with a copy print, walked around all the front gardens in that part of the town and eventually *(Fig. 52)* managed to reproduce the view. The Hunts' home is today, because of re-numbering, No. 4 Kimberley Park Road and by courtesy of the present occupant the Energiatype was precisely imitated. It is peculiarly appropriate that this, among the few really early but still identifiable townscape images in British photographic history, comes from Falmouth; the town where Robert Hunt spent five, intensely formative, years and through the Polytechnic contributed so much to photography in his adopted Cornwall.

1. Cf. Tong 1973 (Hunt as photographer); Pearson 1976 (admirable short memoir of Hunt's scientific work and Cornish involvement).

2. See p. 81 below.

3. See p. 14 above, and Stirling 1981, 1982.

4. Tong 1973, xlix, 'Notes'.

5. *Ibidem,* ix.

6. R. Griffin & Co., Glasgow (1841); facsimile edition, Tong 1973.

7. Captain Charles Thomas (1794−1868), manager of Dolcoath Mine and a lifelong practical exponent of mining education − 22 RCPS (1854), 28−35; articles in WB and RCG during 1855; *Quarterly Mtg. Miners' Assoc. of Cornwall & Devon, 16 Apr 1863* (Truro, 1863), 11−16.

8. Royal Society, Herschel Letters HS.10.85 (see Tong 1973, xviii).

9. York, British Association meeting − Arnold 1977, 211 n.

10. 'The Energiatype', *Athenaeum*, no. 866 (June 1844), 500−01, and no. 869 (June 1844), 575. See also Hunt, *The Practice of Photography* (R. Griffin & Co, London & Glasgow, 1857), 113−5.

11. Lanyon 1984b, Fig. 1.

Fig.51   A View From Our Front Garden

Robert Hunt must have set up his camera, or apparatus, on the lawn of his front garden at what was then No.20 Berkeley Vale, Falmouth — now No.4 Kimberley Park Road — in the late afternoon. No.22 is the neighbouring house in the centre of the view, and the ornamental iron railings stood in the same position until removed for scrap in the 1940s.

'Energiatype' (new print), Hunt, 1841.   (Science Museum)

Fig.52   One Hundred and Thirty-Six Years Later

Taken in the front garden of what is now No.4 Kimberley Park Road, Falmouth, by kind permission of the occupier (back to camera), this view replicates Robert Hunt's of 1841. The tiny yew bush has now grown to a small tree; the iron railings were partly removed in 1940, but some survive across the garden of No.6, the white house, centre. No.4 began its existence as No.20, Berkeley Vale (the Hunt home) and No.6 was then No.22.

Photograph: 35 mm. print, author, March 1987).

Fig.53 St Michael's Mount

William Jenkyns's impressive view of the Mount is taken at ground level on the north-west side; the foreground will be unfamiliar because, since the last century, trees and shrubs have been planted and some extra pathways made. There is no evidence that Jenkyns took interior views, and this one may have been made about the same time as *Fig.54*.

Print (Richards) from lost plate, Jenkyns, c. 1857.   (R.I.C.)

JENKYNS, William
Professional: Penzance (Figs. 53 to 60)

The shape, and early date, of this man's life goes far to support the contention that the photographers of Penzance made up the most interesting group in Cornwall. Mr Jenkyns adopted the improved *nom photographique* by which we remember him, when he forsook the leather trade for the tripod and studio; he was 'the first maker of wet plates in the West of England';[1] he married a widow nine years his senior, with no means of her own (and a daughter); having attracted wealthy patronage he was able to set up business in the centre of Penzance, and to employ an assistant, who married his step-daughter; reputedly, he began to buy and sell real property, unwisely, and to conduct his life in the same fashion; and then he died at the early age of thirty-seven.[2]

His real surname was 'Jenkin' and the probability is that he came from St Blazey, in mid-Cornwall; if so, he was the William Jenkin baptised there on 23 March 1823, son of William and Grace Jenkin. At Madron, the ancient mother-church of Penzance, he was married on 8 March 1847 to Ruth Carter, widow, daughter of a Penzance labourer, herself at the time aged 33 and

APPEAL IN BEHALF OF A NEW CHURCH, AT MARAZION, CORNWALL.

Fig.54   The Old Marazion Church, 1857

A print from an early negative of a (lost) octavo handbill, this woodcut – by one of the Blights ? – headed an appeal, and is itself labelled
'N.W. View of Marazion Church. From a Photograph by Jenkyns of Penzance. June 1857'. The appeal was to raise £1800 for the replacement
of the ancient structure, the town's chapel of ease within St Hilary parish; 'weak and rotten . . . incurably damp and unwholesome' (Reynolds,
T., *The Chapels and Curates of Market Jew,* Marazion, 1963). The appeal succeeded, and the present church dates from 1861.

Print of lost original, after Jenkyns, 1857.   (Author)

having a nine-year-old daughter Ruth. William
Jenkyns, in the marriage registration entry, gave his
occupation as that of a currier, his surname as 'Jenkins'
and his father as 'William Jenkins, tin-dresser'. (After
his death his widow, who presumably knew best,
reverted to being plain Mrs Jenkin.[3])

It must have been fairly soon after the marriage that
Mr Jenkyns (as we may call him) became a photographer. If the account of 'Messrs Jenkyn and
Thomson' practising as daguerreotypists in Hayle in
the autumn of 1853 refers to Hugh Thomson and
William Jenkin, Jenkyn or Jenkyns[4] – and this seems
highly likely – he may have learnt the art from
Thomson and then opened his own business in
Penzance during 1854. We know that in 1856 he had
the rare distinction of appearing, among the five
professional artists listed for the whole of Cornwall,[5]

as 'Jenkyns, W. (photographic), North Street,
Penzance'. This makes him the first recorded, permanently resident, professional photographer in the county
(putting aside the very special case of Robert Hunt).
Mid-1850s, Penzance area, daguerreotypes by Jenkins
presumably exist; the chance of recognising any one of
them is slender.

In the years between 1848 and 1857, William and
Ruth Jenkyns had four children – Mary, Martha,
William and Robert.[6] None was to become a photographer and Mary died in childhood.[7] From the
original home in 'North Street', now known as Causewayhead, they moved about 1858 closer to the
fashionable clientele of Penzance's little Regency
terraces and sea-front, to No. 2 Queen Street, at that
stage popularly and alternatively known as 'New
Road'.

This second house was larger, and it needed to be. In 1856 William Richards, another escaper from the leather trade and Jenkyns's assistant or photograph-colourist,[8] married his employer's young step-daughter Ruth (Carter). Richards had at the time either a small house or a residential workshop at No. 4 Foster Court, an alley off New Street in Penzance. His and Ruth's first two children − William, born 1857; Thomas, born 1858 − were reared at Foster Court, and later he kept the place on as a workshop or extra studio.[9] But by 1861 the Richards had moved into Queen Street, where they were now jammed alongside their in-laws.[10] Ten persons, and this included a new baby John Richards, were fitted into three bedrooms (one room of the house, at least, had to serve as a photographic studio).[11]

William Jenkyns died in 1860; this has to be worked out from converging pieces of evidence.[12] Though, a year later, Richards described himself with partial accuracy as 'shoe-maker',[13] he had been Jenkyn's assistant and stepson-in-law for several years, and in 1862 could be listed as 'photographer'.[14] For the next few years Mr Richards had to support both families through running a business which was in fact owned by his mother-in-law.[15] His story is resumed a little later in these pages.

As for Mr Jenkyns, he would have left a stock of plates; some, illustrated here, can fortunately be dated. Prints of images made in 1855, and earlier, probably exist unrecognised. It is unlikely that he was concerned with either cartes de visite or stereographs, if later in 1860 Richards was making both. Before the compilation of this book, William Jenkyns's name was virtually unknown; Penzance's colourful history has inspired an above-average quantity of books, pamphlets and guides, in none of which is Jenkyns even mentioned. Patchy as this short account may be, and it has been put together with considerable difficulty, it is pleasant to have been able to rescue Mr Jenkyns and a sample of his work from oblivion.

1. Newspaper obituary of Edward Richards senr., 1935 (see p.118).
2. Info. Mr Edward Richards, Penzance.
3. Census 1861, C 1864, etc.
4. See p. 125 below, for Mr Thomson.
5. K 1856, 169.
6. Census 1861.
7. RCG 21 June 1861, p. 5 col. 1 − 'daughter of the late Mr Wm. Jenkins, photographic artist'.
8. C 1864, 27 and 144 − 'artist, 4 Foster Court', but in the sense of one who hand-coloured a photographic artist's work.
9. *Ibidem;* Foster Court is now (1988) called 'Foster Place'.
10. Census 1861; the widowed Mrs Jenkin or Jenkyns was returned as 'housekeeper' (in two senses; she owned or leased the house).
11. Info. Mr Edward Richards, Penzance.
12. His grave has not been located, nor the dated burial entry.
13. Census 1861.
14. H 1862.
15. C 1864, 54 and 130, listed Mrs Jenkin both as the proprietor of the house, and as 'photographic artist'; i.e., at that date she still owned her late husband's photographic business.

William Jenkyns, Augustus Smith and the first photographs in Scilly

Exceptionally, this gazetteer entry has an appended essay in view of the special interest of its theme. The history of the Isles of Scilly, which is quite unlike that of Cornwall, has proceeded by steps or episodes.[1] Modern times began in 1834. During Tudor and Stuart ages the Isles had been leased as a defensive fief to a Cornish family, the Godolphins. Their interest devolved through marriage and descent to the Osbornes, Dukes of Leeds, who in 1831 gave up their tenure with a certain amount of despair and exasperation. The Duchy of Cornwall, proprietor of the archipelago which Henry II seems to have claimed in the 12th century, were stuck. Finally, a tenant was found in the person of Augustus Smith, a Hertfordshire squire, who began a 99-year lease on 20 November 1834.

Augustus Smith was a remarkable man − few today realise quite how remarkable. There is a well-meaning but cursory sketch of his life[2] and recently a more attractive depiction appeared in the guise of a novel.[3] Local mythology would have him as a reforming ogre, dangerous to thwart; a benevolent but misguided despot who could (though rarely) be out-manoeuvred. The remote situation of Scilly and the dispersal of contemporary records, other than his own, have discouraged production of the full and proper biography that a person of his stature should be accorded. As a determined social engineer, disciplined visionary and landed proprietor given to direct and immediate action, Smith was outstanding; circumstances permitted him, frequently, to be much in advance of his own times. Unyielding in pursuing what he deemed to be right, he was inevitably embroiled in battles with authority. Unmarried, he needed a confidante, and he found one in his old friend Lady Sophia Tower, to whom over the years he wrote his most revealing letters.

Fig.55   Tresco Gardens; The Old Church
Often miscalled 'the Abbey', a name best kept for Augustus Smith's 19th-century house, the remains of the medieval priory church of St Nicholas still stand in Tresco Gardens. This is the south aspect, with two gardeners (and two chairs). Today the ivy has been removed and the upper course or so of the stonework has gone, but the view in 1988 is essentially what it was in 1856.
Print, from wet-plate, Jenkyns, 1856.

(Author)

Augustus Smith's monument is the island of Tresco. Here he built 'Tresco Abbey', a sprawling granite mansion of idiosyncratic design, enlarged (often, but in stages) by his collateral descendants the Dorrien Smiths; and also the superb terraced gardens, part-tropical, part-Italianate, created in instalments along a south-facing slope. The foundations of these enterprises were laid in the decade 1840−50. Since this phase, the 'middle period' of his own career, coincided with the start of outdoor photography, and since Smith had made himself familiar with half a dozen technologies and had artistic taste, there has long been the hope that early visual records − other than water-colours − might be found.

Until very recently indeed it was generally believed that the earliest photography in Scilly was co-eval with the Gibson family, beginning not long before 1870. Leaving aside the near-certainty that John Gibson was making images there from about 1866[4] we can now state that William Brooks was there, photographing, in 1870 *(Fig. 25)* and may have paid a previous visit; that William Richards seems to have made 1860-period stereographs in the Isles;[5] and that Robert Preston was

Fig.56 A View in Tresco Abbey Gardens
Augustus Smith laid out his gardens on terraces, across (or up and down) which are paved pathways interspersed with flights of steps. As the gardens grew, there must have been more changes of lay-out than has been realised. This scene is somewhere near the bottom, or perhaps Long Walk, in 1856, but cannot be matched today and the steps must have been re-fashioned. The four decorative urns certainly survive and a sharp eye can spot them now in the Middle Terrace.
Print, from wet-plate, Jenkyns, 1856.   (Author)

Fig.57 Tresco Abbey, Pool and Boathouse
The Abbey, Augustus Smith's granite mansion, is seen from the south-east across the Abbey Pool, smaller of Tresco's two very shallow lakes. Just visible, left of centre, is the boathouse. Because of additions and alterations to the house, and planting of shrubs, this view cannot now be matched. For comparison, and as a tribute to Lady Sophia Tower's accuracy, it can however be compared with her 1849 watercolour from the same angle (King, R., *op.cit.* 1985, p. 35).
Print, from wet-plate, Jenkyns, 1856.   (Author)

Fig.58   Tresco Abbey − the Rock Garden
The narrow extruding east wing of the original house, flanked by curving walls, was rooted upon an exposed granite slope. This slope was intended to be, and by the late 1850s was planted out as, a rock garden. Today the slope is covered with appropriate plants, and a further square tower has been added to the house. A photograph of, perhaps, 1870 − by John Gibson − shows the rock garden in an early stage of its establishment (Whitlock, R., *op.cit.* 1985, p. 11).
Print, from wet-plate, Jenkyns, 1856.   (Author)

photographing, with or for Augustus Smith, either late in 1861 or early in 1862.[6]

Smith was always in Penzance when travelling to and from Scilly, stayed in the town often, and had many acquaintances and friends in Cornwall. If he was at all interested in photography, he is likely to have met both Preston and Brooks, and during the last decade of his life (he died in a Plymouth hotel, on 1 August 1872) he certainly knew John Gibson.

Not long after Augustus Smith had died, Lady Sophia Tower published a selection of his letters. The book was issued as a limited edition and copies of it are rare.[7] In one letter, dated 10 April 1856 and written at Tresco, Smith wrote to her that 'I have a photographic man here, and he is going to try to take off a few views of the rocks and buildings'. There is no further allusion to this in the letters chosen for publication, but we now

know that the 'photographic man' was William Jenkyns and that his views pre-date those of Preston − the next such commission − by a good five years.

Eleven of Jenkyns's plates, probably the lot, from this outing have survived. Until their sale in 1985 they were preserved in the family of William Richards, who may have gone with Jenkyns to Tresco to carry equipment and act as his assistant. Prepared as 'wet-plates', they are all 4 by 5 inches, hand-cut glass of differing thicknesses, and still in their slotted wooden carrying-box. Prints can be made directly from them, and have been for use here.

For the time being, possibly for good, one can claim that these really are the first photographic images made in the, since hugely photographed, Isles of Scilly. Several are near-duplicates. They show, as requested, 'the rocks and buildings' and the best are reproduced.

Fig.59   Tresco Abbey from the 'Penzance Road'
The so-called Penzance Road is a driveway and path that approaches the Abbey from the east, through the gate-posts by the Pool, and thence around to the turreted gatehouse (a turret is visible, right). Fourteen years later, the shrubs had become established, and Jenkyns's view can be up-dated by an 1870 watercolour, made from a point nearer the gate by Augustus Smith's sister Fanny (Mrs Frances Isabella Le Marchant; in Whitlock, R., *op.cit.*, 1985, p. 13).
Print, from wet-plate, Jenkyns, 1856.   (Author)

Perhaps the most appealing is the enlarged detail of Smith himself, holding a spade and standing beside an aloe plant. This *(Frontispiece)* is the great man in his prime. It is also the only surviving likeness of Augustus Smith, as Lady Sophia and other friends would have remembered him. And because she so fortunately preserved his letters to her, we can allot the absolute date of mid-April 1856 to William Jenkyns's Scillonian views and likenesses.

Fig.60   Cromwell's Castle, Tresco
The only (surviving) 1856 plate not made in and around the Abbey grounds, this shows the Civil War fortification and battery on Tresco's north-west shore. On the top of the hill, right, can be made out the remains of another fort, King Charles's Castle (now restored). The slight air of gloom suggests that this was the last image made, late in the afternoon. The stance is on the cliff path a short way north of New Grimsby.

Print, from wet-plate, Jenkyns, 1856.   (Author)

1. Two conplementary histories are: Thomas, Charles, *Exploration of a Drowned Landscape* (Batsford, 1985), and Matthews, G. Forester, *The Isles of Scilly — A Constitutional, Economic and Social Survey . . . from early times to 1900* (George Ronald, 1960).

2. Inglis-Jones, E., *Augustus Smith of Scilly* (Faber & Faber, 1969).

3. Schlee, Ann, *The Proprietor* (Macmillan, 1983).

4. See p. 51 above.

5. See p. 117 below.

6. See p. 110 below.

7. *Scilly and Its Emperor*, by 'S.F.T.' (privately, Uxbridge, 1873).

JORDAN, Thomas Brown
Amateur: Falmouth (Fig. 61)

'March 21st, 1839. Attended a Polytechnic Committee in which Jordan introduced and described his new photogenic inventions. One application of the sensitive paper to self-register barometric observations, the other to diary the sun's light, the aspect of the day &c, very simple and pretty.' So wrote young Barclay Fox, brother of Anna Maria and Caroline, in his Journal.[1] He was witnessing a major step forward. Well might a later Fox point out[2] that Jordan's arrangements 'were the first applications of photography to scientific purposes'.

Mr Jordan, who was born in 1807 at Bristol, settled in Penzance about 1830, where he earned a living teaching art. 'But Nature will out', commented an admirer.[3] 'He was never meant by the great Architect to be a mere teacher of painting. His mechanical genius prevailed ere long; he produced some mathematical and philosophical instruments of surprising workmanship and delicacy' — and it was partly because these productions came to the notice of appropriate friends that Jordan was offered the post of Secretary (paid executive) at the Polytechnic. Here, he was able to exercise his talents as a practical scientist.[4]

One of Jordan's duties, as of all subsequent Secretaries including Robert Hunt, Jordan's successor, was to keep local meteorological records. The invention witnessed by Barclay Fox was made possible by Fox Talbot's method of preparing light-sensitive paper. It was best described by Hunt himself.[5] 'The plan this gentleman adopted was to furnish each (meteorological) instrument with one or two cylinders containing scrolls of photographic paper. These cylinders are made to revolve slowly by a very simple connection with a clock, so as to give the paper a progressive movement behind the index of the instrument, the place of which is registered by the representation of its own image.' Hunt rightly regarded this as being just as much the practice of photography (in 1839, a newly-coined word) as were all the 'photogenic drawings' — impressions of leaves, etc., laid on light-sensitive surfaces — and Jordan was able to carry it out because, a month or so earlier, Fox Talbot had made public the details of preparing the necessary paper.[6] Jordan went on to expand the system of self-registration, including another instrument that provided a daily record of the intensity of sun-light at Falmouth, one that he called the Heliograph.

The precise timing of Jordan's work is interesting. In the first place, Jordan and Hunt were fairly closely associated. Jordan was teaching painting in Penzance about 1830 to 1835 at a period when Robert Hunt was also there, running a chemist's shop with his uncle James Thomas.[7] Hunt was then in London for a year, but in 1837 came back to his native Devonport, moving down to Falmouth in 1840 to succeed Jordan. Fox Talbot's description of preparing the paper — as James Y. Tong points out,[8] very guarded in revealing

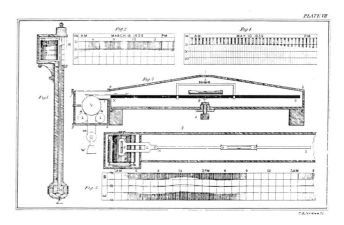

Fig. 61   The New Heliograph
Thomas Brown Jordan's own drawing of his own 'mode of registering the indications of meteorological instruments' using Fox Talbot's prepared photographic paper is here reproduced from the 6th Annual Report of the Royal Cornwall Polytechnic Society. (Falmouth, 1839)

specific method but detailed enough to allow a chemist of Hunt's ability to work out and to reproduce the whole process — was read to the Royal Society on 31 January 1839 and reported on 2 February in the *Literary Gazette*. If Jordan then got the idea of self-registering instruments, he could very easily have obtained guidance from his friend Hunt. In fact he almost certainly did this, because the first announcement of the Jordan invention was made only a fortnight later; to a Polytechnic Committee at Falmouth on 18 February 1839.[9] The initial demonstration witnessed by Barclay Fox took place a month later.

T.B. Jordan published an improved version of his 'Heliograph', with illustrations, in the following year.[10] Meanwhile, he had intended to mount a demonstration on 5 April 1839 at Truro, for the benefit of the Polytechnic's sister-society, now the Royal Institution of Cornwall. As Jordan was unavoidably prevented from attending, the paper was read for him at Truro by Dr Barham.[11]

In 1840 Thomas Brown Jordan resigned his Secretaryship, to the sorrow of the Committee ('We cannot but express our regret at losing the services of Mr Jordan . . . The vacancy occasioned by Mr Jordan's removal to London, your Committee are happy to feel, has been supplied by Mr Robert Hunt')[12] and, though Hunt would already have been known to some of the members, one suspects that the recommendation may have come from Jordan in the first place. Jordan had been appointed Keeper of the Mining Record Office in London — curiously, a post in which Robert Hunt would again follow him after April 1845. In later life Jordan became a successful mechanical inventor; his automatic wood-carving machine, blend of machinery and art, produced items shown at the Great Exhibition and used for decorating the House of Lords, and he then moved into the field of mining and invented a drilling machine.[13] When he retired he went to live at

82

Reigate, photographically significant as the head-quarters of Francis Frith and the home of William Brooks; we know that the latter was in touch with Jordan in 1882, as he informed a meeting at the Polytechnic.[14]

T.B. Jordan died in June, 1890.[15] His 1839 work may not have been in the mainstream of later photographic developments, but it was an important application. The use of Fox Talbot's prepared paper caused great interest, and no doubt gratified the Polytechnic's President, Fox Talbot's uncle Sir Charles Lemon.[16] When this was followed at once by Hunt's enthusiasm, lectures and demonstrations, Jordan can be seen to have contributed directly to the Polytechnic's prolonged support for photography as a popular and competitive art.

1. Barclay Fox, 147.
2. W.L. Fox 1915, 9.
3. Short (anon.) memoir, *Mining Journal* 6 Jun 1857, 399.
4. BC 279–80.
5. Hunt 1841, 87–89.
6. Arnold 1977, chap. 5, 118.
7. Tong 1973, xii–xiii; Pearson 1976, 23.
8. Tong 1973, xiv.
9. 6 RCPS, 184 n.; Hunt 1841, 87.
10. 7 RCPS, 115–6.
11. 21 RRIC (1839), 27, 31.
12. 8 RCPS, xi.
13. See *Dictionary of National Biography* entry.
14. See p. 41 above.
15. Obituary – *The Times,* 9 Jun 1890, p. 6.
16. See p. 144 below.

LANYON, George
Amateur: Falmouth

Mr Lanyon, of Chapel Terrace, Falmouth, was by trade a tanner. His surname is local and he was probably connected with Thomas Halls Lanyon, currier and ironmonger of Market Strand – a currier was also in leather-working – and Jacob Halls Lanyon, draper, with a shop in the same street.[1]

George Lanyon exhibited his own photographs at the Polytechnic in 1862.[2] There is no further record of any entry, but his interest was maintained, and during the 1870s Mr Lanyon's name often occurs as that of a judge for the photographic section of the annual competitions.

1. K 1856, 27; Wa 1864, 67.
2. 30 RCPS, xxv, xxxvi.

LOBB, Charles Renowden
Professional: Wadebridge (Figs 62 to 68)

Charles Lobb was born at Egloshayle, the mother-parish of the town of Wadebridge, on 12 September 1841. His odd middle name is Cornish, and occurs as Renowden, Renawden and Renorden (the last spelling indicates the pronounciation).[1] It was a Bodmin surname of great antiquity, and he had it from his mother Anne Renowden, who married Thomas Lobb at Egloshayle in 1840. Charles Lobb himself married Miss Winifred Rundle in 1865 at the small Roman Catholic chapel at Ruan Lanihorne, near Tregony. He died when he was only thirty, on 14 September 1871; his widow re-married, at the same chapel, a Mr John Reynolds on 4 April 1878.[2]

Not very much is known about his brief working life, apart from the observation that he was mainly concerned with exterior photography and that his images were often of high quality. His career, unfortunately, took place during a gap between the dates of suitable county directories.[3] We know his products mostly as stereoscopic views, probably made early in the 1860s, and some smaller views in carte format. Charles Lobb's preferred area seems to have been the extreme west of Cornwall, though Wadebridge and north-coast views may await discovery.

We do not know if he had any kind of shop at Wadebridge. After his death and before her re-marriage, Mrs Lobb did issue prints with her own name for a brief period, presumably using her late husband's stock.

1. CC 794.
2. Info. Mr Douglas Lobb, Lobb Genealogical Records, Truro.
3. Between K 1856 and K 1873; nothing in H 1862.

Fig.63 St Michael's Mount
The traditional view of the Mount, taken from the lower ground. Note the remains of the small battery with its turreted look-out on the slope, right.
Carte, paper print, Lobb, early 1860s.   (Private colln.)

Fig.62   St Michael's Mount, from its harbour

The title is Charles Lobb's; he was on the end of the granite pier around the harbour and could hardly have missed so spectacular a shot. The vessel seems to be the *Lord Riverston* (a former title of the Earls of Westmeath; was this an Irish trader?) and she is tied up at low water. The slide itself is labelled 'C.R. Lobb, Photographer, Wadebridge'.

Stereograph, Lobb, early 1860s.   (Private colln.)

Fig.64 'Crags and Battlements'
The stance for this striking image would have been three-quarters way up the path shown in *Fig.63*. The eroded granite tor that forms the Mount's east summit is crowned by the terrace around the so-called Blue Drawing-Room, and the east end of the Church. Charles Lobb's view, issued as a carte, is included because very few photographers seem to have made this one.
Carte, paper print, Lobb, early 1860s.   (Private colln.)

LOBB, Nicholas Blake
Visiting Professional: Truro and Boscastle

Nicholas Lobb arrived at Truro in Autumn, 1854, and issued this press notice; 'Photography Portraits taken daily at Mr Mitchinson's Glass Room, Prince's Street, Truro, by Mr. N. BLAKE LOBB, Photographic Artist from 441 Oxford Street, London. Portraits taken from 3s. Parties desirous of obtaining a correct likeness at that price should lose no time as Mr N.B. Lobb's time is limited in Truro'.[1] For three shillings, Ambrotypes (small mounted collodion-positives) are indicated.

Lobb was in fact a native of Truro, born 17 April 1831, son of William Lobb and his wife Mary (Blake). No photographic business is listed at No. 441 Oxford Street — there was a studio, Thompson's, at No. 431 — but then there is also no record of the 'A.1 Photographic Company' which Mr Lobb later claimed to manage.[2] His Truro sojourn was not all that limited; he stayed until at least June of 1855, when he got married. After that, he probably went back to London. In 1859 he was in Cornwall once more, based at Boscastle. Another advertisement[3] asked the reader 'Who Took Your Likeness?' The right answer was 'Why, MR BLAKE LOBB, the Manager of the A.1 Photographic Company, from Oxford Street, London'. On this occasion he offered sixpenny portraits 'done by a new process' — i.e., cartes de visite — and announced arrangements for visiting Tintagel and Delabole, both not far from Boscastle.

According to information given by an Australian descendant in 1984,[4] N. Blake Lobb then moved to Plymouth, where he became a teacher, started a 'Clean Literature Campaign' and opened his own bookshop at No. 38 Old Town Street. He may have married for a second time in December 1881. His death was registered at St Andrews, Plymouth, on 16 December 1887, when he would have been 56.

1. WB 6 Oct 1854.

2. Pritchard.

3. Back cover of *The Camelford Illustrated Magazine and Monthly Advertiser* (Hands & Welch, Camelford), vol. II no. 3, November 1859.

4. Info. Mr Douglas Lobb, Lobb Genealogical Records, Truro.

Fig.65   Logan Rock, Cornwall

The Logan Rock or Stone, a vast granite boulder on the cliffs at Treen, parish of St Levan, rocks or 'logs' slightly when pushed from the south-west side. It did so better before 1824, when Lieut. Goldsmith, R.N., visited it with twelve of his cutter's crew and dislodged it; public outcry soon forced him to put it back, with a forest of scaffolds and tackle, and a lot of expense. Here, either Lobb's assistant or a local guide demonstrates the right push. The view was issued both as a carte and as a stereograph.

Carte, paper print, Lobb, early 1860s.   (Private colln.)

Fig.66   The Longships

Cornwall's most famous lighthouse stands upon a multiple reef lying off Land's End. Wyatt's stumpy tower, its base only 40 feet above water, was begun in 1791. During heavy seas the light was often obscured by water; early in 1870, after he had completed the Wolf Rock light, Sir James Douglass started the replacement seen today, which rises to 114 feet above high water.

The main rock on which the tower stands is Carn Bras. In good weather it is possible to put out from nearby Sennen Cove and even to land on other rocks in the reef. Lobb made such a trip, at some time in the 1860s, and took several views; this is one, *Fig.67* another, and a possible third − with the three keepers standing outside − is shown in Watkiss, R., *Early Photographs − The Land's End peninsula* (White's, Penzance, 1975), Fig.2.

Albumen print, sepia-toned, Lobb, 1860s.   (R.I.C.)

Fig.67 'Longship's lighthouse, Land's End'
The exact title is Lobb's. In this slightly more satisfying composition, issued as a stereograph with the label of C.R. Lobb, Photographer, Wadebridge, the camera has been moved back some yards and the small boat in the previous figure is out of sight. The position of the shadow on the right-hand side of the tower, and perhaps the general state and height of the sea, suggests that *Figs.67* and *66* were taken more or less at the same time.
Stereograph, Lobb, 1860s.   (Private colln.)

Fig.68 Esplanade, Penzance

Charles Lobb's delightfully-composed picture of the Penzance sea-front recalls paintings of the Newlyn School. The Esplanade with its boarding-houses, shops and the Royal Baths − note the 'Bath Inn', for those who preferred to be moistened internally − was the tourist promenade. Charles Truscott and other photographers had their summer studios along here. Just behind the two men leaning on the rail, and below St Mary's Church tower, is No.1 South Terrace, Robert Preston's initial studio and lodgings.

Carte, paper print, Lobb, early 1860s.   (R.I.C.)

LUKE, Francis, jnr.
Amateur: Scorrier

In the 1863 Art Union of Cornwall prize draw at the Polytechnic[1] one of the items available was Mr Luke's photograph, 'Porch of Jedburgh Abbey'. The choice of this distant Scottish detail for a photographic view raises interesting questions. In the list of names, he is specified as 'F. Luke, jun., Whitehall, Scorrier'. His father Francis Luke, occupation unknown, was dead by 1890, and his sister Eugenie married an Edinburgh doctor in 1880.[2] If Francis were an elder brother of hers, in 1863 he must have been in his teens; whether the connection with North Britain began as far back we cannot say.

Francis Luke has already been mentioned in the context of another young amateur, Edward Hawke,[3] whom he almost certainly knew. When we recall that a Camborne amateur whose work also figured in the 1863 draw was W.J. Hambly,[4] who had photographed 'Durham Cathedral', a joint trip to the north seems more probable. The likelihood is increased by the fact that a *third* amateur, Captain John Rule from Camborne, also provided a view of the 'Porch of Jedburgh Abbey' in the same year.[5]

Almost nothing is known about amateur photographic clubs, or circles, in Cornwall at this period. A 'Devon and Cornwall Photographic Circle' is mentioned once or twice in early Polytechnic reports, but with no details, and it was apparently based in Devonport or Plymouth. Despite a certain disparity in ages (Rule and Hambly were probably much older than Luke and Hawke), all these clues hint at the existence of a Camborne-Redruth area excursion for amateur enthusiasts.

1. See p. 17 above.
2. CC 514.
3. See p. 64 above.
4. See p. 61 above.
5. See p. 120 below.

MANSELL, Thomas L.
Visiting Professional

The name 'Mansell' recurs among early British photographers. At Gloucester, there was the photographic firm of A. Mansell & Son, who in 1866 published *The Gallery of Photographs,* a collection of reproductions of celebrated paintings, etc.[1] Somewhat later (1877), Edward Mansell & Co. had their photographic studio at No. 151 Upper Street, N., in London.[2]

T.L. Mansell was among the first of the English topographical and landscape commercial photographers. He was active from the 1850s in both France and England, 'producing notably sharp quality photographs, many of rocks and foliage'.[3] About 1864, Robert Preston of Penzance issued a two-page catalogue of 'Mansell's New Series − Views in Cornwall'.[4] These were distinct from Preston's own series, and the carte views and stereographs by William Brooks that Preston was also selling. We have no other record of a Mansell series, nor do we know when Mr Mansell visited Cornwall, or which part − probably the Land's End area, if Preston was the local trade outlet.

1. Gernsheim 1984, 53 (no. 344).
2. Pritchard, 67.
3. Mathews 1973, 28.
4. BC 1015; see p. 108 below.

Fig. 70 'Samaritan Rock'
One of a series of vast detached slate stacks along the cliffs of St Eval parish, north Cornwall, this forms part of Bedruthan Steps. This stereoscopic slide, blind-stamped 'Photographed by Wm. May, Devonport, is one of a series covering the Newquay to Padstow coast, sold to visitors by G.S. Drew the St Columb bookseller (see p. 22).
Stereograph, May, 1860s.   (Private colln.)

Fig. 69 Completing the Royal Albert Bridge
William May's view is taken from the Devonport side − it is titled 'Royal Albert Bridge from the East' − and shows Saltash, with the curve into Saltash station, in the background. The trolley on the broad gauge lines in the foreground is being used to move stone ballast to complete the permanent way. This cannot be long before the formal opening, and should thus be in the early months of 1859.
Albumen print, stereograph, May, 1859.   (Author)

MAY, William
Visiting Professional (Figs. 69 and 70)

Mr May entered his views of the Logan Rock at Treen, a famous natural curiosity along the coast west of Penzance (see *Fig. 65,* Charles Lobb's view of it) at the Polytechnic's annual exhibition in 1866.[1] His Cornish work is otherwise represented by stereographs, with the legend 'Photographed by W. May, Devonport'. Particularly after 1859, when Brunel's Royal Albert Bridge was open, professional photographers from Plymouth, Devonport and Stonehouse could easily reach the far end of Cornwall. William May was very probably visiting Cornwall earlier than 1866.

'May' is a common name in Cornwall and Devon. In 1873, a William May was a painter and glazier at No. 29 King Street, in Devonport[2] − not necessarily a connection − but in the same year a photographer, Henry John May, was in business at East Street, Ashburton.[3]

1. 34 RCPS, xxxii.
2. K Devon 1873.
3. *Ibidem,* 130.

a milliner, dress-maker and straw bonnet maker. Had the mother Honour died? Edwin Mayell is found at Tavern Hill in 1856[4] and again in 1862.[5] Louisa, however, is not, and had probably married.

Though no directory entry gives any indication that he was engaged in photography, *Fig. 71* is not only plausibly his work, of 1860 as claimed, but must have been taken immediately outside the Mayells' front door. The printed legend on *Fig. 72*, which can be dated to 1863−64, has 'E. Mayell, Photographer' on a crowned circle, surrounding an ornate shield, with the legend 'Tavern Hill, Liskeard'. Mr Mayell is not listed at all after the 1860s.[6] His photographic career may have been fairly brief.

1. P 1830, 151.
2. W 1847, 84.
3. S 1852, 29.
4. K 1856, 58.
5. H 1862, 880.
6. Not in K 1873.

Fig. 71   Tavern Hill, Liskeard

We are looking down Tavern Hill, now Pike Street; the ladder and onlookers suggest some minor excitement, perhaps a fire in an upstairs bedroom. The carte view (labelled 'Tavern Hill, Liskeard 1860') is from an album in the Institution's collection, put together by William Hancock of Liskeard about 1880. The greater part comprises purchased items, Cornish and otherwise, from 1851 onwards, with many showing scenes and buildings in east Cornwall. Edwin Mayell's premises were in this street. He must have come out, set up his camera, and captured the dramatic moment.

Carte, paper print, Mayell, 1860.   (R.I.C.)

MAYELL, Edwin
Professional: Liskeard (Figs. 71 and 72)

The Mayells came from the east of Cornwall. Joseph Mayell was a watch- and clock-maker in St Austell, where his children Letitia and Edwin (twins ?) were baptised in 1812. The family had moved to Lostwithiel before 1830[1] and here on 15 February 1834 young Edwin Mayell, now aged 22 and working with his father, married a Miss Honour Harper. Edwin's and Honour's daughter, Louisa, was baptised on Christmas day of that year.

Joseph Mayell cannot be traced after this time and may have died. Edwin moved to Liskeard, where in 1847 he was working at a shop in Tavern Hill, still as a watch- and clock-maker.[2] As he is described as 'Edwin Mayell junior' an uncle of the same name was perhaps alive. Some five years after this, Mr Mayell was now also recorded as being a jeweller,[3] while his daughter Louisa was listed at the same address as being

Fig. 72   'Mother'

Simple and effective in construction, a Cornish prelude to Whistler's famous oil, Mr Mayell's portrait shows a lady in her fifties. The carte comes from Julia (Dunstan) Yewens's album; she is most probably Mrs Pryor, mother of Julia Yewens's son-in-law Richard, himself also photographed in Liskeard, but by J.H. Colliver *(Fig. 29)*. It is not clear whether Mrs Pryor sat in late 1863 or early 1864, when the children of the two ladies were engaged, or in late 1864 after Richard Pryor's untimely accidental death; but, since she is not in complete mourning, the former occasion is more likely.

Carte, paper print, Mayell, 1863−64.   (Author)

MAYLAND, William(?)
Visiting Professional: Truro

Mr Mayland was another of the early visiting portraitists. He advertised as follows[1] in the summer of 1854; 'Photographic Likenesses — reduced prices — for one week only at Mr Mitchinson's, seedsman. Mr MAYLAND begs to announce that he will be in the above rooms, Monday next the 13th, when in order to place these desirable portraits within the reach of all, the prices will be reduced'. The announcement then went on to say that he had made arrangements to visit Liskeard on 20 August.

Given the date, these must again have been Ambrotypes, the small collodion-positive likenesses. Though the photographer's initial or first name is not recorded, it looks like a youthful venture by William Mayland, subsequently fairly well known. By the end of the decade he was working in Cambridge and in 1862 could exhibit views of interiors, cloisters, etc., of the Cambridge colleges.[2] In later life he appears — assuming, as is likely, that it was the same man — in a central London studio, with the address of No. 236, Regent Street.[3]

1. WB 11 Aug 1854.
2. Mathews 1973, 30.
3. Pritchard, 69.

MAYOW, H.C.
Visiting Professional: East Looe

An advertisement[1] during the summer months of 1855 announced to the citizens, and since the town was in its dawn as a holiday resort to any visitors as well, that Mr H.C. Mayow had made arrangements 'for the purpose of photography portraits in this pleasing and beautiful Style of ART, which will be found worthy of attention, and at greatly reduced prices'. Once again we see some pushing young traveller, cashing in on the novelty of the Ambrotype boom. The location for this treat was given as 'Mrs J. Walters, Church End, East Looe'. Mrs Walters's name is not in any directory as a business[2] and she was probably the proprietrix of summer lodgings. As for Mr Mayow, his surname does occur in the eastern half of Cornwall. If he was not just an enterprising free-lance, we could guess that he was operating out of Plymouth.

1. LG 21 July 1855 (info. Mr John L. Rapson).
2. Not in W 1847 nor S 1852.

MICHELL, William
Professional: St Austell (Figs. 73 to 75)

Mr Michell may be comparatively little known, but he was among the more interesting of Cornwall's early photographers. The surname is not to be confused with 'Mitchell'; both forms are widespread still in the county and probably derive from *Myghal,* the Cornish reflex of the name 'Michael'.

He came from an old-established St Austell background of skilled craftsmen. Benjamin Michell & Co. of St Austell figure as watch- and clock-makers in 1847.[1] Michael Michell, who was presumably Benjamin's son, was in the same line, and also a jeweller, at Church Street, St Austell, in 1852.[2] How precisely all the Michells were related is unclear, but by 1856 William Michell — who must have been born around 1820, if not earlier — had replaced Michael (his brother ?) as the jeweller of Church Street.[3]

The photography began, as was mentioned earlier in this book, in 1846 when William Michell won a prize at the Polytechnic for his entry of daguerreotypes.[4] Whether or not he was then in the family jewellery business, *Figs 73 and 74* show that he moved into printing images from glass plates and into the making of collodion-positives. By the later 1850s, Church Street may have housed a studio; one carte portrait[5] of a lady has an imprint, with a crowned circlet on which is 'Photographed By', around a shield with 'W. Michell, Jeweller, St. Austell'. This is probably earlier than the imprint of the double-headed Imperial Eagle above 'Michell, Church Street, St Austell' on cartes of the 1860s. In 1862, sixteen years after his previous submission, Mr Michell showed further photographs at the Polytechnic.[6]

Difficulty could arise from the inclusion, in the 1846 Annual Report of the Polytechnic (and later), of the name 'W. Michell' among the subscribers; this went on until 1852.[7] The subscriber in question was entered among those living in Truro, but this does not imply a period of Truro residence for the photographer. The person in question was either William Michell, barrister, of Boscawen Street, or William Michell, surgeon, of Lemon Street.[8]

William Michell of St Austell was not a competitor at the Polytechnic after 1862, and carte imprints by the end of the 1860s read 'Michell & Son, Church Street, St Austell'. What happened to father and son is unknown. By 1889 there is no jeweller nor watch-maker of the name of Michell listed anywhere in Cornwall, and the Church Street photography business was then in the hands of Benjamin Julyan, St Austell's next professional photographer.[9]

1. W 1847, 167.
2. S 1852, 52.
3. K 1856, 101; H 1862, 960 ('jeweller & photographer').
4. 14 RCPS, xxv; see p. 20 above.
5. Private colln.
6. 30 RCPS, xxv.
7. See, e.g., 14 RCPS, 62.
8. W 1847, 216.
9. K 1889 ('photographer, Church St.').

Fig.73 The Reverend Trevenen and family, St Ewe Rectory

This is one of two such groups, owned by Mrs Ann Trevenen Jenkin (Mrs R.G. Jenkin, Leedstown), a direct descendant of the Reverend Thomas John Trevenen. Born in 1802, he was the grandson of John Trevenen of Rosewarne, Camborne (1712−75), curate of that parish from 1738 to 1745. In 1836, T.J. Trevenen became Rector of St Ewe, near St Austell. His first wife Mary Ann died after their son Thomas was born and he then (1837) married Susan Angwin Cosserat, from the Channel Islands, by whom he had a further eight children. He died on a visit to Jersey in 1864.

A later Trevenen lady fortunately labelled the back of the frame. Four younger children are present − Sydney William, in Tom Brown's Schooldays attire, b. 1844; Harriet Mary, b. 1845; Emma Jane, b. 1847, and Edmund Ernest, b. 1849. Since Sydney is here about 12 and little Edmund Ernest about 7, the date should be 1856. St Ewe is closer to St Austell than to Truro; by far the most likely artist at this date would have been William Michell. (The pony was called 'Roland', and the dog, 'Don'.)

New print from collodion negative, Michell, 1856.   (Mrs Jenkin)

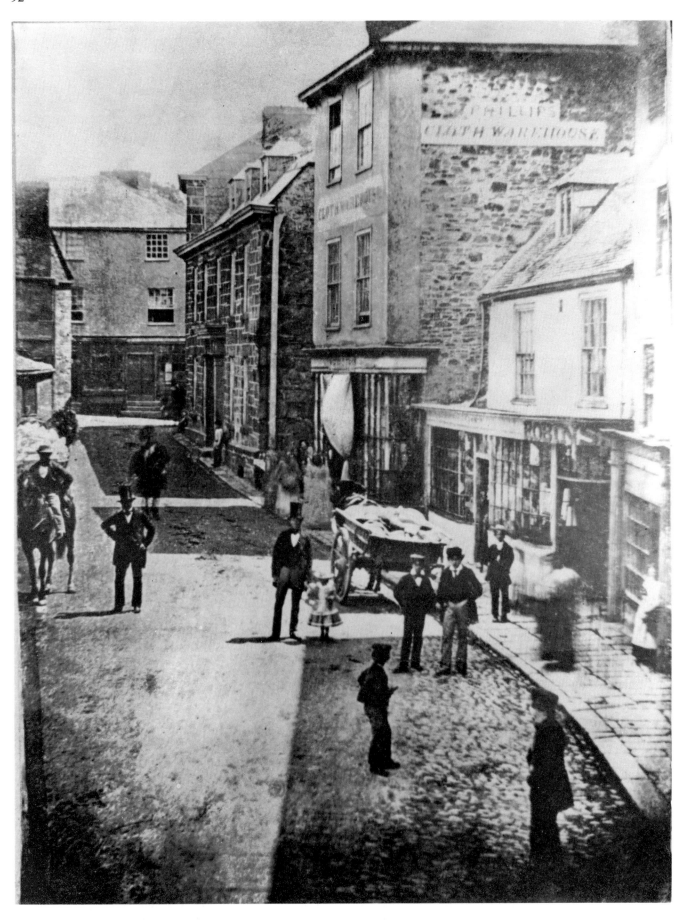

Fig.74   Church Street, St Austell, 1856
William Michell's shop was in Church Street and this view − in which most of the inhabitants are standing and looking at the novelty of the camera and tripod − would have been made from outside the shop. The small child holding the man's hand, by the wheeled cart, is a little boy, a Mr Higman then aged 4, which gives a firm date of 1856 for Michell's photograph.
Copy of whole-plate print, 1856.

(R.I.C.)

1. S 1852, 65.
2. 22 RCPS, xxi.
3. R.I.C. colln.
4. Not in K 1873.

Fig.75   Portrait of a Gentleman

The carte de visite bears Mr Michell's second imprint, with 'Michell & Son' over '6 Church Street, St Austell'. There is no indication as to the sitter, but the likeness is a neat and sympathetic presentation. A date in the later 1860s is likely.

Carte, paper print, Michell, late 1860s.   (Private colln.)

MITCHELL, John
Professional: Truro (Fig. 76)

Mr Mitchell may have had some connection with Frances Mitchell, milliner of Pydar Street, Truro, in 1852[1] if, say, she was his widowed mother. In 1854 he entered some photographic portraits at the Polytechnic, and won a Second Bronze Medal in the Fine Art class.[2] This was an early award, and it places him among the first group of prize-winners in this field.

As a photographer, he cannot be picked up in any directory entry. The carte portrait of Mr Jeremiah Reynalds has as its imprint 'Photographed by J. Mitchell, Artist, Pydar Street, Truro' in a wreath below the Prince of Wales's plume and motto. Another example of his cartes de visite[3] has a different imprint, 'J. Mitchell, Truro', below the shield from the coat of arms of Truro (then a borough). It is unclear whether this second imprint is the earlier or later. Without the scant evidence of these portraits, we should not in fact know at all that he was working in the 1860s.[4]

Fig.76   Jeremiah Reynalds, J.P.

Mr Reynalds was a substantial merchant of Truro, a grocer and tallow chandler with a house in the Malpas Road, a shop in New Bridge Street, and outside interests; he was a borough councillor and magistrate. The statement (*CC*, 797) that he died 'about 1863' is not correct; his 1861 Census entry shows that he was born in 1804, and his tombstone in Kenwyn churchyard records his death on 30 July 1873, aged 69. The most likely year for Mitchell's portrait would be 1865, when Mr Reynalds was Mayor; in July of that year he was in attendance during the visit of Prince Albert Edward and Princess Alexandra. The posture and expression are both entirely mayoral, and we can safely guess that during his year of office he arranged to be photographed on as many occasions as possible.

Carte, paper print, Michell, 1865.   (R.I.C.)

MOODY, James
Professional: Redruth (Figs. 77 to 79)

The Moodys were not Cornish. They came from Derbyshire, a part of England where Cornishmen might be encountered as shaft-sinkers or the installers of pumping engines in the lead mines. In 1859, or earlier, James Moody set up shop as a photographic artist at No. 67 Fore Street, Redruth, the town's main street. The site, now the central post office, comprised a home above a ground floor shop and studio. We know

Fig.77 John Rule Daniell, Esq., Solicitor
The interest here lies less in the subject of the portrait than in the background. James Moody advertised the total redecoration of his studio in Doidge's *Redruth Directory,* published in June 1866 and compiled in the preceding half-year (or more). Accessories now included 'Columns, Pilasters and Balustrades', and we see them in pristine condition, as yet unmarried by children's grubby fingers or kicked by miners' boots. J.R. Daniell (born 1840) cannot long have been admitted as a solicitor; this is before he succeeded William Yewens in the latter's Camborne practice at 13 Chapel Street (cf. *Fig.5*). The imprint on the back (circle, with 'J. Moody, Photographist, Redruth' printed in gilt) is Moody's earliest style.
Carte, paper print, Moody, 1865–66.   (Author)

the date because, on 22 November 1859, Sergeant Jones of the constabulary had cause to apprehend 'James Moody, of Redruth, photographist' for threatening the life of Sarah Curtis.[1] Passing swiftly over this momentary and sad aberration in the life of a family man,[2] we can note that in 1862 and 1866 Mr Moody is recorded as a commercial photographer.[3] In 1867 he entered a frame of his likenesses, as cartes de visite, at the Polytechnic.[4] Though for nearly thirty years the Moody imprint is to be found on carte and cabinet portraits, his output seems to have been almost entirely confined to likenesses; with very occasional, and early, exceptions of some street scenes in and around Redruth.

The Moodys were Nonconformist, presumably Methodist. They were popular and active in a district where music, song and Methodism were intertwined.

James Moody was an accomplished organist; his eldest daughter Maria Jane was the first organist of Redruth Fore Street Methodist Church; others among the, originally thirteen, Moody children sang or performed. Most notable was little Fanny, born on 23 November 1866. A child prodigy, this 'Cornish Nightingale' was taken up when she was 16 by the Bassets, the wealthiest of the local landowning families. Fanny Moody was to attain international fame as a concert singer, the darling of the emigré Cornish on her overseas tours. She married an Irish impresario Charles Manners, and as 'Madame Moody-Manners' she died in Ireland on 27 July 1945, aged 79.[5]

Fig.78 Michael Loam, Esq., Engineer
Mr Loam, born at Ludgvan in 1798, was one of the great Cornish engineers. In the 1830s the Falmouth Polytechnic sponsored a competition to find ways of relieving working miners from the long and arduous task of climbing shafts by means of ladders. Michael Loam's invention, which won the 1834–35 premium of Ten Guineas, was the 'man-engine' – interval stages on a huge rod, driven slowly up and down, on and off which the miners could step from corresponding interval platforms in shafts. First tried at Tresavean mine in 1842, the man-engine was universally adopted. In partnership with his son Matthew, Michael Loam was engineer to many larger Cornish mines (Dolcoath, Clifford United, etc.). By 1866 he was living at Treskerby in Gwennap. He died in 1871.
Moody's likeness has captured the stern, uncompromising face of a man who was at the top of his profession, knew it, and had very little time for amateurs and Mr Fixits.
Carte, paper print, Moody, mid 1860s.   (R.I.C.)

Fig.79 Dr Boase's House, Redruth

James Moody's carte view goes with a series (in carte and larger format) that he made at various times and at various points in Redruth's main thoroughfare; Fore Street, where the Moodys had their home and shop. An early hand has noted on the back 'Dr Boase's House and Site of Red Lion Hotel Redruth'. The posters on the wall advertise such attractions as 'Thurtons Odd Folks'. In 1854 this house, north side of Fore Street, adjoined the London Hotel and the Red Lion. The imprint, 'J. Moody, Photographer' above the plume of feathers and motto, with 'Fore St., Redruth, Cornwall' below, is not Mr Moody's first, but was in use around the mid-1860s.

Carte, paper print, Moody, mid-late 1860s.   (R.I.C.)

James Moody appears in directories until 1883, though he was certainly operating later than that. As indicated above, he is not on record as a landscape photographer; speciality is shown by various of his advertisements, which state that likenesses could if wanted be enlarged to life-size, and painted in oils. His son (? eldest son) John, who was the baritone of the family, acted as his assistant; his career is examined in the next entry.

1. RCG 30 Dec 1859, p. 8.
2. He was bound over for 3 months in the sum of £10.
3. H 1862; D 1866, 20, and advert. p. 5.
4. 35 RCPS, cat. p. 16.
5. See *The Cornish Magazine* (ed. 'Q'), I (1898), 29−36; and *Cornish Life*, 5 pt. 1 (1978), 18−20.

MOODY, John
Professional: Penzance (Fig. 80)

Assuming that his father James, who seems to have retired in the 1880s, had been born in the decade 1810−20, John Moody would himself have been born in Derbyshire in the 1840s. We find him in 1866 − but in a directory almost certainly compiled during the previous year[1] − living at Trefusis Terrace, Redruth, a short walk from the no-doubt crowded Moody home at No. 67 Fore Street; he was listed as 'photographic artist's assistant'.

Fig.80 Mrs Catherine Snow

This carte de visite is from a framed display, in which likenesses of Catherine and Abraham Snow, husband and wife, flank ornate printed memorial cards that record her death on 13 July 1865 (aged 70) and his at the age of 81 on 10 August 1875. The frame must then have been made up after the latter date. Mrs Snow with her brolly leans against a fake pedestal that appears in other portraits from the Moodys' Penzance studio. The ink-stamped imprint (an easel), with 'John Moody − Photographer − Penzance') is the first from Penzance, when the branch studio opened (around 1864?). Either the father James or the son John could have taken this photograph; John Moody may have reproduced it later, when the occasion demanded.

Carte, paper print, Moody, 1864−65.   (R.I.C.)

Probably in the latter part of the 1860s, Mr Moody senior acquired a branch studio in Penzance, at No. 27 Market Jew Street.[2] The establishment was obviously intended to provide a start in life for this son, even if it opened under the name of the Redruth business. There is no suggestion that James Moody himself moved there — he would have begun in the usual way by paying one-day-a-week visits — and by 1883[3] it is John Moody's name that we find attached to the Penzance establishment.

Like his father, John Moody seems to have restricted his work mainly to likenesses, cartes de visite and cabinet portraits. He may well have married and had his own family in Penzance. He was working in the town until, perhaps, the 1890s[4] but cannot be traced later than that. Though evidence of the exact date when John Moody became manager, or partner in charge, of the Market Jew Street studio is lacking, he is included here because of the likelihood that it was before 1870; and, as his father's assistant, he would certainly have been making images in Redruth in the 1860s.

1. D 1866, 32.
2. K 1873, 979 (as 'Jas. Moody, 27 Market Jew St.').
3. K 1883; K 1889.
4. Not in K 1897.

MOYLE, Matthew Paul
Amateur: Helston

Mr Moyle was the son of John Moyle and his wife Julia Hornblower, daughter of a family of engineers from Bromsgrove who settled in Cornwall in the 18th century.[1] Born at Chacewater in 1788, he trained in London and qualified in 1809 as a Member of the Royal College of Surgeons of England. From 1811 he was in practice at Cross Street in Helston, where he died in 1880 after 69 years of medical service.

He is included from the 1850s in the membership lists of the Polytechnic at Falmouth as 'M.P. Moyle, Helston', his name being starred to indicate that he belonged to the Central Committee. Mr Moyle was twice married; firstly to his second cousin Jane Vivian Moyle, daughter of his father's cousin Richard Moyle, medical practitioner of Marazion (as a family, the Moyles produced a large number of surgeons and physicians in Cornwall and Scilly), and then after her death to Frances, daughter of Dr Walter Borlase.[2]

Matthew Paul Moyle was closely associated with the Polytechnic, a society whose 'home area' embraced Penryn and the easily-reached Helston as well as Falmouth. For many years he kept local meteorological records and in 1855 was given a First Class Medal for this activity.[3] Despite geographical isolation, he was a prolific contributor of scientific papers to French as well as to English journals.[4] One, entitled 'On the formation of electro-type plates, independently of any engraving' (did this herald a form of photo-lithography?) appeared in 1841,[5] and one imagines that Robert Hunt would have been particularly interested. The evidence that Mr Moyle was also a

photographer is buried in a solitary allusion of 1855. We are told[6] that the Polytechnic's exhibition included 'some very successful collodion positives from engravings, by Mr Moyle of Helston'. This again looks like a scientific rather than artistic application, but it would be in keeping with an unusually productive private life.

1. CC 600–01.
2. BC 1289.
3. 23 RCPS, xiv.
4. BC 373–4.
5. Not seen; Sturgeon's *Annals of Electricity*, vi (1841), 112–14.
6. 23 RCPS, xxxii.

OKE, William Williams
Professional: Bodmin

This surname (the English *Oake, Oakes*) is found in Devon and mid- and east Cornwall. W.W. Oke & Son, as a photographic business, is first encountered in 1883 at Crockwell Street, Bodmin.[1] This is misleadingly late.

W.W. Oke, son of a man of the same names and his wife Betsey (Worth), was born at Bodmin on 8 November 1827. By the mid-century he was in Fore Street there, a linen and woollen draper.[2] Like his contemporary W. Higgs[3] he took up photography as a side-line, and was named with Higgs in 1860[4] as photographing the Bodmin wedding of John Tremayne and Mary Vivian. Oke is there described as being 'of Bodmin'. A year or so later, he had however moved his drapery business to Lostwithiel.[5] He was in Lostwithiel for some few years; it is possible that he maintained photography during this time as a commercial side-line, but we have no evidence of it.

The return to Bodmin was in the 1870s. Mr Oke may have inherited a house, if so from a Mrs Hannah Oke (not his mother; an aunt, perhaps ?) who in 1852 was a private resident in Boar, or Bore, Street, Bodmin.[6] Photography was certainly resumed. The Institution has several cabinet-size images of detailed stonework from St Petroc's Church, Bodmin, with the imprint of 'W.W. Oke, Photographer, Bodmin'; these were made well into the 1870s, and consequently none has been illustrated. Mr Oke seems to have retired, or possibly died, by the later 1880s. In 1889 another Mrs Oke — one would suspect, W.W. Oke's widow — was listed[7] as a private resident in (Higher) Bore Street.

An intriguing footnote to the 1860 wedding at Bodmin, with its rather early specific mention of the photographic arrangements, is that the bridegroom John Tremayne of Heligan may have had a particular interest. His mother Caroline Matilda (Lemon) was the youngest sister of Sir Charles Lemon of Carclew.[8] Mr Tremayne was therefore a cousin by marriage of W.H. Fox Talbot; whom, of course, he would have known. Was this acquaintanceship responsible for his decision?

1. K 1883.
2. S 1852, 6.
3. See p. 68 above.
4. RCG 16 Nov 1860.

5. H 1862, 900.
6. S 1852, 5.
7. K 1889, 939; also in K 1897.
8. See p. 144 below.

PADDON, Mr
Amateur: Truro

Mr Paddon (initial not given) had one of his photographs in the 1863 Art Union of Cornwall prize draw.[1] At that period, Paddon was very much a Truro name. John Paddon, originally from Penryn, was a Truro publisher in 1820;[2] William Paddon, retired mine agent, lived in Union Place in 1861[3] and there was a Dr John Paddon who practised in the town.[4] Mr Paddon is described as 'of Cornwall Railways'. A younger man from one or other of these Truro families could well have been an official with the railway company. The title of his photograph was 'Musicians Ambulant', an unnecessarily fancy way of describing a band on the move, but one might guess a picture of the band of the 11th (Truro) Rifle Volunteers. Most of the 1859—60 volunteer companies in Cornwall had their own bands.

Possibly relevant is the fact that, in Cornwall's first serious railway accident, which happened in May 1859 when a special train — returning from the Royal Albert Bridge opening ceremony — crashed near Saltash, among those killed was a railway guard named Paddon.[5]

1. See p.17 above.
2. Potts 1963, 313.
3. Census 1861.
4. CC 648—9.
5. Woodfin, R.J., *The Centenary of the Cornwall Railway* (1960), 178.

PALMER, John E.
Visiting Professional: Truro (Fig. 81)

In February 1858 a public notice[1] advertised the dissolution of a partnership between Messrs Palmer and Viney, photographers of River Street, Truro. Four months later the lease of the premises — a twelve-roomed house, shop with plate-glass front, courtlage and stabling, etc, 'occupied by Mr Palmer, Photographic Artist' — was itself advertised[2] by a Lemon Street agent. Was this house No. 32, and was it, after a space of a couple of years, acquired by another Truro photographer Richard Griffiths with his family? The business of Palmer & Viney was not listed at all in 1856[3] and may not have been in existence very long. The notice of the partnership's dissolution adds that 'The business is carried on as before under the personal supervision of Mr Palmer'. Here, at least, we can say that in the period 1858—61 it was re-located in a smaller studio at High Cross, by the western end of the present Truro Cathedral.

'Mr Palmer' was John E. Palmer, a successful commercial photographer based at No. 58 Union Street, East Stonehouse (now part of Plymouth).[4] William

Fig.81 'Mr Richard Tuck, Dentist, Truro'
The carte portrait, so labelled and signed 'Yours sincerely, Richard H. Tuck', bears Palmer's dual imprint of 58 Union Street, Stonehouse, and High Cross, Truro. As the imprint includes a representation of J.E. Palmer's 1865 Polytechnic prize medal, that dates the likeness to 1866 or later — but not much later. Tuck was son and partner of William Richards Tuck, licentiate dental surgeon. The surgery was in Lemon Street, Truro, and the Tucks could have claimed to be Cornwall's leading dentists.
Richard Tuck has either just qualified or, having done so, is contemplating a marriage he can now afford. In 1856 as a Truro schoolboy he won 2s. 6d. in the Polytechnic's competition for schools, with his drawing of that exciting novelty, a railway engine. Here, he is in his mid-20s. As Palmer seems to have passed his Truro branch to Argall by the late 1860s, the date is fairly closely bracketed.
Carte, paper print, Palmer (Truro), 1866—67. (Private colln.)

Palmer, photographer of Lynton in North Devon,[5] may have come from the same family. The surname Viney hardly occurs in Cornwall, but is common in south Devon. What this seems to mean is that Palmer, doing very well in Plymouth during the late 1850s, spotted a likely market in Truro and decided to lease a branch shop there (1857?). Mr Viney was sent down to run it on a manager-partner basis; this arrangement failed, and was wound up. Some other manager (William Palmer ?) was engaged and the business was moved to smaller premises; it was suggested earlier[6] that by 1865−66 Frederick Argall − subsequently in business on his own − was Palmer's last Truro manager.

'Personal supervision', then, probably meant no more than occasional visits from Mr Palmer. He certainly never lived in Truro.[7] He did however maintain an association with Cornwall, apart from attracting a good deal of custom for portraits from Cornish people at his Plymouth studio. In 1865 he was awarded a First Bronze Medal by the Polytechnic at Falmouth for 'his three very fine portraits on opal glass, enlarged by him from ordinary cartes de visite'.[8] The imprint on Palmer's cartes in use from 1866 bears a record of this award, as well as both the Plymouth and Truro addresses; but 1866, or possibly 1867, was the last year of the Truro involvement.

1. RCG 26 Feb 1858.
2. RCG 18 Jun 1858, p. 4 col. 5.
3. Not in K 1856.
4. H 1862, 709; K Devon 1873.
5. K Devon 1873, 616.
6. See p. 28 above.
7. Not in Census 1861, for Truro.
8. 33 RCPS, xxiv.

PARKER, Frederick Townley
Amateur: Camborne

Captain F.T. Parker was among those named as having taken part in a January, 1870, exhibition at Camborne Literary Institution;[1] we learn that he was among the photographic contributors. The chief claim to interest of this, slightly unusual, figure among Cornwall's amateur photographers is that he is mentioned[2] in the *Diary* of Francis Kilvert.

Frederick Parker, born in Italy on 6 February 1832, was the son of a Lancashire M.P. and one-time High Sheriff. He married Miss Louisa Little on 9 November 1854. The Littles were connected by marriage with a family called Hartley; and Mary Hartley (born 1794, daughter of a Mr Harris of Rosewarne, Camborne) was an heiress and rich widow, living after 1824 with her son at Rosewarne. Afflicted by melancholia, she worsened and was declared a lunatic in 1843. Commissioners in Lunacy then appointed successive relatives of her husband's family as 'Committees', that is, resident administrators or receivers of her very large estate. F.T. Parker appeared in this role during 1864.

In 1868, poor Mrs Hartley accidentally set fire to her clothes and was burnt to death, but the Parkers stayed on until 1892, managing affairs for the delicate surviving son, William. Captain Parker was a keen member, and a sidesman, at Camborne parish church; Treasurer of the town's National Schools; and at the time of his death (15 July 1892) also associated with All Saints, Tuckingmill, where he lies buried.[3] No other reference is known to his interest in photography; but it is not impossible that, after his arrival at Rosewarne, he was introduced to the joys of the camera by a gentleman who was his immediate neighbour. That gentleman, another amateur cameraman, was Captain John Rule;[4] Rule's house, Parc Bracket, adjoins Rosewarne's south entrance.

1. See p. 15 above.
2. The dates in Kilvert's Diary are 27−29 July and 5 August 1870.
3. All these details are from: Smith, Barry, *Rosewarne, The Parkers and the Lewises − Insanity, Imbecility and Inter-relationships in a Victorian Family* (privately: Truro, 1984).
4. See p. 120 below.

PAUL, Mr
Visiting (?) Professional: Penzance

In the summer of 1860, readers of the *Royal Cornwall Gazette* were offered the harrowing tale of the unfortunate Mrs Paul.[1] She had finally succeeded, after various attempts, in committing suicide by cyanide poisoning. She was the wife of a Mr Paul, 'photographic artist'; they had been staying in Penzance since December 1859, living at the Duke of Cumberland Inn. 'The husband last year stationed himself at the Logan rock to take views and portraits'. The Logan Rock *(Fig. 65)* was a pleasant wagonette's ride from Penzance. 'Paul' is a common enough Cornish surname. All one can surmise, in this case, is that Mr Paul came from somewhere other than Penzance.

1. RCG 15 Jun 1860, p. 5 col. 2.

PHILLIPS, Mr
Visiting Professional: Liskeard

Rather as Mr Hampton had booked rooms in 1856 at the Union Hotel, Liskeard, the next year a Mr Phillips was advertising at the Albion Inn, Dean Street, in the same town his 'Photographic Portrait Saloon'.[1] His boast was 'Likenesses from One shilling, Taken in any Weather'. It would be unkind to call Mr Phillips simply an itinerant cheap-jack; together with other of the visiting professionals included here, he exemplifies a commercial trend of the 1850s. His outing to Liskeard does however look rather like the down-market end of the portrait trade.

Nothing else is known about Mr Phillips. There is no reason to suppose that he was a London photographer.[2]

1. LG 11 July 1857 (info. Mr John L. Rapson).
2. Not in Pritchard.

PHILLPOTTS, Thomas
Amateur: Feock

The Reverend Thomas Phillpotts was a familiar figure in Victorian Cornwall, best known in Truro and Falmouth. He was born in 1807. His father John Phillpotts of Porthgwidden, a large house in Feock parish, was the elder brother of Henry Phillpotts, a bishop of Exeter, bibliophile, and founder of the (surviving) Bishop Phillpotts Library at Truro.

Thomas Phillpotts was educated at Eton, and duly became Vicar of Feock. His father died suddenly in an omnibus in Regent Street, London in 1849, whereupon the Vicar inherited Porthgwidden. He held the cure of Feock for thirty years, became a Canon of Truro Cathedral in 1877, and in 1881 — a year after the first Mrs Phillpotts died — he married again at the age of 74.[1] Canon Phillpotts himself died at Porthgwidden in July 1880.[2]

He was an enthusiastic photographic amateur, and had a long connection with the Polytechnic. In 1863,

his photograph picked as a prize in the Art Union of Cornwall draw[3] was called 'Robin Hood'. Since the Phillpotts family consisted of seven children, one of them no doubt posed with a long-bow. On other occasions, Thomas Phillpotts's name occurs among the judges for the photographic entries, though he does not seem to have participated in the competitions.[4]

1. CC 733.
2. CC 1904.
3. See p. 17 above.
4. 29 RCPS (1861).

Fig.82 Interior of Camborne Parish Church before renovation
In 1859 Mr J. Piers St Aubyn, the Cornish architect and restorer, was engaged to enlarge and to re-arrange the church's whole interior (cf. *The Ecclesiologist*, vol. 20 (1859), 137 ff.). Work began in 1862 when William Pester Chappel was Rector; the west gallery was removed, and the 17th-century wagon roof was replaced with pine cladding.
Piper's studio was almost opposite the parish church. He may have been asked to make this picture for the architect, or by Canon Chappel as a record before the work began. For some years it was thought that this view was by Robert Preston; but the existence of contemporary versions with Piper's own label makes the ascription certain.
Half-plate albumen print mounted, Piper, 1859−61.   (R.I.C.)

PIPER, William
Professional: Camborne (Figs. 82 to 91)

In the year 1861, William Piper was aged 32 and gave his place of birth as Abbotsham, Devon.[1] This is

a small parish near Bideford. No Anglican baptism in 1829−30 referring to him can be found, and later events suggest that he was a Methodist.[2] From various clues[3] we learn that he established a photographic

Fig.83 Captain James Thomas of Bolenowe
This venerable Methodist − mine agent, farmer and local preacher − was born at Bolenowe, Camborne, in 1778. As a boy, he walked to Gwennap Pit to hear Mr John Wesley's last sermon there (on Sunday 23 August 1789). His life was divided between his farm at Bolenowe and (mostly) Dolcoath Mine; he was a younger brother of the Charles Thomas in *Fig.4*. He died at home, aged 89, on 26 January 1867; in his last years he was frail, and confined to his bedroom and study. Piper's likeness, which was also made into a bust-only carte de visite, implies a visit to the Camborne studio − note the old gentleman's heavy topcoat. A likely occasion is 1860, when James Thomas's nephew Charles, then managing agent of Dolcoath, visited Ireland to inspect mines and (as the exchange of surviving cartes de visite shows) went down to County Cork in order to see two of his cousins. Captain James was surely persuaded to get his likeness taken by Piper, so that his nephew could deliver copies to the distant sons; Captain William Thomas (b. 1807) at Cusheen Mine, and Charles (opening a barytes mine at Brandon). Collodion positive in case, Piper, 1860.   (Author)

studio and shop in Church Street, Camborne, in 1858; it is likely that for a year or so before that he was in Redruth. Mr Piper was returned as 'photographic artist' in 1861,[4] as a photographer with his own business in 1862[5] and four years later as running his own photographic works − studio, facilities for printing and copying, etc.[6] The business continued until his death in 1890, and from about 1880 or a little beforehand there was a branch shop at Hayle.[7] Some of Piper's negatives may have passed to W.J. Sandry, a later Camborne photographer; the shop was taken over by Messrs Major and Darker, one of four in Cornwall that they owned in 1893.[8]

William Piper's background, and personal history, has long been wrapped in obscurity and it has taken a great deal of investigation to find it out. The present writer some years ago suspected, because of the large number of cartes de visite and other portraits (all by

Piper) dating from 1859 and preserved in his own family, that William Piper might have 'married into Camborne' and thus acquired, ready made, a considerable number of local customers. This proves to have been the case. In 1857 Piper married a Miss Eliza (Elizabeth Jane) Mayne of Illogan, aged 20.[9] Their first child, Charles James, was born on 7 May 1858 and baptised on 29 May, details being registered at Redruth Wesleyan Methodist Chapel. Eliza was the third child of an Illogan miner James Mayne and his wife Susanna (Thomas); she was the eighth child of Captain Charles Thomas, senior, of Knavegobye *(Fig.4)* and a niece of Captain James Thomas *(Fig.83)*. From 1858, this enormous Camborne mining family had its own photographer.

Fig.84 'My Mother-in-Law'

We can be certain, looking at this formidable lady, that this is one portrait for which William Piper did not dare to charge. Susanna, eighth child of Captain Charles Thomas senr. *(Fig.4)* and niece of Captain James in the preceding figure, was born in 1807, and married James Mayne, an Illogan miner of Brea village, on 25 November 1828. She was a devout Methodist. A sampler, replete with Christian sentiment, that she worked aged 14 is still owned by her great-granddaughter. Susanna Mayne's daughter Eliza Jane had married William Piper in 1857, and here she sits, wrapped in that magnificent shawl. The carte bears Piper's early imprint (about 1861). Note the painted background, especially the false book-case. Did Piper's rival James Moody have this in mind when, in 1866, he advertised the redecoration of his own Redruth studio as including 'Book Cases (solid, not painted)?' Mrs Mayne died in 1891; here, she is in her fifties. The expression on her strong face can only be called enigmatic.
Carte, paper print, Piper, early 1860s.   (Author)

The Pipers had a number of children. Some were named after the Thomas side of their ancestry (Charles, James, Ellen), implying deference to Mrs Piper and to William's mother-in-law. The second son Frank born in 1860[10] and a daughter Matilda aged 6 in 1871[11] may

MR PIPER PHOTOGRAPHER CAMBORNE CORNWALL.

Fig.85 Dr George Smith

George Smith of Trevu, Camborne, son of a mine carpenter in that parish, was born in 1800. With the family of his wife Elizabeth Burrall Bickford he was concerned in the safety-fuse manufactory of Bickford, Smith & Co. at Tuckingmill; the successful promotion of the Cornwall Railway; and Methodism. An ardent preacher, he wrote a three-volume history of that church, and published numerous Old Testament and Wesleyan commentaries. A Fellow of the Asiatic Society and honorary LL.D. of the University of New York, in all his busy life he was central to a large and happy family at Trevu, and to a circle of old friends who held him in the highest affection and esteem.

Dr Smith died in August 1868; not long before, he had preached the funeral address of one of his closest friends, Captain Charles Thomas jnr. of Dolcoath. This carte portrait was preserved in the latter's presentation copy of Smith's *The Cassiterides* (1863). The occasion of its making must have been the 1862 Wesleyan Methodist Conference held at Camborne, when such cartes de visite were widely exchanged as mementos. Later portraits of Smith (e.g., by F. Jones of 146 Oxford Street, W.; in operation (so Pritchard) 1862–1868) show a markedly older face.

Carte, paper print, Piper, 1862.   (Author)

Fig.86 'Three Generations'

The grandmother is Julia, Mrs William Yewens, born 1805 and mother of J.P. Dunstan in the daguerreotype *(Fig.5)*. Beside her stands her elder daughter, born 17 July 1830 as Julia Vivian Dunstan; on 17 August 1864 she married Richard Pryor, who was killed in November of that year *(Fig.29, by Colliver)*. Their son Richard Aitkin Pryor was born on 20 June 1865. In this group, little Richard is 4 or 5 months old and his young mother, not unexpectedly, wears mourning. The date is thus around Christmas, 1865.

Carte, paper print, Piper, 1865.   (Author)

indicate the names of William Piper's Devonshire parents. In 1881, Frank Piper was also a 'photographic artist'[12] and since he was then aged twenty-one he was presumably given charge of the branch at Hayle.

William Piper's first ventures may have included such Ambrotype likenesses as that of his wife's great-uncle *(Fig.83)*, but from 1860 he was making cartes de visite in quantity for most of Camborne's well-to-do. In the notice of the 1859 jubilee celebrations at Camborne's Literary and Scientific Institution, the occasion of Robert Hunt's lecture and display,[13] it was stated that 'Mr Pike of Camborne sent a case of photographic likenesses'.[14] It so happens that a Roman

Fig. 87   Mr T.T. Whear, Camborne

Thomas Trevarthen ('Tom') Whear was, in Arnold Bennett's sense, a bit of a Card. His friend Piper has caught this, in the pose, expression, and fondling of a too-heavy watch chain. Born in 1832, Tom was the seventh child of Samuel Whear, schoolmaster; was trained as a printer's compositor; and, aged 19, set himself up as stationer, bookseller and agent for the Caledonian Life. Later he became an auctioneer. In 1861—62 he published several skilfully-composed booklets of Cornish dialect, and from 1864 was embroiled (on the anti-Radical side) in a ferocious Camborne row about the pros and cons of the Local Government Act. He died in 1879, leaving his widow Sarah the printing works. Here, Tom Whear is in his thirties, on the make as usual, and probably still in the middle of his battles with the Reverend Samuel Dunn, 'Roaring Sammy', and the Camborne Reformers. We can guess 1866.

Carte, paper print, Piper, 1866.   (Author)

Catholic family called Pike, prominent mine venturers, was present in Camborne at that period, but 'Pike' is clearly a misprint for 'Piper'. William Piper never showed any work at the Polytechnic; possibly he felt that he did not need the additional promotion. We know that he occasionally took outside views (cf. *Fig. 90*), and it would be interesting to find some showing the area's mines, if only above-ground. He seems to have made and sold stereographs, mostly of Camborne and district but also some taken in The Lizard area, during the 1870s if not before; neatly identified in handwriting, these have no printed labels, but can be safely attributed to him.[15]

He died, at Camborne, on 11 March 1890 aged 61, and was buried in the parish churchyard (no headstone) five days later.[16] This was not inconsistent with a life

in Methodism; many of Eliza Piper's, fervently Wesleyan, forbears and cousins lie in the same Church of England burial ground. Given this religious attachment and all his influential relatives by marriage scattered throughout the mining district, it is odd that William Piper played no part in Camborne's public life. He cannot be traced in any elective position, or

Fig. 88   Mrs Josiah Thomas

Charlotte Augusta Dunstan, two years younger than her sister Julia, Mrs Pryor *(Fig. 86)* was born in 1832, and married Captain Josiah Thomas at Treslothan, Camborne, on 23 October 1856. Her carte portrait is included as an exercise in dating. William Piper's studio is as for *Fig. 86* (1865—66) with the pedestal table also used for Tom Whear *(Fig. 87,* same general date), but the carpet has been changed. The legend at the bottom of the carte is now 'Piper — Camborne', not the earlier 'Piper. Photographer. Camborne. Cornwall' seen, for example, in *Fig. 85* (1862). The imprints on Augusta Thomas's carte are repeated in *Fig. 91,* known to have been made late in 1869. Therefore we are between 1866 and 1869.

Augusta and Josiah Thomas had ten children. She wears a wedding ring, is still in her thirties, and is dressed in mourning (black bombazine trimmed with black braid frogging). The third child, George Marsingall Thomas, was born in 1861, but died on 30 November 1867. Christmas of 1867 or, more probably, early in 1868 is thus the indicated date.

Carte, paper print, Piper, 1868.   (Author)

Fig.89   Mine Captains at Cook's Kitchen, Tuckingmill

These gentlemen are dressed to go underground. Top left is 'Cappen Charlie', Charles Thomas, agent at the mine from 1854 until his death (as its manager) in 1896. Born 13 June 1831 at Roskear, Camborne, he was a great-nephew of both James Thomas *(Fig.83)* and Charles Thomas senr. *(Fig.4);* his father William was a brother of the better-known Captain Charles Thomas, 1794–1868, manager of Dolcoath. Top right is someone identified in pencil as 'Capt. Frank Gilbert' – unlikely, since Francis Gilbert was a much older person and at this time almost an invalid. It is most probably the mine's other agent, Capt. S. Davey. Below stands Arthur Budge, Camborne merchant, here as a friend or visiting shareholder, this is an unusual group, and one wonders what William Piper was doing at the mine.

Carte, paper print, Piper, 1867–68.   (R.I.C.)

Fig.90   The Old House at Knavegobye, Camborne

This rambling eighteenth-century structure, demolished about 1910, was the home of Captain Charles Thomas senior *(Fig.4)*. He married in 1794 and moved here from Bolenowe at that time. Mrs Susanna Mayne, William Piper's mother-in-law *(Fig.84)*, was born here, along with her brothers and sisters. After her father's death in 1847, her brother Captain Charles Thomas of Dolcoath moved half-a-mile south to his own new home at Killivose, but various relatives used the old house until the end of the century.

Numerous prints, half-plate size, exist of this view. It was re-issued (copied) about 1920 by W.J. Bennetts, Camborne, quite improperly stamped as his own copyright. An early, mounted, print which belonged to Captain Josiah Thomas (1833–1901) has pencilled on the back 'Capn Chas T's Old House 68'. It was almost certainly taken by William Piper, and the date of 1868 is acceptable.

Unascr., albumen print, mounted, Piper, 1868.   (Author)

indeed beyond the setting of his business. None of the Pipers can be found, in Camborne or Hayle, by the end of the century.

1. Census 1861.
2. Two 'William Pipers' only had Anglican baptisms at the right period; both at Pancrasweek many miles away, both in 1830.
3. Imprints and advertisements.
4. Census 1861.
5. H 1862.
6. D 1866, advert.
7. K 1873; K 1883; K 1889 (and imprints).
8. K 1893 – Camborne, Falmouth, Penzance, St Austell.
9. Info. Mr David Thomas, Camborne; location unknown, but probably Tuckingmill Methodist Church.
10. 30 April 1860; baptised 24 Aug 1860 at Camborne Methodist Church.
11. Census 1871.
12. Census 1881.
13. See p. 15 above.
14. RCG 9 Sept 1859.
15. Preserved, continuously, in author's family colln.
16. *Cornish Post & Mining News* (Camborne), 14 Mar 1890, p. 7 col. 5; Camborne Parish churchyard register.

PIPER W(illiam?) H.
Visiting Professional: Truro

A press notice in 1856[1] announced, below the usual heading – 'Photographic Portraits. For A Short Time Only' – that a certain Mr W.H. Piper 'recently from London, begs to announce that he has opened Mr Mitchinson's Glass Room, Princes Street, Truro, for taking Portraits . . . and trusts by strict attention and skill to merit public support. N.B. Specimens to be seen at the establishment.' Here is another young man, a travelling Ambrotype or collodion positive merchant, trying his luck in a Cornish town during the summer months.

While it is tempting to see this as an early stage in

Fig. 91 A Visit To Dolcoath

The final Piper image, a carte with the imprints already established as covering the latter part of the decade to 1870, shows Edward Morris; one of a family that started the stockbroking firm of William Morris & Sons (after various mergers, finally taken over by Quilter, Goodison). On the back is written 'Edward R. Morris Xmas 1869 Miner's Costume', and family tradition has it that young Mr Morris went down Dolcoath just after this was taken. The original was kindly lent for copying by Justin Brooke, Esq., Marazion.

Carte, paper print, Piper, 1869.　　　　　(Private colln.)

the career of William Piper of Camborne, who is first encountered in Redruth in the following year (1857), there is no real warrant to do so. The Camborne photographer's name had no middle initial 'H', nor is there any evidence, or claim, that he had worked in London. Mr W.H. Piper, on the other hand, is much more likely to have been the 'William Piper' in business in the Walworth Road, London S.E., from 1862 to 1866, and again in 1873–75 at No.146 Walworth Road.[2]

1.　RCG 1 Aug 1856.
2.　Pritchard, 76.

POLKINGHORNE, William
Amateur: St Columb

The Polkinghornes were for many years the landlords of the Red Lion Hotel, a large inn at St Columb Major.

They achieved notoriety through James Polkinghorne (1788–1851). Six feet two inches tall and built to match, he dominated Cornish wrestling, and in 1826 after an historic bout with Abraham Cann of Devon – depicted, in Cornwall, as a dirty fighter and cheat – Polkinghorne claimed the title of 'Champion of England'.[1] His son William took over the Red Lion in the 1840s.[2] When he died in 1879 a newspaper obituary[3] described him as 'one of the first persons to have photographs of Cornish scenery'. This, slightly ambiguous, statement ought to imply activity in the 1850s. St Columb, a small market town, looks to both Wadebridge and Truro, and Polkinghorne might have found fellow-enthusiasts at either. It remains unclear whether he simply displayed photographs at his inn, or took them himself. As he was Chairman of his local government Board, and was actively involved in promoting various technical and industrial concerns, it is reasonable to suppose that he was also an amateur photographer.

1.　BC 504; CC 57, 127, 1442.
2.　K 1856, 106.
3.　Western Morning News (Plymouth) 6 Jan 1879, p. 3 col. 1.

POLKINHORN, Thomas W.
Professional: Penzance (Fig. 92)

Mr Polkinhorn – a shadowy figure – was a Penzance man, born there about 1813. His wife Mary was a year his senior, and in 1861 they had two sons, Edwin (21), a solicitor's clerk and Alfred (10) at school.[1] The Polkinhorn (Polkinghorn, Polkinghorne) family is still widespread; its members have regarded themselves, historically, as originating at the farm of that name in Gwinear parish.[2]

In 1861 Thomas Polkinhorn described himself as a 'writer and photographic artist'. Unless he was a freelance journalist, no evidence of his literary output can be traced.[3] He lived at No.2, Chapel Row, a little street off St Clare Street in Penzance, and the studio would have been a ground-floor back-room.[4] In a directory of 1864 Mr Polkinhorn, in addition to the photographic business, was a commission and emigration agent, acting for the Liverpool and London, and the Albert Medical Insurance Co.[5]

There is no commercial listing for him in 1873, or later.[6] One might almost be inclined to think that the Polkinhorns had taken advantage of their own agency and emigrated; in fact, the family had suffered a partial disintegration. Mrs Mary Polkinhorn must have died between mid-1861 and mid-1863; for in August of the latter year 'Thos. W. Polkinghorne, photographic artist of Penzance' is recorded[7] as having re-married, at St Andrew's, Plymouth. The second wife was apparently also called 'Mary'; and in 1889 Mrs Mary Polkinhorn, surely by that date a widow, kept a lodging-house at No.78 High Street, Penzance.[8] Edwin Polkinhorn probably became a solicitor's managing clerk and by the end of the century figures among the town's private residents.[9]

Fig. 92 'Married Life'

Mr Polkinhorn's studio at Chapel Row, off St Clare Street, lay well out of the centre of Penzance; it would have been hardly known to the patrons of Preston or Richards. We can see that the interior is barely furnished. The carte de visite has no imprint, only a blind-stamp 'Polkinhorn. Penzance'.

The couple, both around thirty, are plainly dressed — he has no watch-chain, she no jewellery — and his suit seems to hang uncomfortably. This is the down-market end of Penzance photography. Are they small farmers in town for market-day, or poor but respectable artisans? Yet, in Polkinhorn's not very gifted hands, the camera still cannot lie. The tenderness of his hand on her shoulder, his awkwardly protective stance, and the serenity in her face as she clutches the straw bonnet, all proclaim their mutual affection.

Carte, paper print, Polkinghorn, mid-1860s.   (Private colln.)

T.W. Polkinhorn's output seems to have been confident to modest cartes de visite. In view of the personal history outlined above, his photographic career may have been a short one.

1. Census 1861.
2. *One And All* (monthly; Penzance), May 1868, article.
3. But nothing is listed in BC and CC.
4. H 1862, 940.
5. C 1864, advert., p. 28.
6. Not in K 1873 or P 1876.
7. RCG 14 Aug 1863, p. 5 col. 5.
8. K 1889, 1121.
9. K 1902, 257 (at No.31 Morrab Road).

POOLE, Samuel
Professional: Truro (Fig. 93)

Mr Poole's career in Cornwall — five years or more — is nowhere directly recorded and the story has been painstakingly put together from scattered clues. The starting-point is a solitary, much faded, carte de visite, a likeness of an elderly man in a chair,[1] with on the back a blurred ink-stamp 'Poole & Son, River St. Truro'. No 'Poole' occurs in any capacity trading in Truro in 1853 and 1856[2] nor is anyone of this surname listed for River Street — or indeed Truro itself — in the 1861 census enumerators' returns. One immediate implication would be that 'Poole & Son' was a business name, but not that of a residential concern, and that the business was carried on in rented rooms, the Poole or Pooles in question being elsewhere on the 1861 census night.

The next stage is the occurrence of 'Preston & Poole' as the trade name of a photographic partnership, the first half being Robert Preston, whose career is known in some detail and who is discussed here in the next entry. The first record of Preston & Poole is from 1862, probably collected in late 1861,[3] and the only address given is not in Truro at all, but at No.1 South Terrace, Penzance, where it is known that Robert Preston was lodging and renting a studio space from 1860 or the end of 1859. On the other hand, as we shall see, Preston did apparently live in or near Truro, to which his parents had moved, in the 1850s.

Carte imprints are also puzzling. Earliest may be one[4] showing a circle with the words *E Lumine Vita* ('Out of Light, Life') surrounded by a nimbus of fine rays, above 'Preston & Poole. Penzance'. This was replaced by another with the plume of feathers and coronet of the Prince of Wales, above the circlet (lower half wreathed) with *E Lumine Vita* around its rim and an ornate 'PP' within the circlet; below is 'Photographed by Preston & Poole', and below that either 'Penzance' or 'Truro'. Lastly, certainly used in 1865 and perhaps in 1864, we find the plume and coronet above 'Preston and Poole' with 'Penzance and Truro' below. For the period after 1862, a Penzance directory of 1864 — compiled in 1863[5] — lists Messrs Preston and Poole as photographic artists, but with no address; nor is either person contained in the list of Penzance residents and house-owners. An address of the studio, with its 'admirably lit Galleries', emerges only in the advertisements[6] and proves to be No.1 South Terrace, where Preston was a lodger.

From the evidence so far, and building on our much more detailed knowledge of Robert Preston's career after 1860, it would be possible to deduce the following. A family called Poole had a photographic studio, probably rented ground-floor accommodation, in River Street, Truro, about 1859−60 (the carte de visite was introduced to Cornwall not earlier than 1858−59). By 1860−61 'Poole' was linked, as the second of two names, with Robert Preston who was then in Penzance. From that time the joint concern was regarded as

Penzance-based, but with an alternative or subsidiary studio in Truro.

If we turn to Devon, Samuel Poole is listed as a photographer at No.6 Southernhay, Exeter, in 1873[7] and in the same directory there is a Samuel Poole at No.4 Somerset Place, Teignmouth. Since these are the only photographers with this surname mentioned in any Cornwall or Devon directory at the period, it is a fair guess that this person – or one of the two, if (say) a father and son are represented by the 1873 entries – was the Poole of Truro a decade earlier. This guess does in fact turn out to be correct.

Samuel Poole senior was listed in 1850[8] as a dye-master with his dye-works at Exe Island, Exeter. A dyer's trade involves familiarity with chemicals and the transfer of images and is a suitable background from which to expand into photography. Mr Poole began his photographic sideline at No.6 Southernhay, probably a little before 1860, and was recorded there in 1864 and 1867.[9] But in the latter year – as in 1873 – there was another Samuel Poole, photographer, at Somerset Place, (West) Teignmouth. He was in fact the son, who by 1867 had returned from Truro to his native Devon. The evidence for this comes from the imprint on the carte, *Fig.93*, kindly provided by friends at a late stage in the search.[10] In purple ink, it reads 'S. Poole, Teignmouth' above the Plume of Feathers and motto, and then 'of the firm of . Preston & Poole, Penzance . and . Truro. Photographers to their Royal Highnesses . The Prince and Princess of Wales.' Since at no stage in the Cornish record is the initial or forename of 'Poole' given, this links the Teignmouth and Truro Pooles as one man, Samuel Poole junior. It also tells us that the date is after the end of 1865, when Preston apparently obtained this Royal appointment.[11] The pre-1865 partnership is not likely to have outlasted Samuel Poole's removal to Teignmouth for very long; *Fig.93* is obviously an 1866 product, in the year in which the partners must have separated, since the partnership is not mentioned in Poole's 1867 directory entry.[12]

The later history of the two Pooles will be taken up by another pen[13] but, in brief, Poole senior (the dyer) continued in Exeter until about 1882. Samuel Poole junior was a photographer at both Somerset Place and No.19 Wellington Street, Teignmouth, until 1899 and died early this century. It is known that he was aged 29 in 1870.[14] We can thus suppose that about 1859, when he would have been 18 and when his father had begun his Exeter photographic side-line, Samuel Poole junior was taken into partnership ('Poole & Son') and despatched to Truro, in order to give him a start in a rented studio. As a youth, he would have been in lodgings anywhere in the area. This Truro branch – in competition with rather larger concerns – survived only because Robert Preston, who in 1859 had come into some money on his parents' death and was looking for an opening, injected himself (and presumably some

Fig.93 'Holding Tight'
This richly caparisoned infant, presumably (though by no means visibly) male, sits well on his pot-bellied little steed. Mother, rather than Nurse, grasps the bridle firmly, but her concentration is beginning to slip. The background is too faint to tell us much, but we are more likely to be in Teignmouth than in Truro. This, not very impressive, example of Samuel Poole's work is at least earlier than 1870, and can be included here for the sake of completeness.
Carte, paper print, Poole, about 1866.   (Author)

capital) into a new partnership. It was in effect a Penzance photographic business, with Preston as the senior partner to Samuel Poole junior; Poole was left to look after the Truro studio, the precise arrangements – as we shall see – leaving Preston free to use another, sole, imprint for certain of his Penzance products. In the winter of 1865–66 the arrangement broke up when Samuel Poole moved to Teignmouth; he was then 25 and would have been commercially independent of his father in Exeter. In making this reconstruction, it is worth pointing out that, apart from one confusing directory entry in 1864 and whatever may be inferred from carte imprints, we have no other evidence for Poole & Son, later Preston & Poole, as Truro photographers for a good six years.

1. R.I.C. collection – too faded to reproduce.
2. Not in S 1853 nor K 1856.
3. H 1862, 940 and advert.
4. Author's colln.
5. C 1864, 130.
6. C 1864, adverts p. 11.
7. K Devon 1873, 616.
8. W Devon 1850, 158.
9. K Devon 1864 and 1867.
10. Mr and Mrs L. Hewitt, Gwithian.
11. See p. 110 below.
12. K Devon 1867.
13. Mr Robin Fenner's *An Illustrated Directory of Devon Photographers 1850–1925* (in preparation: forthcoming).
14. Info. Mr Robin Fenner, Tavistock.

Fig.94   Penzance — The Corner of Green Market and Causewayhead

This is Robert Preston's earliest dated Penzance view, confirming that he was in the town by 1860. Most original prints were sepia-toned; one, in a contemporary frame, has on the wood back a seal — within a double-outline lozenge, the Plume of Feathers above the three-line legend 'R.H. Preston. Photographer. Penzance'. On the mount itself has been written, at the time of framing. 'The Green Market. Photod in 1860'.

There is no reason to question this date. The large building (left), the Three Tuns Hotel, has HEMMINGS along the front of the porch with HOTEL continued on the visible side. George Hemmings, the licensee, died in 1859, but his family must have continued in his place since the licence was not transferred to Thomas James until 15 April 1864. (Note Brooks's similar view, *Fig.19,* which is after the latter date and shows James's name.) The old granite Market Cross is visible (right) at the start of Causewayhead, below the auction poster on the wall; the portico beside it housed a water-shoot.

Albumen print, sepia-toned, from plate, Preston, 1860.   (R.I.C.)

PRESTON, Robert Hawker Peniel
Professional: Penzance (Figs. 94 to 101)

Robert Preston's maternal great-grandfather was Robert Hawker the Calvinistic divine, who had left the Church of England to minister for a half-century at his own church (Charles Church, Plymouth).[1] His son James Stephen Hawker, the photographer's grandfather, was known as 'Jacob'. He qualified as a doctor, but then in 1810 took Holy Orders. After curacies at Altarnun in east Cornwall and, supposedly, for a brief spell at Madron, the mother-church of Penzance, Jacob Hawker became Vicar of Stratton in north-east Cornwall (1833), where he died in 1845.

Jacob Hawker had a large family.[2] The eldest son, who was to become a national figure, was Robert Stephen Hawker — poet, mystic, acquaintance of Tennyson and other notables, Vicar of Morwenstow and inventor of the service of Harvest Thanksgiving.[3] A sister, one of Jacob's five daughters, was Mary Hodson Hawker, who had been named 'Hodson' after a benevolent aunt Mary, Mrs Thomas Hodson. Mary Hawker first married a Colonel Sidley, and after his death, re-married Mr John Preston, gentleman and amateur painter, who came from The Grange,

Fig. 95 *'The Cornish Fishwife'*

Robert Preston's 'Royal Series of Cornish Views' was launched by himself at Penzance, outside the Preston & Poole partnership, about 1863−64 − 'Royal' is to remind us of Preston's involvement in HRH Prince Arthur's visit in 1862. These neat carte-format mementos had their own circular label − wreath, 'Royal Series of Cornish Views' over a crown, rectangle across the middle with the specific title of the item, 'Robt. H. Preston, Photographic Studio, Penzance'. The series included coastal scenery and antiquities from his own and William Brooks's cameras, but he knew enough not to omit the expected. Viewers of this wholly artificial picture would be invited to identify the old lady with Dolly Pentreath. The exploitation of the Mounts Bay beaches and the harbourside scenarios of Penzance, Newlyn and Mousehole had already begun. In Preston's series, the Cornish people themselves were being launched into a career of touristic exposure.

Carte, paper print, Preston, 1863−64.   (Private colln.)

Sheepscombe, near Painswick in Gloucestershire.[4] The Prestons, an old landed family, are today represented in nearby Tetbury by Sir Kenneth Huson Preston (b. 1901).

John and Mary Preston had four children, the first three being baptised at Sheepscombe (Robert Hawker Peniel, 1838; Catherine Frances Mary, 1839; and Cranham John George, 1841). The family then moved to Cheltenham, where Elizabeth Ann was baptised in 1843. After a few years they moved again and by the 1850s had settled in Cornwall, it is believed[5] in the Truro area. Both Preston parents died about 1859 or a little earlier, though their burials have not been traced.[6]

John Preston had private means, and as a painter he remained a gentleman amateur. There must be a suspicion that, among the many Prestons listed as artists or portraitists for the 18th and 19th centuries, other members of this family are included.[7] Robert Hawker Peniel Preston, named in part for his famous uncle the Vicar of Morwenstow,[8] inherited not only his father's artistic bent but, it has to be supposed, an elder son's share of the family wealth.

Fig. 96 *John Thomas Blight, F.S.A.*

The best-known photographic likeness of Blight, the Penzance author, antiquary and illustrator, is that reproduced in John Michell's *A Short Life at the Land's End* (1977), 35. Dated to 26 April 1870 and taken about that time, it shows poor Blight as he then was; virtually unhinged and suffering from delusions and paranoia. In 1871 he was committed to the County Asylum. His death was long assumed to have occurred in 1884 but, as we now know (Michell 1977, 63), he actually died on 23 January 1911.

Preston's portrait is much happier. Blight, born on 27 October 1835 at Penzance, is hardly thirty. The carte imprint, one that antedates the (post Botallack) Preston version with its Royal Appointment, is one of the three-line 'R.H. Preston' varieties that he used independently of the 'Preston & Poole' stampings. Blight's purpose in having this taken may have been to send a likeness to Robert Stephen Hawker, Vicar of Morwenstow (and Preston's own uncle), with whom Blight long corresponded after their meeting in 1856. John Michell's book well describes their up-and-down relationship. Admirers of John Blight and his work will welcome the appearance of ths sensitive image.

Carte, paper print, Preston, 1863−65?   (R.I.C.)

Having sketched this family background, it can be said at once that Robert Preston, J.P., was both the longest-lived and commercially the most successful of Cornwall's early photographers. His name, appended to views, is frequently cited by local historians, but until now there has been no published outline of his life and work, nor has the fact that he was R.S. Hawker's nephew been known. Something of his initial career has been reconstructed already, in the context of his partnership with the Poole family. Assuming that both his parents had died in or about 1859, providing him with funds, we know that at this date he moved to Penzance, where the rest of his life would be spent. One reason for this was suggested in a speech he made in 1887,[9] after his election as Mayor of Penzance; he then said that his mother Mary (Hawker) had been born 'under Madron Church bells', her father Jacob being at the time the curate.[10]

Preston's first-known Penzance photographs date from 1860. In the following year, he was recorded[11] as 'Robert H. Preston, lodger', aged 24, photographic artist, born in Gloucestershire, and living at No.1 South Terrace. The owner of the house was a Mrs Ann Andrews, a widow of 81, and her maidservant Mary Grenfell. South Terrace, on the Penzance sea-front, is a row of early 19th-century marine villas; No.1 occupies the corner with Morrab Road and the shape of the back of the house suggests that Preston rented the ground floor for a studio and accommodation.

By 1862, the well-connected young photographer was in the ascendant. It is possible to deduce that he must have met Augustus Smith (in Penzance), among many other interesting people of the day. Early in September 1862 Smith entertained members of the visiting Cambrian Archaeological Association in Scilly, and for their benefit opened a stone cist in a barrow on the island of Samson. As President of the Royal Institution of Cornwall, Augustus Smith read a short paper describing this excavation in May, 1863; this was published in 1864, with a fine wood engraving showing both cist and upraised lid, signed 'J.T. Blight'.[12] In fact Blight never visited Scilly in his life, and it has recently been discovered that the wood engraving is a very accurate copy of a whole-plate photograph, probably made in the late autumn of 1862.[13] Together with other views of Tresco, it formed a batch sent from Penzance for the Royal collection in 1865. These can be distinguished from others made in Scilly (1861?) by William Richards, who mainly used a stereoscopic camera,[14] and Robert Preston is much the most likely person for Smith to have commissioned on this occasion.

In May of 1862 Preston took a number of photographs, for sale, of a visit to Cornwall by Prince Arthur, the later Duke of Connaught, Queen Victoria's twelve-year-old-son.[15] By the next year the Preston repertoire embraced 'Views of Architecture and Landscape, for Stereoscope or Album.'[16] At this period, it has been suggested that John Gibson was working with Preston, and that William Brooks must also have been

friendly with these two young men. It may be of significance that when, later, Gibson opened his branch studio in Penzance after his return to Scilly, it was in the ground floor of the (vanished) Royal Baths building, not far from No.1 South Terrace where presumably Gibson and Brooks had used Preston's facilities.[17]

By 1864 Robert Preston had arranged to market Brooks's views alongside his own, and was also issuing in carte format his new 'Royal Series of Cornish Views' (Fig. 95). Life in lodgings was, however, beginning to pall. That August, at Madron church, he married Miss Harriet Ann Snell Body, daughter of Thomas Body, gentleman, from Callington.[18] Harriet was twenty-one; the bridegroom was not quite twenty-seven; and their marriage partnership was to continue happily until Robert Preston's death sixty-nine years later. Preston registered himself as 'photographer' and his late father as 'John Preston, gentleman'. Where in Penzance or Madron the young couple set up home is not yet established.

The next year, 1865, Preston achieved the singular coup of being permitted to record officially a second, and more important, Royal visit; the Cornish tour of Albert Edward and Alexandra, of great appeal because they were also present as Duke and Duchess of Cornwall. The climax was the carefully managed descent of Botallack Mine, the pictorial record of which (Figs. 97 to 99) is discussed below. Since Mr (later Sir John) St Aubyn, proprietor of the Mount and host to the Royal pair, was probably responsible for nominating Preston to make the photographs, we can suppose the St Aubyns knew Preston from previous visits to St Michael's Mount.

Between about 1860 and early 1866 Robert Preston used two quite separate series of imprints for his carte views, souvenirs and portraits, and the whole-plate studies that he sometimes sold ready framed by J.C. Uren and others. One series relates to 'R.H. Preston, Penzance', and the other to 'Preston and Poole' in partnership at Penzance and Truro; there is no doubt about their contemporaneity. The agreements underlying all this are now irrecoverable; but there is an inference that Preston, aside from any partnership agreement with the Pooles, was in a legal position to operate on his own. It is likely, as we saw earlier,[19] that Samuel Poole left Cornwall for good in 1866. Before this date the joint Preston & Poole imprint had featured, above any monogram or legend, the Plume and Coronet of the Prince of Wales. Though, strictly, this is a badge of the Prince of Wales as such, and should not be confused with other ancient devices proper to the Duchy of Cornwall, the 'Feathers' have long been employed throughout Cornwall as a patriotic emblem[20] and were indeed used by a number of other early Cornish photographers. After the 1865 Royal visit, however, Preston may have obtained some form of appointment. From the end of 1865, or possibly early in 1866, his single new imprint read 'Robt. H. Preston, Photographer TO THE PRINCE AND

PRINCESS OF WALES, PENZANCE'. Abandoning the Plume of Feathers, he surmounted his legend with the Royal Arms.

Preston acquired new premises about 1870, at No.23 Market Jew Street in the centre of Penzance, the raised part known locally as The Terrace.[21] Though he was doing too well to need the additional promotion of prizes, he did in 1870 show examples at the Polytechnic of his 'patent process called photo-crayon', probably a form of hand-coloured portraits.[22] In 1875 he bought Polmennor House at Heamoor, then in a rural setting on the northern side of Penzance, though he does not seem to have lived there. Three years later he purchased the adjoining Polmennor Farm, and subsequently the farm of Tresvennack in Paul and some other properties. In 1881, leaving whatever home he and Harriet had occupied since their marriage in 1864, he acquired Alverne House, a fine granite residence west of the Greenmarket (later the Camelot Restaurant of the 1970s).[23] It had a large garden at the rear, and a later date the Prestons leased the farther portion of this for the building of three shops just below the present Savoy Cinema.

Investment and return on this scale must suggest not so much inherited capital as business profits and acumen. The Prestons were now substantial Penzance folk, with a growing family. Robert Preston became a councillor of the Borough, and then an alderman, and was elected Mayor for the year 1887–88. During his term of office he played a leading part (for which all Cornish people can be grateful) in the purchase of Morrab House and its grounds, now the home of the private Penzance Library standing within the delightful Morrab Gardens. Preston bought the whole property for £3120, and at once re-sold it to the Borough Council for the same figure.[24]

In 1880 he had joined the committee of that venerable body, the old Penzance Natural History and Antiquarian Society, and for the session of 1898–99 he served as its president. His retiral address was 'a highly interesting account of a tour through Brittany . . . illustrated by numerous fine life-like photographs' (on the epidiascope?). He must also have held other minor offices in Penzance, and from 1888 he served as a magistrate.

Robert Preston died at Penzance on 29 January 1933. It would be hard to say when his last photograph was taken. Local views with the blind-stamp 'Preston – Penzance' were being reproduced and sold after the first World War, at a time when one or more of his sons could have been concerned. On his death, Mr Preston – aged 94 – was claimed to be England's oldest photographer. He had been born one year after William IV's death and had almost outlived three further reigns. The funeral[25] was attended by three sons (Robert, George and Harold) and two sons-in-law. Dr Robert Preston and a family solicitor from Stroud were executors. Harriet, Mrs Preston, outlived him. She also died aged 94 on 21 May 1938[26] and to the family

mourners was added her own brother Mr C.S. Body of Devonport.

The Penzance concern ceased. Of the sons, Harold Preston became a professional photographer. He opened in High Street, Sidmouth, Devon in 1917 and was still in business there in 1926.[27] If George Preston, like his brother Robert, became a medical man, was he the Dr George Preston, M.R.C.S.E., of Port View, Saltash,[28] two of whose (amateur) photographs appear in a 1905 history of that town?

Robert Preston's work, notably in the shape of the images made during his first quarter-century, is of special value because his circumstances apparently permitted him to photograph what interested him, and because his main interest lay in exterior studies. Penzance was never dull; during so long a life he must have met an exceptional range of people, and have recorded with an artist's eye a Cornwall that changed gradually from a now-forgotten world to modern times. We can only regret that he was not left any kind of memoir. Cornish historians could also reproach themselves that this present entry is the first, if condensed, account of so interesting a career. Robert Hawker Peniel Preston retains an unchallengeable position, as the premier cameraman of Victorian Cornwall.

1. See entry in D.N.B., and also Fleming, Guy, *Hidden Fire – Plymouth: Its Christian Heritage* (Plymouth, 1986), chap. 4 with illus.

2. F.G. Lee's *Memorials of the Rev. R.S. Hawker* (1876) gives an incomplete family tree, omitting Mary Hodson Hawker, who seems to have been the youngest child.

3. Byles, C.E., *The Life and Letters of R.S. Hawker* (1905) – which includes Robert Preston's name in the acknowledgements; Brendon, Piers, *Hawker of Morwenstow* (1975).

4. Info. Mrs Evelyn Batty, Oxford, great-granddaughter of Catherine Preston.

5. Info. Mrs Batty.

6. At neither Kenwyn nor St Mary's cemeteries (fully listed).

7. 'Captain' Thomas Preston, painter, d. 1759; E. Preston, portraitist, in London 1842–43; H.J. Preston, landscape painter in 1855–67.

8. The name 'Peniel' appears to be Welsh.

9. *Cornishman & Cornish Telegraph,* 17 Nov 1887.

10. Though the fact of this curacy must be accepted, no record of it can be found; it may have been very brief.

11. Census 1861; see also C 1864, 62, 130, and p. 11 of adverts.

12. *46 Ann. Rep.,* R.I.C., appendix VI (Truro, 1864).

13. Royal Archives, Windsor; this will be separately published.

14. See p. 117 below.

15. *RCG* 23 May 1862.

16. C 1864, p. 11 of adverts.

17. The 1870s Gibson studio is shown (a William Richards view?) as Fig.50 in: Bird, Sheila, *Bygone Penzance & Newlyn* (Phillimore, 1987).

18. Madron registers, Marriages 1864, fol. 46, entry No. 92.

19. See p. 107 above.

20. Common in 1860–period Rifle Volunteers devices (cf. *Fig.48*), and as 'Three Feathers' and 'Plume of Feathers' inn signs.

21. K 1873; K 1883.

22. 38 RCPS, cat. p. 15.

23. Information from Mr and Mrs P.A.S. Pool, who lived at Heamoor and have made a special study of this; see Watkiss 1975b, Fig.36 (1907).

24. Noall, Cyril, *The Penzance Library 1818–1968* (Penzance, 1968), 18 – for Preston's involvement (not mentioned by Noall), info. Mr Pool.

25. *Cornish Evening Tidings*, 30 Jan & 2 Feb 1933.

26. *Ibidem*, 23 & 24 May 1938.

27. Info. Mr Robin Fenner, Tavistock.

28. K 1902, 292 & 513; see also Porter, P.E.B., *Around and About Saltash* (Dingle, Saltash, 1905), pp. 127, 181, by 'Dr G. Preston'.

Robert Preston and the Royal Visit to Botallack, 1865

A descent of the Boscawen shaft, a long incline going under the sea, at Botallack Mine, St Just, was arranged as a part of the visit of Prince Albert Edward and Princess Alexandra to Cornwall in July 1865. Details of the occasion are preserved in contemporary press accounts.[1] Robert Preston's photographic record brought him much publicity and large sales.

Previous reproductions in print of Preston's images do not make it clear that, having followed the Royal party across country from Penzance to Botallack on the morning of 24 July 1865, Robert Preston took at least four separate views of the start of the descent. At the mine, where the wheeled skip let down on a cable normally took only 6 or 7 persons, the Royal party alone numbered fourteen. Three, perhaps four, separate trips were necessary. The visitors included the Prince and Princess; Mr John and Lady Elizabeth St Aubyn from St Michael's Mount (the hosts for the occasion), with Lady Elizabeth's mother Lady Townsend; John St Aubyn's younger brother Edward; the Duke and Duchess of Sutherland, the Duke of St Albans, the Earl of Mount Edgcumbe, Lord and Lady Vivian, and Captain and Lady De Grey.

The classic view, with the Prince and Princess about to go down, is shown here as *Fig. 97*. Versons, in whole-plate format and in a smaller, cut, format centred on the Royal party, were sold widely all over west Cornwall.[2] The Royal Institution of Cornwall has examples of both, and a very fine print of the larger version (the bottom margin clipped slightly) was sent to the Royal Archives at Windsor.[3]

Preston must have then taken the second party to descend, but no clear print of this has been found. He then photographed the third party, which consisted entirely of the remaining gentlemen, and did so twice. The first of the images *(Fig. 98)* was included in *Trounson 1981*, as Fig.8, but is there wrongly identified as the second descent. The other image (here, *Fig. 99*, from a Preston print in its contemporary frame and mount) is of special interest because it must have been made almost immediately after the first, and had not previously been recognised as such.

1. Noall 1972, 71–5.

2. Smaller format; see, e.g. Noall 1972, 103.

3. Kindly confirmed by Miss Frances Dymond, Curator.

Fig.100 Her Royal Highness in Mining Dress
After the Royal visit to Botallack most of the party went on to see Land's End, but the Princess was fatigued and returned to the Mount. Here she is, in front of a doorway (to the Blue Drawing-Room) on the terrace by the Church, where Preston could best catch the afternoon light. This was issued as a commercial carte; below is printed in script 'H.R.H. the Princess of Wales in the Mining dress worn by her Royal Highness in the descent of Botallack Mine July 24. 1865'. The imprint on the back is the Plume of Feathers and motto, above a four-line 'Preston and Poole. Penzance. and. Truro — Copyright'.

Carte, paper print, Preston, July 1865.   (R.I.C.)

Fig.97 The Royal Party at Botallack; First Descent
This, more than any other single image, consolidated Robert Preston's reputation. The skip is about to descend the inclined Boscawen Shaft, down to the 235-fathom level (about 2400 feet of inclined rail). Captain John Boyns, manager, was already underground and the elderly suited person, top hat in hand, may be the Purser. In the front of the skip are Mr St Aubyn and the beautiful Danish princess, whose charms have already reduced to jelly the hearts of the rugged St Just men. Behind them is Lady Elizabeth St Aubyn; then, side by side, a gentleman with no hat and another lady, either the Vivians or Sutherlands. The Prince of Wales is behind the lady and Captain John Rowe acts as brakesman. The full unclipped print, as shown here, includes front of the skip and the blurred figure (left) standing by it. Note the bushes and greenery decorating the wooden stage housing.
Albumen print from plate, Preston, 24 July 1865.   (R.I.C.)

Fig.98   The Third Descent − Getting Ready to Go

The second party down the shaft (not illustrated here) would have comprised Lady Townsend, Lady de Grey, and either the Sutherlands or the Vivians − whichever were not in the first skipload. This would have left the Duke of St Albans, The Earl of Mount Edgcumbe, Captain de Grey and Edward St Aubyn. Here they are, with another mining official (rear, left, next to young Edward in his peaked cap), and Captain John Rowe standing, about to don his helmet and resume his brakesman's seat. The despatching party have put on their top-hats. Note the front of the skip, which is still raised, and not yet tipped down to engage the rails.

Albumen print from plate, Preston, 24 July 1865.   (R.I.C.)

Fig.99   The Third Descent − Just Off

Comparison with *Fig.98* shows that this was made only minutes later. Captain Rowe is in the skip, the despatchers have backed into the housing and the skip's front has been lowered. Not hitherto known, this fine print in sepia tone, 143 by 156 mm, is mounted in a glazed gilt frame with 'J.C. Uren, Carver, Gilder, &c, Penzance, 1867' pencilled on the back of the mount. Printed on the mount is 'Preston & Poole, Photographers, Penzance' with, below the view, THE VISIT OF THE PRINCE AND PRINCESS OF WALES TO CORNWALL and, below that, 'The Royal Party at Botallack Tin Mine, July 24th 1865'. Mr Uren would have prepared numerous such mounted and framed copies for sale, in which the actual photograph could have been chosen from three, four or more of the relevant Preston images.

Albumen print from plate, Preston, 24 July 1865.   (Private colln.)

Fig.101   'The Princess and the Mineral Hammer'

In this delightful study Princess Alexandra has been posed against the battlements on the terrace, and invited to shoulder her souvenir hammer from Botallack. Beautiful as ever, she looks tired, and no wonder; one hopes that this was Preston's last photographic request. It is doubtful whether this particular image was ever issued commercially.

Paper print, carte format, in album, Preston, July 1865.

(Royal Archives, Windsor Castle. Copyright reserved. Reproduced by gracious permission of Her Majesty Queen Elizabeth II.)

RASHLEIGH, Jonathan
Amateur(?): Fowey

The evidence for Mr Rashleigh's involvement in photography is circumstantial, not direct, but sufficient to warrant his inclusion. A member of the Fowey family of Rashleighs of Menabilly, he was born in 1820, and inherited Menabilly when he was fifty-one, on the death of his brother William. He was married twice; to Mary Pole Stuart in 1843, and after she died, to an Irish lady, Jane Pugh.

Mr Rashleigh had private means. He was High Sheriff in 1877, and for many years was a keen member of the Polytechnic at Falmouth, serving on the society's Committee over a long period, and acting as a Vice-President from 1872.[1] Educated at Harrow and then a tutor's before going to Balliol, he lived partly in London — where he held some minor public offices — and partly in Cornwall. He contributed articles to the *Numismatic Chronicle,* and died in 1905.[2]

Among the Rashleigh material at Cornwall County Record Office is a large bound album, compiled at some stage in the mid-1860s, that contains over a hundred photographic prints. These are pasted in, and most have been dated and identified in pencilled notes.[3] The coincidence of the locations — Menabilly and other large houses in Cornwall, Harrow School, Aldenham Abbey (home of the Stuarts, his first wife's family), Balliol and other colleges, etc. — with the known life-story of Jonathan Rashleigh shows that it must have been his own compilation. Some of the photographs are bought items, including an interesting set of whole-plate prints by R.P. Yeo[4] made at Cotehele, near Callington, of the house and its contents. Others show family groups and social visits, including several to the Fox family at Grove Hill, Falmouth. These are half-plate albumen prints, many sepia-toned, and clearly the work of a private photographer. Unless some other member of his family was responsible, there is a very strong presumption that Jonathan Rashleigh himself was the cameraman.

1. 73 RCPS, 20 (the writer's own bound run of RCPS originally belonged to Mr Rashleigh, with his Menabilly book-plate).
2. BC 546.
3. Accession No. D.D.R(S) 107.
4. See p. 139 below.

RICHARDS, William
Professional: Penzance (Figs. 102 to 104)

The story of William Richards has been partly covered in the entry for his wife's stepfather, William Jenkyns,[1] but a good deal more must be added.

Mr Richards was born at Penzance in 1835.[2] The likelihood is that he was a son of William Richards, currier, of No.2 Alverton Street.[3] In 1864 Penzance supported no less than fourteen curriers, serving over sixty boot- and shoe-makers, harness-makers and dealers in leather goods.[4] We know that William Richards began his working life in the fine leather

Fig.102   Self-Portrait

William Richards's descendants own a set of glass plates 4¾ by 6½ inches, in the slotted box in which they have been kept for over a century. They are in excellent condition, are all family portraits, and two show a young man and his wife. The man is Mr William Richards himself. He would have taken the likeness of his wife Ruth, and then arranged for her (or his mother-in-law) to operate the camera and lens in respect of his own. The carefully fixed expression — is there a tiny hint of anxiety? — suggests that he has ordered Ruth Richards to take it slowly, and not to jog anything.

Mr Richards was born in 1835. Here, he is certainly not much, if at all, older than thirty. The formal dress, the watch-chain and the general air of responsibility proclaim him as being now in command at No.2, Queen Street.

Print, from original plate, Richards, c. 1865.   (Richards colln.)

trade[5] and it was conceivably in this occupational context that William Jenkyns, photographer and one-time currier himself, first met him; did Jenkyns once work for, or with, Richards senior?

Like William Jenkyns, Mr Richards would have learnt, or taught himself, photography in the later 1850s. When Jenkyns died in 1860, and William and Ruth Richards moved into No.2 Queen Street, Penzance, home of her widowed mother, they had three children[6] — William junior (4), Thomas (3) and the baby John. A decade later, Thomas and John are not mentioned — had they died young? — but Frederick (aged 7), George and Edward had come along.[7] William junior was apprenticed to a Penzance mason.[8]

When mother-in-law Jenkin and her three surviving

Fig.103 New Grimsby Channel, Tresco, Isles of Scilly
Following the little Prince Arthur's visit in 1862, Edward Rowe the Penzance bookseller forwarded an assortment of views, photographs and stereographs to the Palace (*West Briton*, 30 May 1862). The Queen and Prince Albert had visited Scilly in 1847, and the account of Rowe's gratifying commission makes particular mention of stereographs of some beautiful views afforded by the Scilly Islands 'which have recently been taken by a skilled photographer and will soon be ready' — i.e. were in existence, in Penzance, as prints but not yet been put on sale as slides.

The 'skilled photographer' cannot have been Preston, who is mentioned prominently by name as having photographed the Prince. Rowe had sold the J.W.G. Gutch series, but Gutch did not visit Scilly and as far as we know did not bother to take stereographs. William Jenkyns died in 1860 (if not 1859), and May 1862 is too early for Gibson, who used a plate camera, to have worked in Scilly; while William Brooks was not in Penzance until 1864 (or 1863). This leaves us with Charles Lobb, and William Richards, who was certainly active in 1862 and unlike Lobb worked from Penzance. The stereographs sent to Windsor have disappeared; the 1862 Penzance and Scilly views have not, are in an album in the Royal Archives, and are all 2¾ by 3 inch prints — the normal stereograph size, if (as seems likely) these are single prints from stereoscopic pairs. Richards is by far and away the best candidate.
Stereograph, Richards (?), early 1862.   (Private colln.)

children by her marriage to William Jenkin or Jenkyns had disappeared from the scene, the Richards had Queen Street to themselves, and kept it for over a century. William junior eventually returned to the photographic fold and took over the business from his father. He died aged 80 in 1937; having married young, he actually outlived his own son Edward, third of the Richards photographers, who was born in 1875 but died in 1935 aged 60 — with a long record of photography in west Cornwall, and the award of a diploma from the Polytechnic at Falmouth.[9] The family business had passed to Edward's two sons, Edward (junior), born in 1911, and his brother Reginald

eighteen months the younger. When at last in 1977 the firm of 'William Richards, Photographer' closed its doors, it had been in existence longer than any of its kind in Cornwall. Assuming that William Jenkyns (step-great-great-grandfather to the Richards brothers) began to trade in views about 1852, we can allow them century and a quarter of solid photography.

The bulk of the surviving Richards negatives, and they include many fine turn-of-the-century shipwreck and lifeboat studies, are now in the recently catalogued collection at the Penzance Library, Morrab Gardens. Among various very early glass plates and prints therefrom it is not really possible to be sure which were inherited from Jenkyns and which were made by William Richards. A box of plates of family likenesses (from which *Fig.102* has been chosen) is certainly Richards's work. Most recently, examination of albums in the Royal Archives at Windsor Castle suggests that among the selection sent from Penzance in 1862 — discussed in connection with Robert Preston's early years[10] — a number of small views are single prints from stereoscopic pairs, date from 1861–62 (or earlier) and were not made by Brooks, cannot safely be attributed to Preston, and in all probability are William Richards's products. *Fig.104* comes from this group, and *Fig.103*, from another source, is by analogy also considered to be a Richards stereograph. Since hardly any of Cornwall's early photographers have left us images in which they themselves appear, it is particularly welcome to have William Richards's self-portrait.

1. See p. 74 above.
2. On the evidence of Census 1861.
3. S 1852, 41.
4. Listed in C 1864.
5. 'Shoemaker' in Census 1861, and see p. 76.
6. Census 1861.
7. Census 1871.
8. Info. Mr Edward Richards, Penzance.
9. Obituary, *Cornishman* (Penzance — undated, but in 1935).
10. See p. 108 above.

RICKARDS, Robert Francis Bute
Amateur: Constantine

Mr Rickards, born at the Cape of Good Hope in March 1812, was the son of Robert Rickards, formerly an official member of the Council of the Honourable East India Company's Bengal Presidency and from 1813 to 1816 the M.P. for Wootton Basset. Educated at Balliol, Mr Rickards was ordained in 1839. He served as curate in two Devonshire parishes, and on 17 October 1856 was inducted as Vicar of Constantine.[1] In the course of his career he took up the hobby of photography. In 1857, he exhibited six of his views of Constantine at the Polytechnic,[2] in whose programme and report his surname was predictably misprinted as 'Richards', the usual Cornish form.[3]

Sadly, he was accidentally killed on 2 November 1874 while inspecting repairs on the roof of his church.

Fig.104 Market Jew Street, Penzance

Penzance's main street enters the town from the Marazion (or Market Jew) end; the large building with its classical front is the Market House, in front of which (1872) the statue of Sir Humphry Davy was placed. The vehicles parked, right, are the horse buses in their so-called 'Eastern Omnibus Station'. The lengths of street at the sides of, and behind, the Market House made 'Market Place', and the shop front of Symons (Dispensing and Practical Chemist — later, Symons & Guy) can be made out at No.1, left of the Market House.

The original albumen print, in its Royal Archives album, is a 2¾ by 3 inches print with rounded top corners, almost certainly from a stereoscopic pair. As explained in the caption to *Fig.103*, it is on balance most likely to be by Richards.

Albumen print (from stereo. pair?), Richards(?), before 1862.

(Royal Archives, Windsor Castle. Copyright reserved. Reproduced by gracious permission of Her Majesty Queen Elizabeth II.)

He left behind a widow and eleven children (they had thirteen in all).[4] With what now seems almost indecent haste — even if one can understand the spur of need — all his effects were auctioned at the Polytechnic Hall, Falmouth, on 24 November. They included 'a library of upwards of 2000 volumes . . . magic lantern, transit instruments, etc.'.[5] Though he published a few articles, they were entirely devotional, and he played no other part in early Cornish photography.

1. BC 570.
2. 25 RCPS, xxx.
3. And elsewhere as 'Rickard', also a Cornish surname.
4. Henderson, Charles, *A History of the Parish of Constantine in Cornwall* (1937), 68; also CC 805.
5. BC 570.

Fig.105   Captain and Mrs Athanasius Pryor and Family
On the back of this carte de visite is written 'Captn. Atheneus Pryor's (Lanner) Family Group 1866'. The print itself was copied from its negative a little later, since the imprint proclaims Matthew Row's award of 'the only Prize given for Carte Pictures at the Polytechnic in 1867'. Pryor's title of 'Captain' was a courtesy; he was in fact an assayer, rather than an agent, operating at Lanner Moor, and his baptismal name was Athanasius. The extremely formal group, in which the schoolboy sons have been scrubbed and told to stand up straight and keep still, exemplifies the new social standing of Cornish mining's managerial class in the 1860s. Athanasius junior (back row, centre) eventually became land steward to John Charles Williams, Esq., Burncoose, Gwennap. One hopes that the other lads went into mining. The Pryors, on a larger scale, made up an influential family in the area. In 1862 Francis Pryor was manager of some eight mines, with his son W.H. Pryor a surface agent at two of them, and Richard Pryor had charge of another five.
Carte, paper print, Row, 1866.   (R.I.C.)

ROW, Matthew
Professional: Redruth (Fig.105)

In Cornwall, Mr Row's surname is more usually spelled 'Rowe', or even 'Rawe', which reproduces one way of pronouncing it; but the shorter form is still in use. Matthew Row began life as a gilder and painter. His earliest imprint (stamped, not printed) describes him as a 'Photographer and Gilder'. In 1866, he was noticed as a photographic artist in Penryn Street, Redruth.[1] The next year his entry of a set of cartes de

visite won him a prize at the Polytechnic's exhibition.[2] In 1868, he was exhibiting again, this time in the class for Professionals,[3] with some 'frames of portraits', and more were submitted in 1869 and 1870.[4]

Mr Row was never more than a competent portrait photographer in a small town, but he did well enough during the 1860s to move his studio to a more central location. By 1873, his premises were in Buller's Row, Redruth, up at the east end of the town.[5] More of his work was shown at the Polytechnic in 1875,[6] including 'an original design for a memorial card', a Victorian curiosity where the portrait of the deceased could be re-photographed, as a carte, inside a wreath with cross. There is no record of Matthew Row by 1876, or later,[7] but we do not have the date of his retirement or death.

1. D 1866, 77 ('carver, gilder, toy-seller and photographer').
2. 35 RCPS, 15 — prize of 10s.
3. 36 RCPS, 18.
4. 37 RCPS, 34; 38 RCPS, cat. p. 16.
5. K 1873.
6. 43 RCPS, cat. p. 25.
7. Not in P 1876 and K 1883.

RULE, John
Amateur: Camborne (Fig. 107)

John Rule was born at Camborne in 1801,[1] and was the eldest surviving son of Captain John Rule (senior) and his wife Anne Bennett. His father (1752–1834) was a well-known mine agent, and at the time of his death was the manager of Dolcoath Mine. John Rule (junior, as he was usually distinguished) went underground at Dolcoath when he was fourteen[2] and became an agent in the mine in his early twenties.[3] In 1824 he left for Mexico, worked for many years in the complex of silver-mines centred on the Real del Monte, and finally became a Commissioner of Mines in 1832.[4] In May 1834 he came back to Cornwall on prolonged leave — at the time of his father's last illness — and on 16 January 1835 he married a Miss Philippa Tocker of Gwinear, who was slightly older than himself. The Rules then returned to Mexico;[5] but in February 1843 John Rule resigned his positions and once more returned, this time for good, to Cornwall.[6]

He bought a large house, Parc Bracket, in Camborne, and engaged in sporadic consultancy work. He was a member of the Royal Geological Society of Cornwall, to whose *Transactions* he contributed,[7] and also of the Polytechnic at Falmouth; here he was soon invited to join its main Committee. In directories of the period[8] he is listed as 'John Rule, Esq., Parc Bracket' and as a private resident. Philippa, Mrs Rule, died at Bath on 20 February 1861, probably while taking a cure.[9] There were no children of the marriage. John 'Mexico' Rule, as he was called far and wide, died at Parc Bracket on 12 May 1866 and was buried beside his wife in Camborne parish churchyard. His age at

Fig.106   Captain John Rule of Parc Bracket
Half-length portrait, signed 'T. Boldan' (?), and painted about 1850−55 at Parc Bracket, Camborne; after Captain Rule's death this was left to his cousin Julia Vivian Yewens *(Fig.86)* and is now owned by her great-great-grandson.
(New photograph, author, 1987).

death was variously give as '82' or '83'.[10] The strain and heat of years in Mexico may have taken their toll, but he was in fact only 64. His younger brother William, who had been with him in Mexico, came back to Camborne after 1843 and took up residence in Camborne Veor, once their father's home.[11] When John Rule (junior) died, Parc Bracket was sold by his executors to a third Camborne mining man who had worked in Mexico, William Rabling (1806−70).[12] Today the house is the local Conservative and Unionist Club.

John 'Mexico' Rule was related to many of the other Camborne people mentioned in this book. His mother, and the mother of Mrs Julia Vivian Dunstan or Yewens *(Fig.86)*, were sisters; it was Julia Yewens who, as a cousin, inherited the oil portrait of Rule *(Fig.106)* painted in the 1850s. Through the Bennett family, John Rule was related to the various Thomas mine-captains associated with Dolcoath *(Figs.4 and 83)*; and his own sister Susanna Rule (b. 1800) was the mother of the lawyer John Rule Daniell *(Fig.77)*. John Rule may have been alone at Parc Bracket in his final few years, but he was in his native town, and it is odd that among all these connections no-one seems to have known his true age when he died.[13]

His hobbies included mineralogy, and playing the violin.[14] To these must, it seems, be added photography. In the 1863 Art Union of Cornwall draw, two

of the photographs listed were 'Happy As A King' and 'Porch of Jedburgh Abbey', both taken by 'John Rule, Esq.'.[15] The significance of the latter title, with its hint of a trip to the North in the company of other amateurs, has already been mentioned.[16] It is true that there were other John Rules in Cornwall, but no other 'John Rule, Esq.' subscribed to the Polytechnic; we know that another Camborne amateur, Mr Hambly, had an 1863 photograph of Durham Cathedral, and the second 'Porch of Jedburgh Abbey' view was by Francis Luke at nearby Scorrier.

This leads on to another interesting possibility. Captain John Rule senior and his wife Anne were both painted in oils, at or soon after the time of their marriage in 1796. The originals have long since vanished. Both portraits were however photographed and the resulting carte prints, with William Piper's earliest mark (oval strap: 'Piper, Photographic Artist, Camborne'), were given to various related Camborne families for their own albums. Piper may of course have undertaken the photography, in this case about 1859−60; but is it just conceivable that John 'Mexico' Rule himself, in the context of his new pastime, made the images of his parents' portraits himself, and then got the nearby Piper to produce prints for family circulation?

Fig.107   Captain John Rule (senior), of Camborne Veor
The original portrait in oils, long since lost, was probably commissioned in 1796, at the time of John Rule's marriage to Anne Bennett; he was then forty-four, and there was a matching oil of his wife. Surviving as a small print mounted in carte format, with William Piper's earliest imprint on the back, the actual image may have been made around 1860 by John Rule (junior) − bringing thus together his father's portrait and his own photographic hobby − and then getting Piper to make multiple prints. At least three such copies can be traced.
Paper print on carte, Rule(?), about 1860−62?   (Author)

1. Baptised at Camborne, 2 May 1802.

2. *Trans. Roy. Geol. Soc. Cornwall* (Penzance), I (1818), 225.

3. At Dolcoath in 1822 he was 'Capt. J. Rule jnr.'.

4. Todd, A.C., *The Search for Silver; Cornish Miners in Mexico* (1977).

5. Todd, *op.cit.*, 88, 91.

6. Todd, 142; BC 607.

7. In 1846 and 1850 — BC 607.

8. W 1847, S 1852, K 1856.

9. Her gravestone, Camborne parish churchyard.

10. BC 607; RCG 17 May 1866, p. 8.

11. Todd, *op.cit.*; CC 850, 932, 1158.

12. CC 780.

13. Julia Yewens's memorandum book has 'Cousin John Rule died May 12th 1866 aged' (date crossed out) '83'.

14. Tuck, W.R., *Reminiscences of Camborne* (Truro, n.d. = 1880), 19.

15. See p. 17 above.

16. See p. 87 above.

STEPHENS, John Counsell
Professional: Falmouth (Fig.1 & 108)

J.C. Stephens would have been born about 1815—20; his baptism is not recorded in any Anglican register in Cornwall and Devon, the name 'Counsell' is not apparently a Westcountry one, and we must assume he came from elsewhere.

He has been already mentioned, briefly, as a daguerreotypist.[1] He won a First Prize at the Polytechnic in 1849, as an amateur entrant in the Fine Arts section, with some daguerreotypes,[2] and a Third Prize in 1851 with a similar exhibit.[3] The list of subscribers to the Polytechnic includes, from 1848 onwards, a 'J. Stephens' with an annual subscription of 5s.[4] but the surname is widespread in Cornwall and this was not necessarily the same man.

Assuming that he was in Cornwall by 1849, the first known address for Mr Stephens was at West End, Redruth, in 1855; from here he was advertising photographic likenesses, frames included, for 4s. 6d. upward, and a portrait drawn on stone 'from an excellent Daguerreotype likeness' of William Richards, surgeon.[5] Mr Richards had died in June 1855.[6] It therefore looks as if Redruth was Mr Stephens's place of work from 1849 to 1855.

Between then and 1859 he moved to Falmouth. The Perran Foundry interior *(Fig.108),* probably his work, may imply a Falmouth base because of the Fox family connection with the foundry; *Fig.1,* of the 1859 Falmouth Polytechnic meeting, surely points to an on-the-spot cameraman. There is ample later evidence for these guesses. In 1862 he was listed as working from High Street, Falmouth,[7] confirmed by a press report[8] of the disastrous fire of 1862 that destroyed thirty houses in the High Street between the Town Hall and Market Strand including 'a small and very old house occupied by Mr Stephens, photographer'. The home was however at Berkeley Place where, sadly, four-year-old Bessie Counsell Stephens died shortly before Christmas 1862.[9]

Mr Stephens found a new shop in Church Street, much closer to the Polytechnic.[10] Here he practised as a photographer, picture frame maker, and dealer in pictures and fine art materials. This must be seen alongside his other involvements. We know that he acted as manager, and then as secretary, of the Art Union of Cornwall. His standing at the Polytechnic was indicated by a further appointment in 1866[11] as an Assistant Secretary. He continued to exhibit, entering cartes de visite in competitions in 1865 and again in 1866.[12]

Mr Stephens's commercial history suggests minor expansion. By 1865 the business had become 'J.C. Stephens & Co.,' but without any indication as to who was his partner or assistant. After the period in Church Street, he returned to No.42 High Street by 1873,[13] though rather unexpectedly is not listed in any directory after this date. Two carte portraits which give every indication of dating from around 1880 bear imprints of 'Stephens, Photographers' (in the plural) and 'Stephens and Siddons, Photographers, 42 High Street, Falmouth'.[14] They must reflect the closing phase of his career. Mr Siddons — probably not Cornish — is mentioned nowhere else, and there is no record of him as a photographer, framer, colourist or anything else.

J.C. Stephens was a photographer in Cornwall for over 30 years and had these close associations with the Polytechnic. In 1866, for example, when Dr Le Neve Foster was appointed Secretary, Stephens was at once made 'Assistant or Deputy', otherwise 'assistant local secretary', and as well as being given a First Bronze Medal for his frames of vignetted portraits was also awarded a complimentary First Silver Medal 'for managing this department'.[15] Despite this, not much is known about him, and one hopes that more may emerge.

1. See p. 20 above.

2. 17 RCPS, xxiii.

3. 19 RCPS, xx.

4. 16 RCPS, 47.

5. WB 20 July 1855.

6. CC 803.

7. H 1862, 843.

8. RCG 18 Apr 1862.

9. RCG 26 Dec 1862, p. 5 col. 1.

10. Wa 1864, 77.

11. W.L. Fox 1915, 45 (wrongly as 'J.G. Stephens').

12. 33 RCPS, xxiv; 34 RCPS, xxxii.

13. K 1873.

14. Info. Mr Winfrith Scutt; City of Plymouth Museums & Art Gallery, album (accession no. 1986, 687), pp. 23—4.

15. 34 RCPS, x, xv, xxxii and lix.

Fig.108 Interior of a Foundry Workshop

The original of this striking image is a plate, 6 by 8 inches, in the Institution's collection; unidentified but of Cornish provenance. The consensus of informed opinion is that it may represent the smiths' shop at Perran Foundry (see Barton, D.B., *The Cornish Beam Engine* (Truro, 1965), 154 & pl. xxiv). This famous foundry was started in 1791, alongside the navigable tidal inlet of the Fal at Perran Wharf, by the Fox family of Falmouth. Progressively during the early 19th century shares were acquired by the Williams family, who completed their domination by 1858, the Foxes then concentrating on Falmouth Docks.

In this view, important gentlemen in top hats are standing near a vertical engine (boiler and valve gear). Is this 1858, or a year either side of it, and is the occasion so depicted an aspect of the take-over?

There were not many photographers at the time, in the area, likely to have been on hand. J.C. Stephens was closely associated with the Polytechnic (and thus known to the Foxes); he was at the supposed date either in Redruth or, perhaps already, Falmouth (see *Fig.1*). Perranarworthal is far too distant from Penzance to suggest William Jenkyns's involvement.

Print from original plate, Stephens(?), late 1850s.   (R.I.C.)

TALBOT, William Henry Fox, F.R.S.
Visiting Professional (Fig.109)

W.H. Fox Talbot remains the most famous of all the early British photographers. His personal history and his role in the development of processes, and in the art itself, are too well chronicled to require even a summary here.[1] He was born on 11 February 1800. His father William Davenport Talbot had married Elisabeth Fox Strangways, a daughter of the Earl of Ilchester, and her sister Charlotte Anne later married Sir Charles Lemon, F.R.S., of Carclew near Truro. Fox Talbot's Cornish connection centred upon his distinguished uncle by marriage. Its extent has not been entirely explored, nor is there any detailed list of the specifically Cornish items among the thousands of Fox Talbot photographs held in the Science Museum, London.[2]

Given the Lemon relationship, and Sir Charles's friendship with Robert Were Fox's family and long presidency of the Polytechnic, we can assume Fox Talbot knew something of the background to photographic research in Cornwall. T.B. Jordan publicised his use of Fox Talbot's prepared paper;[3] in 1840 Robert Hunt and Fox Talbot were vicariously in contact through Herschel and the following year in correspondence.[4] Fox Talbot made a visit to Carclew in August 1841. Whom, apart from his cousins, he then met is not known, but it was surely on this occasion that — through his Uncle Charles — an entire album of Talbot calotypes was conveyed as a gift to the Polytechnic.[5]

Fig.109   View from Mount Edgcumbe

This striking image, not apparently published before, shows one of the little shore batteries at Mount Edgcumbe, by Plymouth Sound, looking east across the mouth of the Tamar at Devonport and the handsome granite range of the Royal William Victualling Yard. It is in composition so close to another version, with figures (cf. Buckland 1980, 165), as to allow the same date; probably September 1845, when Fox Talbot was on a visit.

Print, from original, Fox Talbot, 1845.

(Science Museum)

Fox Talbot made a number of images at Carclew. Three were published by Andrew Lanyon[6] as 'The First Cornish Photographs?' — as they must be, unless it can ever be shown that Hunt's own Falmouth 'Energiatypes' *(Fig.51)* precede them, even by a few weeks. Two more Carclew views, both dated to 30 August 1841, are accessible in print.[7]

William Davenport Talbot had sadly died when his young son was only five weeks old; Lady Elisabeth in 1804 re-married, to Captain Charles Feilding, R.N. In 1831 their daughter Caroline, Fox Talbot's step-sister, married a Cornishman, Ernest Augustus Edgcumbe (Lord Valletort, heir to the Earl of Mount Edgcumbe). This provided an additional reason for the photographer to visit Cornwall; and on one such trip, probably that made in September 1845, he made a number of images at Mount Edgcumbe. One of them is well-known and

has been reproduced.[8] That shown here *(Fig.109)*, by courtesy of the Science Museum, is not encumbered with human figures and — while looking at the Devonport side of the Tamar mouth — was taken on Cornish soil. It may aptly be included as a small tribute.

1. Arnold 1977 and Buckland 1980 are both excellent monographs.
2. Many of them (trees, foliage, woodland scenes) cannot now be geographically located.
3. See p. 81 above.
4. See p. 71 above.
5. W.L. Fox 1915, 11; where is this album now?
6. Lanyon 1984b, Figs.2–4; see also Arnold 1977, Fig.42.
7. Buckland 1980, 142–3.
8. Buckland, 165 — also as Arnold, Fig.43; add Buckland, 191.

Fig.110   A Temperance Society Outing on the Strand

The Strand, at Bude (or 'Bude Haven', as it was generally called in the last century), forms the bank of the tidal estuary. Harry Thorn's panoramic view shows the annual procession of the Bude Band of the Temperance Society, banner in the forefront, as the members walk to the Summerleaze downs for the children's sports. This pleasant outing would have been followed by a grand (temperance) tea in the Parish Hall. Details of the setting are explained in the caption to the next illustration.

Carte, paper print, H. Thorn, c. 1860.

(Thorn family colln.)

THOMSON, Hugh
Visiting(?) Professional: Hayle and Truro

'During the last fortnight' stated a newspaper account, dated from Hayle in October of 1853,[1] 'a number of persons have availed themselves of the visit of Messrs Jenkyn and Thomson, photographic artists, to secure correct and beautiful likenesses of themselves and families. Great satisfaction has been given by the lifelike appearance of the portraits, which for warmth of colour, beauty of design, and forcibility of style, cannot be surpassed. They show the perfection of the improvements in Daguerreotype as practised by these talented artists'.

This reference is of particular interest in that it appears to mark the photographic debut of Mr 'Jenkyn', or William Jenkyns of Penzance.[2] Mr Thomson is presumably the man who, six months later, proclaimed in an advertisement[3] that portraits would be taken daily 'at 15 Frances Street, Truro, by Mr Hugh Thomson at prices from 4s. 6d. each. Specimens to be seen at the rooms'. Frances Street, the western continuation of River Street, was fairly new and 'the rooms' would have been a hire of space in a private home or boarding-house, rather than a shop. The price of the portraits suggests collodion glass plates rather than daguerreotypes.

Mr Thomson remains unidentified. There are plenty of Thomsons in the world of early photography,[4] but this one need not have come from further than, say, Plymouth. From the nature of his 1853 sojourn in Hayle, he would seem to have been what photographic historians call 'a travelling Daguerreotypist' — hardest class of all to trace.

1. RCG 28 Act 1853.
2. See p. 74 above.
3. WB 14 Apr 1854.
4. E.g., Pritchard, 91 (for the 1870s).

THORN, Harry
Professional: Bude (Figs.110 to 113)   and

THORN, Samuel, jnr.
Professional: Bude (Fig.114)

The Thorn family originated in the north-east corner of Cornwall — the parishes of Kilkhampton and Launcells — in the 16th century and probably earlier. Parish registers show plenty of Thorns in the adjoining Devonshire parishes. Samuel Thorn, master carpenter, was baptised at Launcells on 8 February 1809 and married a Miss Ann Horrell (another east Cornwall

Fig.111   The Strand at Bude Haven

Taken a year or so later than *Fig.110*, but from more or less the same standpoint − note the wall and gate, left foreground − this depicts aspects of the town's economy. The buildings no longer exist; they were demolished gradually between 1904 and 1950. From left to right, we see a house with bay windows, occupied by Mr Hooper (partner in the adjoining business with Mr Hockin, presumably linked with the merchants Hockin of Hartland Quay, Devon). The stores and warehouses catered for local farmers and builders. The huge baulks of timber were brought by sea from South Wales; they were floated up the Neet, Bude's tidal river, and later taken to a yard at the rear to be sawn into the sizes required by house-builders. In view of their lengths, and the modest proportions of local shipping at this period, it is possible that the baulks were not actually carried on ship-board. Most general cargo was shipped to Bude in the summer, when weather conditions were most favourable and it can be presumed that the baulks of timber were towed on voyage, strapped together to form great rafts. Carte, paper print, H. Thorn, c. 1862.   (Thorn family colln.)

surname) at Stratton on 22 October 1835. His business in Bude, or 'Bude Haven' as it was then known, employed several men and he is believed to have had a shop in what is now The Crescent.[1]

Samuel and Ann Thorn had many children. Harry (never 'Henry') is thought to have been born in 1838, though there is no record of his baptism. He committed suicide at Bude on 30 October 1876 and was buried there on 7 November, his age being given as thirty-eight.[2] Harry was the first photographer in the family, and was listed as a 'photographic artist' in 1861.[3] Ten years later his address was No.17, The Crescent. This must have included a studio, the rest of the Thorn family being in a house at the back, No.16b.[4] The last record for Harry Thorn as a photographer dates from 1873.[5]

Samuel junior, the baby of the family, was born in 1853, and joined his elder brother as a part-time assistant in 1863, when he was only ten.[6] He, too, was listed as a photographer by 1871.[7] Early Thorn images, carte views and portraits, and apparently

stereographs too, bear the imprints of either 'H. Thorn' or 'S. Thorn'. It is not clear how early the separate S. Thorn imprint came into use. It is fairly certain that Samuel would have used older negatives to make prints under his own name after Harry's death in 1876, and Samuel Thorn appears in directories for a long period.[8]

To add to the potential confusion, a third Thorn − a second 'S. Thorn' − joined the family business. This was a sister, Sarah Pain Thorn, baptised in May 1843, and after her death just before she was ninety buried at Bude on 4 June 1932. Samuel Thorn had died on 27 January 1898. Sarah was then left to carry on the concern, which in fact she enlarged. An 1889 advertisement[9] for Sarah Thorn's 'Photographic and Stationery Establishment, The Crescent' mentions her sale of views of North Cornwall and Devon, with sea views and portraits; and branch outlets at Boscastle and Tintagel, places beginning to attract summer visitors in substantial quantity. The same notice draws attention to Thorn's Circulating Library, and to 'Horses and

5. K 1873 (incorrectly as 'Henry' Thorn).

6. Info. the Thorn family.

7. Census 1871.

8. K 1883, K 1889, K 1893; K 1897, 46, lists him as 'photographer, stationer and library'.

9. Weighell's *North Cornwall Guide*.

10. See p. 65 above.

11. Spencer Thorn, Jeweller & Bookshop; F.J.R. Thorn, Painter & Decorator; various other Bude Thorns, see telephone directory.

Fig.112 Bude Haven, Cornwall

One half of a stereoscopic pair, so titled and with H. Thorn's label, this albumen print reveals that the Thorns, too, entered the profitable world of the stereographs. It is the same estuarine inlet as in the previous two views — a few baulks of timber can be made out on the bank, right — but taken from a point, and angle, nearer to the sea. Just above the bend of the river, the low white building bears a full-length sign, Bude Hotel.

Stereograph, H. Thorn, late 1860s.   (Private colln.)

Carriages Let on Hire'. This last reminds us that many of the excitements depicted in the photographic views could only be reached with some difficulty along minor roads. Sarah Pain Thorn was still active around 1900, editing a small local paper *(The Bude Gazette and Visitor's Guide)* and using the large family stock of photographs for postcards. Thorn's Library, as it was called, was at Nos.17 and 18, The Crescent. In the early years of the present century the business passed to a Mr Jake Harrison (also a photographer) who had been acting as Sarah Thorn's manager. Classic Thorn views of shipping, the coast and scenic views were still being issued by him as postcards.

The high quality of the Thorn photographs, most of which began commercial life as half-plate sepia prints for albums, is striking. The Haymans apart,[10] the Thorns had very little competition and knew their area intimately. Like the Gibsons in Scilly, they specialised in wrecks, storms and lifeboats. Insufficient attention has been given to the pictorial chronicle built up by this old-established family, one still very much to the fore in Bude's commercial life today.[11]

1. Info. the Thorn family, Bude (with family tree); S 1852, 60; H 1862, 786.

2. RCG 11 Nov 1876; CC 987 ('aged about 30').

3. Census 1861.

4. Census 1871.

Fig.113 Robert Stephen Hawker at his Vicarage Door

R.S. Hawker, Vicar of Morwenstow (and uncle of Robert Hawker Preston), was photographed by both Thorn brothers on various occasions. This, the best-known image, shows Hawker in his sea-boots and fisherman's jersey, welcoming the world. Its date is indicated in a letter by Hawker to his friend W. Valentine: 'Aug. 6, 1864 . . . I inclose another Photo. But the one done by Thorn in an attitude standing at my door sells very fast at Bude'. Hundreds of copies were sold, and the carte must have been often re-issued. The original was made by Harry Thorn; the Institution has a version with an imprint of 'ST' in a crowned circlet, and 'S. Thorn, Portrait & Landscape Photographer, Crescent, Bude Haven'. As Samuel Thorn was only aged 11 in 1864, this re-issue would be as late as 1876, after Harry Thorn's death; when, of course, his younger brother took over the negatives and the business.

Carte, paper imprint, original by H. Thorn, 1863−64.   (R.I.C.)

Fig.114   Bude Haven: Ivy Cottage and the Breakwater

The main series of classic Thorn views, covering Boscastle, Tintagel and the remote north coast was well as Bude itself, seems to begin in the latter half of the 1860s. Most of them − half-plate format, sepia-toned and designed for pasting into albums − have a small 'Thorn. Bude' blind stamp. In the Institution's collection there are a number, but along the basal margin of each is a small neat handwritten legend; the title (as above) and then 'S. Thorn'. Samuel Thorn was still only 17 by 1870, but had worked with his older brother Harry since he was ten and was undoubtedly quite capable of using a plate camera. He must be among Victorian Cornwall's youngest photographic artists. There is no reason to doubt that he could have taken, and did take, the above. Well composed, it shows Ivy Cottage (which still stands) with its complement of visitors. A gentleman in straw hat examines the dinghy, and some small boys are doing something at the water's edge; two larger vessels are berthed out at low water.

Half-plate albumen print, sepia-toned. S. Thorn, late 1860s.   (R.I.C.)

TOPLISS, Mr.
Visiting Professional: Redruth

'Mr Topliss, Artist from London. Begs respectfully to call the attention of the inhabitants of Redruth and the neighbourhood to his new style of Collodion Photographic Portraits, taken in one or two seconds in all weathers. Mr Topliss being a portrait painter of twenty years experience flatters himself that these portraits will be found artistically posed and lighted, and coloured in a natural pleasing manner. In Redruth for a very limited time. Specimens of the various sizes and prices, from 3s. upwards, to be seen at Mr Tregaskis's, Redruth'.

This informative notice [1] confirms once more that the familiar little cased collodion-positive likenesses were usually the work of visiting artists. The reference to hand-colouring, a desirable extra, is of interest. The premises in question will have been those of James Tregaskis, one-time printer and bookseller at St Day,[2] who by 1856 had moved to Fore Street, Redruth, and built up a substantial business.[3] His shop and works were the 'Ticketing-Paper Office'; he had the contract to print the slips or forms used in the local mode of auctioning tin ores at the Redruth Ticketing Office. We know nothing more of Mr Topliss.

1. WB 20 Jun 1856.
2. P 1844.
3. K 1856; D 1866, 83.
4. Not in Pritchard.

TREBILCOCK, J(ames?)
Amateur: Falmouth(?)

In the Polytechnic's 1845 exhibition, one entry aroused very particular interest. The Judges on Natural Philosophy, etc., a long list of names headed by Robert Were Fox, were enthusiastic. 'To specimens of Daguerreotyped Portraits, they have given a First Bronze Medal. The portraits exhibit a distinctiveness and pictorial effect, which could not have been arrived at, but by long trial and skilful management'.[1] There is surely an implication that some of these portraits were of persons known to the Society's judges or committee. Who took them? A little further,[2] among the prizes awarded in the Mechanical Inventions and

Improvements category we find the entry (under 'Miscellaneous') 'Daguerreotypes, Mr J. Trebilcock'.

The next year the same person submitted further specimens of the same[3] but the novelty had subsided somewhat; 'Daguerreotypes, Mr Trebilcock. 10s.' This is all we know. He is not among the lists of the Polytechnic's annual subscribers. He is also not recorded in any form of business or trade in 1847;[4] there is no Trebilcock in this context listed under Penryn, Truro or Falmouth in 1852 either.[5] The guess would be that he was a private gentleman. This notion is supported when we find a Mr James Trebilcock living at No.110, Killigrew Street, Falmouth, in 1864, with no other occupation cited.[6]

1. 13 RCPS, xviii.
2. *Ibidem*, xxiv.
3. 14 RCPS, xxv.
4. Nowhere in W 1847.
5. S 1852.
6. Wa 1864, 79 & 95.

TREBILCOCK, William Barrett
Professional: St Day (Fig.115)

W.B. Trebilcock, son of a John Barrett Trebilcock, was baptised at St Clement near Truro on 31 August 1834. He occurs in only one directory entry,[1] as a photographer in the village of St Day in 1866. There was probably a general family connection. Paul and Richard Trebilcock were glaziers and oilmen at Carharrack; William Trebilcock and Sons, builders in the same place; and a Captain Davies Trebilcock, mine agent, lived at Lanner. Carharrack is very near St Day and Lanner not far distant.

Mr Trebilcock did not enter work at the Polytechnic, was not a talented artist, and is known only from a few cartes de visite. In 1867 he was in a spot of trouble at Truro Police Court.[2] 'A photographer of St Day named Trebilcock' was fined for assaulting a female domestic with whom he had formerly been keeping company. Nor was this all. After such adverse publicity, the ambience of St Day − a tightly-knit village, replete with places of worship − proved too hot to hold him and he removed himself to Truro. Here, he found employment in Pydar Street, possibly as an assistant to the larger photographic business of the Griffiths family.[3] But in 1872 he was again charged, this time with indecent assault upon a 12-year-old and an 11-year-old.[4] 'Evidence of other cases' was adduced by the constabulary and Mr Trebilcock was sentenced to six months' hard labour. His photographic career was over.

1. D 1866, Gwennap sect., 9, 18 and 26.
2. RCG 2 May 1867.
3. See p. 53 above.
4. RCG 20 and 27 Apr 1872.

Fig.115   An Unknown Youth
This is among the very few surviving Trebilcock carte portraits. Given the isolation of St Day and the relative poverty of that village, the sparsely furnished studio with its painted back-drop seems appropriate.
Carte, paper print, Trebilcock, c. 1865−66.   (Private colln.)

TREGASKIS, William (?)
Amateur: Falmouth

A problem in identifying some of the amateur photographers mentioned in the Polytechnic's Annual Reports is that the surname alone may be given, without initials or place of residence; and concurrent press reports usually copied whatever prize-list was handed out.

In 1869, 'Mr Tregaskis' entered a case of photographs in the Amateur class and won a Second Bronze Medal.[1] There is no reason to see him as the Redruth printer Mr James Tregaskis, at whose premises the visiting London professional Mr Topliss could for a short time be found in 1856.[2] In the setting of Falmouth, this amateur is far more likely to have been his younger brother William. Born in 1832, William Tregaskis was also a printer, and a publisher, with a shop at No.19 Church Street, Falmouth.[3] Early in his career he had worked in London. In 1858 he had taken out a provisional patent for the invention of an improvement to a printing-press.[4]

The evidence of mechanical interest, the London experience, and the proximity of his Church Street shop to the Polytechnic Hall (and to the photographic establishments of J.C. Stephens and J.F. Trull), are no more than clues. In combination, they point to William Tregaskis as the most likely identification for this amateur prize-winner.

1. 37 RCPS, 34.
2. See p. 128 above.
3. Wa 1864, 79 and 89; CC 1026.
4. BC 749.

TREMBATH, Edwin
Professional: St Just in Penwith (Figs.116 & 117)

Trembath is the name of a farm in Madron parish, next to Penzance, and the surname derived from it occurs mostly in the Land's End area. Richard Trembath's general stores and carpenter's shop was a feature of St Just early in the last century.[1] Edwin Trembath was presumably his son.

His is another of those instances, as with his contemporary W.J. Trevaskis, where geographical remoteness meant omission from directories. Mr Trembath is first listed as a photographer in 1873,[2] at a period when the family stores were in Fore Street, St Just. This is quite misleading. There is ample evidence, nearly all in the shape of local portrait photography, that Edwin Trembath was active in this respect in the early 1860s, if not indeed a year or so before 1860;[3] until the mid-1860s, this was probably in a part-time capacity.[4] It is fairly certain that he took his own views of Botallack at the time of the 1865 Royal visit (*Fig. 116*), and his use of the Royal Arms as part of his first-known carte imprint may reflect this. Other, but so far unattributed, views of St Just and district at this period may equally be his work.[5] Quite securely his is the 1868 portrait of the two Ballantynes (*Fig.117*), and there is an 1869 group of four St Just worthies.[6]

Mr Trembath was in business until late in the last century, moving in the 1880s from Fore Street to a new studio in Bank Square, St Just.[7] Some of the Trembaths are known to have emigrated, a common feature in this predominantly mining town.[8] The last flicker of the business was in 1939[9] when Miss Hetty Trembath — an unmarried daughter? — was listed as a photographer, still at Bank Square.

1. S 1852, 58; K 1856, 119.
2. K 1873.
3. Info. Mr Clive Carter, Sancreed (from a dated album).
4. In H 1862, 988, Mr Trembath was a 'painter and glazier'.
5. Variously in Watkiss 1975a, Watkiss 1975b.
6. Watkiss 1975a, 37.
7. K 1883; K 1889; K 1893.
8. Info. Mr Clive Carter.
9. K 1939, 539.

TRESIDDER, John Nicholas
Amateur: Falmouth

Dr Tresidder was born at Falmouth in March, 1817. He was a son of Nicholas Tolmie Tresidder (1791–1861), attorney of Church Street. His mother had been a Miss Genn, which made N.J. Tresidder a cousin at one remove of another amateur photographer, W.J. Genn junior.[1]

He would also have known his contemporaries in the Fox family. Robert Barclay Fox, brother of Anna Maria and Caroline, was born in 1817 as well. A journal entry for 1840[2] notes how he and Caroline were taking a September walk along the beach and 'unhappily broke in on the sacred privacy of a loving pair seated in a cavern intertwined like vine stalks . . .

Fig.117 'Ready For Deep Down'

In 1868 the famous novelist R.M. Ballantyne (1825–94) was in Cornwall, where he produced his '*Deep Down — A Tale of the Cornish Mines*. During August he and his wife moved to 'Alma Villa', now Penrose House, at St Just, and later that month or early in September they made a descent of Botallack. They were lent the outfits used during the 1865 Royal visit. Mrs Ballantyne, looking a little nervous, wears the Duchess of Sutherland's protective dress, and Robert Michael Ballantyne is rigged out like a mine-captain. The carte has an imprint of 'E. Trembath, Photographer, Fore Street, St Just', below the Royal Arms backed by a trophy of standards. The original was kindly lent by Mr Eric Quayle, author of *Ballantyne the Brave; A Victorian Writer and His Family* (London, 1967).

Carte, paper print, Trembath, 1868.   (Private colln.)

Fig.116   Botallack; after the Royal visit

Pearce's winding-engine house at Botallack hoisted the skip from the incline shaft. In this picture, late on July afternoon with a hint of sea mist dulling the sunlight, we can see the remains of the foliage decorating the wooden housing of the skip gate, bottom centre. The Royal visit is over and almost everyone has gone home. Since Robert Preston, having recorded the visit *(Figs. 97 to 99),* then returned to the Mount in the wake of Princess Alexandra *(Fig. 100),* it is clear that someone else took this view. St Just is barely two miles away and Edwin Trembath would have come out to see the Royal party, here or at Land's End (or at both places). Surely he is the un-named photographer in question. Unascr., paper print, Trembath(?), July 1865.

(R.I.C.)

Recognised 2 old acquaintances, Miss Kirkness and J. Tresidder'. The girl-friend would have been Margaret Anne Kirkness, one of the daughters of an Orkney packet-ship commander, John Kirkness, who had settled in Falmouth.[3] John Tresidder, five years later, married Miss Elizabeth Barnicoat, daughter of a Customs officer. He then went into service in India as a surgeon, retiring in June 1877 from the Indian Medical Service in the rank of surgeon-general. The Tresidders bought a house in Alleyn Park, Dulwich, where he died aged 71 in May 1899.[4]

In 1862, Mr J.N. Tresidder, H.M.I.M.S., contributed a number of views to the Polytechnic's exhibition which 'possessed great interest, from the circumstances of their being taken by himself in India, and of many of them being views of scenes and places in which occurred remarkable events connected with the late Indian mutiny'.[5] The 32nd Cornwall Regiment, later The Duke of Cornwall's Light Infantry, had been nobly involved in the Siege of Lucknow in 1857 and there was much interest in the county. Mutiny and post-Mutiny photographs from India do exist, but they are not common and none of these known were made by Cornishmen. In 1863, though by then out of Cornwall, Dr Tresidder supplied 'more beautiful photographs' for the Polytechnic's annual exhibition.[6] One would much like to know what happened to his albums.

1. See p. 49 above.
2. Barclay Fox, 208.
3. CC 464.
4. CC 1068 and 1868.
5. 30 RCPS, xxv, xxxvi.
6. 31 RCPS, xxxiii.

Fig.118   The Reverend Thomas Aubrey
The lower margin of this carte de visite bust portrait is signed 'Revd Thos Aubrey' in ink across its lower margin. As the text entry describes, it was probably taken in 1863 when Mr Aubrey opened the new Leedstown Methodist Church; less probably in one of the several years afterwards when he attended, before his death in 1867.

Carte, paper print, Trevaskis, 1863.   (Author)

TREVASKIS, William John
Professional: Leedstown (Fig.118)

Leedstown — older, Leeds Town — is a crossroads village on the route from Helston to Hayle. It was named after Dukes of Leeds, as successor landowners in the district through marriage into the Godolphin family;[1] and it has long held members of the Trevaskis family, whose surname comes from the farm of Trevaskis standing close by in Gwinear parish.

When the first Methodist church for the area, at Gwinear Downs, became too small and decrepit for the Leedstown Wesleyan Society, it was decided to build a new chapel in Leedstown proper; this was opened early in 1863. In October there was a ceremony to mark the completion of the building, which was conducted by the Reverend Thomas Aubrey from Wales. Mr Aubrey was a Wesleyan Methodist minister, though there is no clear explanation for his presence; he did not serve in any of the Cornwall circuits and the invitation must have been personal. It was noted that 'for several years afterwards' Mr Aubrey made annual visits to take Chapel Anniversary services, which would have been held in either February or October.[2]

Mr Aubrey died in 1867.[3] A carte portrait, with the signature of 'Revd Thos. Aubrey', has the imprint of 'W.J. Trevaskis, Photographer, Leedstown'. Because Leedstown is a not very prominent village, Mr Trevaskis is first recorded as a photographer in 1883.[4] The Aubrey likeness cannot be later than 1866 and was more probably taken in 1863, which places Mr Trevaskis's career in a good twenty years before we find him listed.

W.J. Trevaskis was, in a geographically-constrained way, a sound and successful local photographer. The family continued their close association with the Chapel — the photographer himself was a Trustee in 1890[5] and in the 1963 centenary celebrations the senior Trustee was, appropriately, Mr H.N. Trevaskis — and the business, which was run from the Leedstown house now called 'An Gernyk',[6] managed to expand. From 1889 Trevaskis had a branch studio at Nettles Hill in Helston.[7] Carte de visite imprints of the later 1870s, or the 1880s, announce[8] that he was at Leedstown on Mondays, Thursdays, and Saturdays; Porthleven, Tuesdays and Wednesdays; and Breage on Fridays.

Fig.119 St Germans Church
The magnificent, mostly Norman, church of St Germans in south-east Cornwall is regarded as successor to the seat of the pre-Norman Celtic bishops of Cornwall. It stands in the grounds of Port Eliot, home of the Earls of St Germans (the Eliot family). Tripe's plate view, 13 by 11¼ inches, goes with some surviving Devonport studies and is presumably in the mid- or late 1850s.
Plate-sized albumen print, Tripe, c. 1855.
(Copyright; reproduced by kind permission of Plymouth City Museums and Art Gallery)

(Porthleven and Breage are 7 and 5 miles respectively from Leedstown.) Business continued into the early years of this century — it is not known when Mr Trevaskis himself died — and was then revived by his daughter Miss Polly Trevaskis, who was listed as a photographer at Leedstown up to the start of the last War.[9]

1. See also p. 76 above.
2. *Centenary Brochure* (privately, Leedstown, 1963).
3. Info. Revd. Thomas Shaw.
4. K 1883.
5. Info. Mr Cedric Appleby, St Erth.
6. Info. Mr Richard Jenkin, Leedstown.
7. K 1889; K 1893; K 1897, 130.
8. Private colln.
9. K 1935, 91 and 533; K 1939, 539.

TRIPE, Linnaeus
Visiting Professional (Fig.119)

Captain Linnaeus Tripe, of Devonport (1822–1902), has in recent years emerged from undeserved oblivion, and is now recognised as having been among the really important 'Imperial' photographers of the last century, specialising in what one can only call massive views. Two papers by a descendant[1] have drawn attention to his work. When examples of Tripe's images do reach the market, they now command massive — one might almost say, astronomical — prices.[2]

In the late 1850s he published albums of views, as albumen prints and stereographs, through the agency of the Madras Presidency in India, in which he was described as 'Government Photographer, Madras Presidency'.[3] He had an army career in the mainstream of his life, and when he retired from the Indian

Army, he did so in the rank of major-general (1 September 1875).[4] In due course the full extent of his photographic career will doubtless be established.

Linnaeus Tripe's curious surname may possibly be the same, with variant spelling, as 'Tribe', still found both in Cornwall and the Plymouth area. He did undertake some Devonport photography and nine negatives of unusually large size, about 13 by 11½ inches, are now owned by the City of Plymouth Museums and Art Gallery. Only one of them indicates a trip into Cornwall — a fine view of St Germans church, close to the railway line and easily reached from Plymouth.

1. Dewar, Janet; 'Linnaeus Tripe: Critical Assessments and other notes', *The Photographic Collector*, 5 no.1, and 'Linnaeus Tripe's Photographs: Notes Towards an Index', *History of Photography*, 8 no.1 (1984).
2. Sotheby's Belgravia sales — 29 March 1985, in which four Tripe prints realised £4620, £2420, £3850 and £1980.
3. Gernsheim 1984, nos.91–99.
4. See *Army Lists* of the period.

TRULL, James Frederick
Professional: Falmouth (Figs.120 & 121)

Where Mr Trull came from is unknown. His surname does occur in Cornwall, perhaps breaking down from names like 'Trehill' or 'Trewell', but could also be English, derived from such forms as Truehill. He was in Falmouth, probably by 1861. In 1862 he was listed with photographic premises at Church Street,[1] and earlier that year he was announcing[2] a new branch studio ('for First Class Carte de Visite portraits') at Mrs Cosbey's, No.26 Lemon Street in Truro. This was intended for the summer-months trade 'in a new and spacious gallery built expressly for the purpose'. During August Mr Trull's visiting day was changed to Wednesdays only, and a month later, thanking his Patrons, he closed for the winter.[3]

By 1864, as well as the Church Street shop, Mr Trull had started a private studio at his own residence, No.89 Killigrew Street.[4] Business was good. He entered samples of his work at the Polytechnic in 1863, 1864 and 1865[5] and then in 1868 he was awarded a First Bronze Medal.[6] This prize was duly announced on his carte imprint, along with his ability to make 'Direct Solar Enlargements'. The main premises were still at No.45 Church Street in 1873.[7] J.F. Trull is not however listed in directories after this[8] and presumably retired in the later 1870s.

His output was not only portraiture. He took views in the Falmouth area and issued them in carte format. The two illustrated here have a simple imprint of 'J.F. Trull, Church Street, Falmouth' and are certainly earlier than the 1869, or end of 1868, version that includes his Polytechnic medal. We can guess, fairly safely, that they were among the series of 'very fine photographs' he entered at the Polytechnic in 1863.

1. H 1862, 243.
2. RCG 18 Apr 1862.
3. RCG 29 Aug and 5 Sept 1862.
4. Wa 1864, advert. p. 40.
5. 31 RCPS, xxix; 32 RCPS, xix; 33 RCPS, xxiv.
6. 38 RCPS, xxxi.
7. K 1873.
8. Not in P 1876, K 1883.

TRUSCOTT, Charles
Professional: Truro and Falmouth

Charles Truscott (baptised on 18 April 1820) and his brother Walter were sons of Lewis and Elizabeth Truscott of St Stephen in Brannel, the medieval church-town on the edge of the china-clay district. The Truscotts were a very large mid-Cornwall family, one that has produced no less than three Lord Mayors of London.[1] Charles himself was trained in London, somehow becoming a youthful member of the Oxford and Cambridge Photographic Association.[2] In 1855, as a 'photographic artist, of London' he returned to Cornwall ('for a short time only') in order to take likenesses at Mr Mitchinson's, Truro.[3] John Mitchinson, a Cardinham man, appears often in these pages. He was a well-known seed merchant and nurseryman of Truro — later, with branches elsewhere — whose 'Glass House' in St Mary's Street could be hired as a temporary photographic studio.[4]

Mr Truscott's venture was successful and the following year, thanking his public for their very liberal and unprecedented patronage, to which one hopes his numerous Truro relations had contributed, he opened his own studio in East Bridge Street.[5] He was married, with several children, and a passing

Fig.121 Falmouth and Pendennis
It is not easy to work out precisely from what point this was taken; probably an attic window, or roof, at the north end of the High Street. This may be a little later than the previous figure. On the right, down the slope from Pendennis and against the skyline, the large isolated building is the Falmouth Hotel, commenced in 1863 and finished a few years later.

Carte, paper print, Trull, mid-1860s.   (Private colln.)

Fig.120 Pendennis Castle
At the period when Mr Trull made this view, the 16th-century granite fortress of Pendennis Castle was still part of Cornwall's coastal defences, and was used as the headquarters of the Royal Cornwall and Devon Miners, the local militia regiment of coastal artillery. The one-storied building with porch and window, now removed, was probably a guard room.

Carte, paper print, Trull, 1863(?)

(Private colln.)

reference[6] suggests that he had a house at Campfield Hill. By 1861 he had moved[7] to St Nicholas Street, with his wife Susanna and their five children, ranging from Charles junior aged 10 to a baby of five months.

By now he was doing sufficiently well to consider starting a summertime branch studio on the Esplanade, or sea front, at Penzance; he may have decided to imitate Robert Preston[8] who had gone there to conduct the lion's share of the, originally Truro-based, Preston and Poole concern. Unhappily the hand of God then struck, for the first but by no means for the last time in the Truscott saga. In January 1863 there was a mighty storm across Mount's Bay; one Saturday morning at 8 o'clock his studio on the Esplanade 'recently erected at great expense' and standing near the old Royal Baths was entirely destroyed by great waves. All the contents and part of the building were washed into the sea.[9]

The studio appears to have been replaced,[10] but meanwhile the Truscotts had decided to leave Truro. Their dwelling and shop was advertised for sale in May 1862; on 21 November 1863, while they were actually moving out, a fire broke out and destroyed 'the photographic rooms'[11] − the fire brigade saved St Nicholas Street from conflagration − because, supposedly, tar for the house's exterior was being melted in an adjoining store. With what had been saved, and the insurance money, the Truscotts moved to their new home at No.9, Berkeley Vale, Falmouth. Here, Charles commenced a partnership with his younger brother Walter.[12] They had a business establishment at No.40 Church Street, 'The Polytechnic Portrait Rooms', not far from the Polytechnic Hall, where however their rival John Counsell Stephens had been very firmly entrenched for some few years. Here the Truscotts set up as Art Photographers specialising in landscape and architectural images. They could also offer permanent enlargements, miniatures and from Walter's brush life-size oil portraits on canvas.[13]

The subsequent history of the Charles Truscotts is far from happy. After 1870, the business was not a success. Charles had embroiled most of his offspring (Charles junior, James, Walter and Fanny Maria) in his photographic and artistic concern. The strain of the enforced mixture proved to be too much. Family squabbles of a most unedifying nature broke out. In 1876[14] Charles junior and James packed up and left. The distribution of the stock, or profits, or goodwill, or all three was not agreed; and in Falmouth County Court James was sued by his brother Walter and sister Fanny Maria. A settlement was reached, Walter and Fanny Maria remained in Falmouth with their mother, and Charles Truscott senior and his brother, Uncle Walter to this litigious brood, left for Truro.

In Falmouth, the Truscotts are not mentioned in an 1876 directory, and we know that by 1883 the shop at No.40 Church Street was occupied by a fresh rival, William Marsden. Nevertheless it seems that Charles and Walter decided to leave Truro and come back to Falmouth. Walter, the artist, may have done so first.

He had his own house in Berkeley Place; we are not told whether he himself had married. It is possible that he found a new post, as artist and assistant, to yet another photographer, W.H. Dunstan,[15] who in the middle of all these moves had bought the former Truscott home at No.9 Berkeley Vale.

By 1879, probably the year of the return, Charles Truscott had a new house in Killigrew Street, Falmouth. He began again on his own, employing at 25s. a week an assistant called Walter Barwick. A certain dilatoriness in paying the weekly wage brought Mr Truscott into the County Court, where he was obliged to give Barwick the £3.18s.0d. that he now owed him.[16]

None of the other Truscotts figure in Falmouth's commercial life at this stge, and the younger ones must have left the town. A final and melancholy note of difficulty is struck by a short press report in 1883.[17] So-called 'Police intelligence' from Falmouth informed the, mainly Truro, readership that Charles Truscott, photographer of Killigrew Street, had been charged with setting fire to his own premises. Had poor Charles, faced with a mountain of unsettled bills (and, by 1883, a town packed with more successful competitors), remembered that Penzance storm twenty years earlier, when the insurance money paid for a new studio on the Esplanade? Alas, many have tried the simple device of arson for realising a policy and making a fresh start. Few have succeeded. Of the subsequent fate of Charles Truscott − he would have been 63 at this time − we remain in ignorance.

1. Francis Wyatt Truscott in 1879; most recently Sir Denis Truscott GBE, in 1957−58.

2. Duly mentioned on his carte imprints, 1870s.

3. WB 31 Aug 1855.

4. Census 1861 (he was then 37).

5. WB 28 Nov 1856.

6. RCG 23 Nov 1860 ('gathered from his garden in the Campfield, a dish of strawberries . . . Mr Chas. Truscott, Photographic artist').

7. Census 1861; H 1862, 616.

8. See p. 108 above.

9. RCG 20 Jan 1863.

10. C 1864, advert. (this may refer to late 1863).

11. RCG 23 May 1862, p. 8 (sale); RCG 27 Nov 1863, p. 8 (the fire).

12. Charles was operating in Truro still in Feb. 1864 (RCG 19 Feb 1864, p. 6).

13. Imprints on cartes; arrival after Wa 1864 was compiled.

14. RCG 27 May 1876, p. 3.

15. See p. 48 above.

16. RCG 25 Mar 1881, p. 7.

17. RCG 13 Jun 1883.

TRUSCOTT, Walter
Professional (?): Falmouth

Walter Truscott, younger brother of Charles, was baptised at St Stephen in Brannel on 3 August 1822. When he was twenty-two, and living at St Blazey − perhaps with Mr William H. Truscott, grocer of that town, if he was a relative[1] — Walter put a notice in the newspaper offering to send anyone, on receipt of thirty 1d. postage stamps, 'instructions to enable any person to take Portraits, Landscape Views etc., with ease and certainty by the above valuable and interesting art' (of photography).[2] Perhaps he had been in London with his brother, and was trying to sell a précis of one of the photographers' manuals of the period.

Tuition by post is not a very promising line, and by 1864 Walter, who may in the interval have been living off his wits in similar ventures, joined Charles Truscott at Falmouth. His own history is largely gleaned from involvement with the turbulent world of the Charles Truscott family; we can deduce that, after some years touching up his brother's photographic likenesses and selling any original works of art, he went with Charles to Truro in 1876, a year in which he was recorded[3] as an artist and portrait painter at No.13, Berkeley Place. The fact that he had his own house may suggest that he was married. It is only a conjecture, but certainly a legitimate one, that Walter Truscott changed allegiance and between 1876 and 1879, if not before, joined the photographer W.H. Dunstan — who had acquired Charles Truscott's former home — as an assistant.

Walter's direct involvement in professional photography is not certain. The sale of instructions by post only just qualified him as a commercial participant but, since he claimed to know enough to teach others, and since he was for a period a partner in a proper photographic business, we can suppose that he did use a camera (if only in the service of Art) and sell the resulting images to customers.

1. K 1856, 102.
2. WB 22 Sept 1854.
3. P 1876, 49.

VEALE, Mr R.
Amateur: Falmouth

Mr Veale, described only as being 'of Falmouth Docks', had a photograph chosen as a 10s. prize in the 1863 Art Union of Cornwall draw.[1] It was entitled 'Choir of Angels'. He cannot be found in either Falmouth or Penryn in the most likely directory of the time[2] and was perhaps a young bachelor. The Veales originally came, in the main, from Penzance, Madron and Gulval.[3] One possible connection with the Fox family and the Polytechnic may lie in the fact that some of the Veales were, like the Foxes, members of the Society of Friends or Quakers.

1. See p. 17 above.
2. Not in Wa 1864.
3. S 1852, 40; CC 1133–36.

VINEY, Mr.
Professional: Truro

All that we know of Mr Viney is that his connection with the Truro branch establishment set up by J.E. Palmer of Plymouth ended early in 1858;[1] and that it can be inferred that, perhaps for a year before this, Mr Viney was Palmer's resident manager in Truro. Presumably he came from Plymouth. As a guide, we can note that in the area telephone directory for 1971, there were three Vineys, all from Plymouth; in 1986, eight, seven of them from Plymouth. Ninteenth-century records point to a Plymouth and South Hams background.

1. See p. 97 above.

WHITFORD, William, jnr.
Professional: Camborne (Fig.122)

Mr Whitford is a case, and there may be others, of an entirely genuine commercial photographer whose name slips through the catch-net of directory and gazetteer sources. Without his single carte view, labelled 'Photographed by W. Whitford, Jr., Camborne', we should be unaware of him in this capacity.

The Whitfords were and are a Camborne family. Richard Whitford was a painter and glazier in 1847.[1] Five years later the business had passed to William Whitford,[2] a son or less probably a brother. William's own son, a second William, was baptised at Camborne on 1 June 1822[3] and in due course opened his own premises in what was called De Dunstanville Terrace — the north, lower and original end of Basset Road. Like his contemporaries Edwin Docton in Padstow and Matthew Row in Redruth he started as a painter and gilder, and was listed as such in 1856 and 1862.[4] Like them, he took up the camera; in Camborne, after 1858, probably aided by William Piper and Piper's greater experience.[5]

In 1873 the original family business still appears as William Whitford, Painter, Cross Street; the son's is William Whitford junior, Painter, Basset Road.[6] The shop and house at the latter address, with ornate front, little pebbled garden and partially glassed roof, survived well into this century and ended as a small fancy-goods shop. Mr Whitford junior may have functioned as a part-time photographer only during the 1860s.

1. W 1847, 25.
2. S 1852, 11.
3. Info. Mr David Thomas, Camborne.
4. K 1856; H 1862, 807 (in 'New Street', i.e., Basset Road).
5. See p. 99 above.
6. K 1873.

Fig.122 North Roskear Mine
The solitary instance of Mr Whitford's work is this carte format view, clearly in the Camborne mining area and identified by the late Mr A.K. Hamilton Jenkin. North Roskear Mine was north-west of Tuckingmill, on the west side of the Red River, and this image was probably taken from what is now East Hill, Tuckingmill, later the main A30 road.
Carte, paper print, Whitford, early 1860s. (R.I.C.)

WILSON, George Washington
Visiting Professional (Fig.123)

G.W. Wilson was born in Banffshire, Scotland, in 1823, son of a crofter who had spent 24 years as an artilleryman in the Napoleonic wars. He left school at twelve, and after some years as an apprentice to a house-builder — during which his considerable talent as a draughtsman was nurtured — moved in 1846 to Edinburgh, where he became a professional artist. Probably through the influence of D.O. Hill (of Hill and Adamson fame), secretary from 1830 of the Scottish Academy, Wilson took up photography, though he always considered himself an artist firstly and a photographer secondly. In August 1849, after a trip to the London galleries, he settled in Aberdeen.[1]

George Washington Wilson's career from this point onwards was one of unrelieved success, and he must be accounted Scotland's principal commercial photographer. In worldly terms, he became both rich and widely known. The combination of the camera and the eastern Highlands inevitably brought him into contact with those photographic enthusiasts, the Queen and the Prince Consort, and in 1873 — after some years of calling himself 'Photographer to the Queen' — he obtained a warrant of appointment from the Lord Chamberlain. Wilson was a prolific supplier of illustrations for printed books. In 1855 he published a practical guide to the collodion process[2] and between 1857 and 1871 his albumen prints, mostly of North British scenery and ruins, figured in many publications.[3]

His firm, which became in 1872 'G.W. Wilson & Co.', when a Mr George Brown Smith joined him in partnership, was an early marketer of stereoscopic views. The series containing these must have been very large. One view, of the Land's End, bears in its printed legend the details 'No.311. G.W. Wilson, Photographer, Aberdeen'; earlier numbers tend to be from Scotland (e.g., No.62, 'The Pass of Ballater') but in a range of over a thousand there is a 'middle' group indicative of the south-west — No.298 shows 'Interior of Exeter Cathedral'.

With many of the great 19th-century photographic concerns, there was an increasing use of agents or staff

Land's End—Cornwall.

Fig.123 Land's End, Cornwall

All commercial series of stereoscopic slides dealing with Cornwall had to include two subjects — St Michael's Mount and the Land's End — and George Washington Wilson's catalogue was no exception. This view, taken by the great Aberdonian in person, shows the ultimate headland of Land's End proper from the south-west.

Stereograph, Wilson. 1861.   (R.I.C.)

photographers; it is not certain that James Valentine of Dundee, himself a notable landscape cameraman, or Francis Frith of Reigate ever visited Cornwall personally, despite the hundreds of Cornish views that both of them reproduced for sale. Between 1861 and 1864, however, Mr Wilson did tour Britain extensively, laying the foundation of his reputation for first-class stereograph and album views, and some of his photographic booklets[4] (such as one of 1866, featuring Gloucester Cathedral) arose from these travels. His biographer assures us[5] that he visited Cornwall in 1861, 'where unusually poor weather and fog denied him many of the subjects he would have wished for'. A half-plate album view of Botallack Mine, similar in composition to *Figs.22 and 29,* arose from the visit,[6] and the Land's End stereoscopic view *(Fig.123)* must be of the same date.

George Washington Wilson, afflicted in his later years by an illness possibly connected with the chemicals necessarily used in his business, retired in 1888 and made over the concern to his son; he died in March 1893. Some forty-five thousands of his glass plate negatives, after passing through various hands following the sale of the firm in 1908, are happily now held by Aberdeen University Library.[7]

1. See Taylor, Roger; *George Washington Wilson, Artist and Photographer 1823–93* (Aberdeen University Press, 1981).

2. Gernsheim 1984, no.753.

3. Gernsheim, *op.cit.* — see Index.

4. Gernsheim, *op.cit.* (nos.302–313).

5. Taylor, *op.cit.,* 86.

6. R.I.C. collection.

7. Taylor, *op.cit.,* vii–viii.

WILTON, William Henry
Professional: Penryn

Though as a borough it was far older than Falmouth, Penryn was and still is subsidiary to its neighbour with the sea-port and docks. In the 1860s there were too many photographers in Falmouth for any Penryn competitor to expect much business. The Wiltons were a local family, of tradespeople, first recorded in the mid-century.[1] In 1864 William and Thomas Wilton (brothers ?) were 'house decorator and photographer' — which was which, unspecified — in Broad Street.[2] The only later reference is to William Henry Wilton, 'photographer, Broad Street'[3] and there is no mention of him at any later date. Mr Wilton was not a competitor at the Polytechnic, nor are instances of his work (carte portraits ?) as yet known.

1. S 1852, 37 (Elizabeth Wilton, Milliner, Broad St.).

2. Wa 1864, 144.

3. K 1873.

YEO, Richard P.
Visiting Professional (Figs.124 & 125)

Richard Yeo would have been born between 1820 and 1830. The surname is common in Devon; he was almost certainly a Plymouth man and probably a Nonconformist.[1] His first Cornish appearance was, as mentioned before,[2] in 1857 at John Colliver's Methodist Temperance hotel and coffee-house in Liskeard. By 1861 he had acquired his own premises at No.15, The Octagon, Plymouth, and his earliest dated photograph from this address is of September 1862.[3]

Mr Yeo undertook a good deal of work in Cornwall, with a high standard, interesting subjects and a preference for whole-plate views. His commercial studies of Cotehele, and its antiques and trophies of arms, contained in Jonathan Rashleigh's album[4] belong to the early or mid-1860s; much the same date as that of *Fig.124.*

In 1864 Richard Yeo sent various views of the Polytechnic, including one of Lanhydrock outside Bodmin, another Cornish mansion.[5] In 1868, exhibiting within the class for Professionals, he submitted views of the Cheesewring, a natural curiosity of granite rocks; of Trethevy Quoit; St Cleer's Well, and some localities in Devon.[6] The range of subjects is revealing. In 1868 the Polytechnic's annual exhibition began on 29 September. This tells us, with fair certainty, that Richard Yeo was the un-named photographer who, six weeks before, had joined the Royal Institution of Cornwall's annual outing to 'objects of much antiquarian interest in the neighbourhood of Liskeard'.[7] The excursion comprised about 120 ladies and gentlemen. We are told that they went to the Cheesewring, the cromlech at Trethevy and St Cleer's holy well. Yeo could have travelled by train from Plymouth's Millbay station in order to be in time to accompany the excursionists from The Parade, Liskeard, a short walk only from the railway stop.[8] A press report[9] confirms that 'a photograph was taken of

140

Fig.124   Saltash Railway Station
This is quite a well-known view − there is a very good print in the Royal Archives collection, sent to Windsor in 1865 − but it is not made clear that it is almost certainly R.P. Yeo's work. A broad gauge Cornwall Railway train is about to cross the bridge (note the horse-box at the rear). On the opposite, down, platform a train is pulling out, leaving a group of people by the signal, and the down-side station building has posters including an advertisement for Heal's Bedding. The view was made from some adjoining house, probably from an upstairs window. Shadows indicate early afternoon; the up train is perhaps the 2.50, leaving Truro at 1.09. The date of 1862 is usually given to this image by railway enthusiasts.
Plate, albumen print, Yeo, 1862.   (R.I.C.)

the Cheesewring and its surrounding swarm of human beings'. This is also mentioned in the Institution's own report[10] '. . . the Cheesewring, which was photographed while the President and Officers, with others, were grouped about its base with good effect'. The Institution still has its own archive print of this momentous occasion *(Fig.125)*. The mount lacks name or imprint, but the foregoing remarks all point to Mr Yeo as the artist.

1. No Anglican baptism can be traced.
2. See p. 45 above.
3. H 1862, 685; info. Mr Robin Fenner, Tavistock.
4. See p. 117 above; these are marked 'R P Yeo'.
5. 32 RCPS, xxxix.
6. 38 RCPS, cat. p. 17.
7. JRIC, II (1868), ann. rep. no. X, xxi.
8. 1865 G.W.R. timetable; Plymouth 7.00 a.m., Liskeard 7.53 a.m.
9. RCG 20 Aug 1868.
10. See n. 7 above, xxiii.

YEO, Stanley B.
Visiting Professional(?) (Fig.126)

Richard P. Yeo is known to have had a brother called Stanley[1] and it is possible that they were originally partners. Given the apparatus required to make his favourite whole-plate views, Richard Yeo would have needed an assistant in the field. One has the impression that R.P. Yeo was the artist, S.B. Yeo the marketing man. Stereographs are known, most of them scenic views made in Devon and Cornwall, a few of them artistic subjects and even the odd comic one.[2] What they have in common, in place of a printed label, is handwritten titling, serial numbers in the case of scenic views, and the initials 'S.B.Y.'. It seems not very likely that the Yeos would need to buy in other people's stereographic views for a, local and informal, range when they were producing their own. To assume that the one shown here was taken by Stanley Yeo, rather than by his brother, is only to give 'S.B.Y.' the benefit of the doubt; but, on that basis, it is included.

Fig.125   A Swarm of Human Beings

Richard Yeo's set piece, which must have taken some time to arrange (and in which a few participants have become bored and are not keeping still), shows a good many excursionists on the Royal Institution of Cornwall's visit. The Cheesewring is a weathered granite tor, a natural curiosity; it is not particularly easy to climb to the top, though some younger visitors have done so. The Institution's President on this occasion — he must he here, though one cannot identify him — was John Jope Rogers, Esq.

Plate, albumen print (sepia-toned), Yeo, August 1868.   (R.I.C.)

1. Info. Mr Robin Fenner, Tavistock.
2. Private colln.

Fig.126   St Michael's Mount

In no way exceptional as a photographic image, the view of St Michael's Mount at low water — causeway across, left centre; part of Chapel Rock visible, right centre — occurs as a stereoscopic slide, the back of which is marked in ink '37. St Michaels Mount. Lowe Water, S.B.Y.' These details are enough to attribute it to Richard Yeo's brother Stanley, and it is included as an example of his work.

Stereograph, sepia-toned, S.B. Yeo, 1860s.   (Author)

Fig.127   A Visit to a Summer Residence

This very early view, given to the Institution by the late Mr A.K. Hamilton Jenkin, historian of Cornish mines and miners, shows the Gonvena 'count-house' (mine office) of Wheal Leisure mine, Perranzabuloe.

The building was used as a summer residence by the James family. Jane, daughter of Sylvanus James, married in 1819 (as his first wife; she died in 1822) Alfred Jenkin, Mr Jenkin's great-grandfather. The original is a collodion positive 4½ by 3¾ inches, held in a gilt metal frame with oval opening. This would tend to place it in the 1850s, and the mid-1850s might be thought to fit the garb of the two ladies. There is no indication as to the photographer. It is not impossible that it could have been the work of J.C. Stephens (p. 122), who seems to have been making Ambrotypes in Redruth about 1855. Both the James and Jenkin families were mainly connected with that town.

(R.I.C.)

SOME UNIDENTIFIED PHOTOGRAPHERS

In the gazetteer section a proportion of the 'views and likenesses' chosen for illustration cannot be directly ascribed to named photographers, but have been included because circumstantial evidence, or reasoned argument, seems strong enough to allow the attributions put forward. On the same approach, various other early photographs, where there is absolutely no evidence as to who made them, have had to be excluded. It is more than possible that between 1850 and 1870 professional photographers of whom we have no record visited Cornwall and made images, though the results are more likely to have been preserved at home than left in Cornwall. This leaves for consideration a small group of photographs, obviously early from style or aspects of subject, and probably taken by 'native' artists because they are mostly views of obscure places that visitors would have been unlikely to have reached. In no case does it seem possible to indicate authorship.

The three shown here – *Figs.127 to 129* – are representative. They date approximately to 1855, 1860 and 1865. One might hazard a guess that John Counsell Stephens, William Michell, and one of the Dyke ladies were the photographers, but that remains a guess.

Principally for those interested in Cornwall's photographic history, one can also give a preliminary, selective, list (again with some informed guesses) of other unascribed early images which can be seen in print. The publication references are expanded in the *Bibliography*, p. 160.

Barham 1977
  Title: 'Mail coach, Market Strand, around 1860'.
  p. 65 lower: 'Broad gauge engine *Mazeppa*' (E. Hawke ?).

Noall 1972
  p. 84:   'Botallack dressing floors' (G.W. Wilson, 1861?).

Noall 1978
  p. 19 top: 'Madron Parish Church c. 1860' (Piper ? Richards?).

Noall 1979
  p. 81 top: 'St Ives Harbour before 1867' (Ashton ?).

Osborne & Thomas 1986
  p. 10:   'Trelowarren Street 1867−74' (Piper? Whitford ?).
  p. 44:   'Centenary Chapel Choir about 1860'.
                  'Tregajorran Chapel Orchestra about 1860'.

Tangye 1978
  pp. 26−27:   'Portreath Harbour 1860−70'.
  p. 30 lower: 'The "Welsh" Fleet about 1860−70'.

Trounson 1981
  Fig.1:   'St Just United Mine about 1863' (Trembath ?).
  Fig.2:   'St Just United Mine and Cape Cornwall'.
  Fig.6:   'Botallack, Timber Staging' (Preston?).
  Fig.96:   'Wheal Leisure, Perranporth, 1850s'.

Watkiss 1975b
  Fig.3:   'Market Jew St., Penzance, about 1851' (Jenkyns ?).
  Fig.23:   'Marazion Town Crier' (carte, about 1860).
  Fig.27:   'Le Grice family, Trereife' (ambrotype).
  Fig.99:   'Mining at St Just' (Trembath ?).
  Fig.100:   'Mine Captains & Venturers, c. 1865' (Trembath ?).

Watkiss 1975b
  Fig.34:   'C.V. Le Grice and family, Trereife' (ambrotype).
  Fig.41:   'William the Fourth Inn, Madron' (Preston ?).
  Fig.74:   'Capt. Tonkin of Newlyn, 1850s' (ambrotype).

This list could be expanded from other Cornish local histories, not necessarily those primarily concerned with early views. It omits those cases where photographs reproduced in this present volume have previously been published with no ascriptions, or

Fig.128 Dr Arthur Austen Davis

A.A. Davis, medical practitioner of Fowey, is seen in the original uniform of Cornwall Artillery Volunteers as Hon. Assistant Surgeon to No.3 Battery, Fowey. An original carte, signed 'A.A. Davis', is pasted into his copy of B.A. Milne's *Historical Record of the 1st Cornwall Artillery Volunteers* (Plymouth, 1885), owned by his grandson Capt. Arthur B. Davis of Fowey.

Dr Davis was enrolled on 14 December 1859, resigning his position on 18 April 1861 when he was promoted to brigade staff surgeon. The uniform (for all ranks) had been designed by Lord Vivian, then lord-lieutenant. Blue wool jersey frock, the bottom, collar and cuffs braided in red, with the battery title, Fifteen Bezants and Cornish motto on the breast. Reaction against Lord Vivian's sensible garment arose in 1860 − the 8th (Hayle) Battery, raised 5 March 1860, refused to wear it − and in November 1860 officers were allowed to substitute the tunic (which most had already acquired and were wearing).

This portrait must then have been taken between mid-December 1859 and November 1860. Dr Davis probably chose to be immortalised in his martial outfit at Christmas 1859. One of the early Truro or St Austell photographers can be held responsible.
Carte-format albumen print, 1859−60.   (Author)

wrong ascriptions, or insupportable claims of date (usually far too early!). Of those listed above two of the most important are 'Portreath Harbour 1860−70' (in *Tangye 1978;* probably about 1859−60) and 'Wheal Leisure' in *Trounson* 1981 (with comment 'It may date from the 1850s, but it is reputed (but unlikely) to be as old as 1840'). This, too, is in the late 1850s. Both of

144

them may be from the same hand as *Fig.127* here. Unless all three are due to J.C. Stephens in his initial, Redruth period (1849 to late 1850s — this is a possibility), then a significant early Cornish photographer, operating in the area of Redruth and points northward, remains to be named.

Fig.129 Sir Charles Lemon, F.R.S. and niece at Carclew

Sir Charles, as President of the Royal Cornwall Polytechnic Society and uncle by marriage to William Henry Fox Talbot, has been mentioned often in this book. Cornwall owed much to him for his encouragement of science and invention and his early championship of mining education. He was born in 1774 and died at Carclew on 12 February 1868. His sister Louisa had married a soldier, George Hart Dyke, and the Dyke nieces were constant visitors to Uncle Charles.

The original is an approximately quarter-plate (3½ by 4½ inches) albumen print pasted on cartridge paper, signed below 'Believe me Yrs affectly L.A. Dyke.' Sir Charles, who sits below the centre of the balustraded steps (below the windowed terrace at Carclew with its portico) is elderly and frail. His companion must be his niece Louisa Ann Dyke, born 14 November 1807; and the date should be, perhaps, about 1865. This is an amateur portrait. Given the family's longstanding interest and involvement in photography, another of the Dyke nieces (or nephews) may very well have been the artist.

(R.I.C.)

ADDENDUM

LLEWELYN, John Dillwyn
Visiting Amateur

As this book was in proof, one important extra name was kindly supplied (by Ms Jeanette Rosing). Mr Llewelyn, son of a distinguished Welsh scientist, married Emma Talbot, a cousin of William Henry Fox Talbot, and was himself made an F.R.S. in 1836. He practised virtually every variety of early photography.[1] It is now known that he made a visit to Cornwall in 1852, and took calotypes of St Michael's Mount and of other places in the Land's End area. An exhibition of his work in recent years claimed him, no doubt correctly, as 'the first photographer in Wales'.[2]

1. Arnold 1977, esp. 148–150.
2. Catalogue, Welsh Arts Council (1980).

APPENDIX I

TABULATED DETAILS OF PHOTOGRAPHERS, 1839—1870

A: *Resident professionals and amateurs*

(Name; dates & places of births & deaths if known)	*(Status)*	*(Business or home address; any branches; dates of careers as photographers)*
1. ARGALL, Frederick Ernest b. d.	P	Truro, High Cross 1866—1893(+)
2. ASHTON, Edward b. St Ives(?) d. St Ives	P	St Ives, Tregenna Hill (earlier, Hayle ?) c. 1865—c. 1890
3. BARNETT, William b. d.	P	Falmouth, Market St. c. 1861—1873
4. BERINGER, Fidelis b. Germany, 1823 d.	A	Penzance, Market Place 1860s
5. BERINGER, John b. Helston (?) d. Helston	P	Helston, Meneage St. c. 1860—c. 1900(+)
6. BROAD, William Henry b. Bodmin, 1831 d. Liskeard (?)	P	Bodmin, Honey St. c. 1858—c. 1870
7. BROOKS, William b. Maidstone, 1828 d. Ilford, 1918 (?)	P	Penzance c. 1863—1870
8. BURTON, James b. London (?) d. London (?)	P	Hayle; also St Ives, Tregenna Hill c. 1869—c. 1871 (?)
9. CHENHALL, James b. Redruth, 1845 d. Redruth, 1910(+)	P	Redruth, West End 1865—1910(+)
10. CLINTON, Charles William b. Devon, 1842 d. Truro, 1900+	A	Truro, Vivian Tce. 1860s
11. COLLIVER, John Henry b. 1826 d. Liskeard, 1903	P	Liskeard, Market St. 1858—1880(+)
12. COX, Henry b. d.	A	Cadgwith, Serpentine Works 1860s—1870s
13. DAWSON, James b. Devonport, 1837 d. Truro	P	Truro, River St. and Pydar St. 1860—1883(+)
14. DOCTON, Edwin b. Padstow, 1830(?) d.	P(?)	Padstow, Middle St. 1850s
15. DUNSTAN, William Henry b. Falmouth, 1820 d.	P	Falmouth, Berkeley Vale 1868—1880(+)

16.	GENN, William James b. Falmouth, 1846 d. Australia, 1870	A	Falmouth, Woodlane Tce. 1860s
17.	GEOFFROI, Henry Malcolm b. France d. Penzance	A(?)	Penzance, Regent House 1850s – 1870s (?)
18.	GIBSON, John b. Aran Isles, 1827 d. St Buryan, 1920	P	Isles of Scilly (earlier Penzance) 1860s – 1910
19.	GILL, John b. Cornwall ? d. (before 1926)	A	Truro 1850s – 1860s
20.	GREGORY, Henry b. d. Falmouth (?)	A	Falmouth 1860s
21.	GRIFFITHS, Richard Price b. Anglesey, 1819 d. Newquay, 1906(+)	P	Truro, River St. (later Newquay, Commercial Sq.) 1861 – 1900(+)
22.	GUTTERES, Frederic E. (Rev.) b. d.	A	Falmouth, HMS Russell 1858 – 1861(+)
23.	HAMBLY, Samuel Symons b. Egloshayle d. Egloshayle	A	Egloshayle, Sladesbridge 1860s
24.	HAMBLY, W.J. b. Camborne (?) d.	A	Camborne 1860s
25.	HARDING, Lewis b. 1803 d. 1893	A	Polperro 1854 – 1870(+)
26.	HART, Thomas b. Falmouth, 1820s d. Landewednack, c. 1910	P	Plymouth (few years), then Falmouth, Up. Berkeley Place 1859 – 1870
27.	HAWKE, Edward b. Gwennap (?) d.	A	Gwennap, Tolgullow 1860s
28.	HAWKEN, Thomas Edward b. Lostwithiel, 1836 d.	P	Lostwithiel, Queen St. c. 1856 – c. 1873
29.	HAYMAN, Henry b. Launceston (?) d. Launceston	P	Launceston, Church St. c. 1858 – 1890
30.	HIGGS, William Henry b. Lanlivery, 1827 d. Bodmin, 1870s	P	Bodmin, Fore St. c. 1859 – 1870s
31.	HOCKING, Samuel b. Camborne (?) d. Camborne (?)	A	Camborne, Market Place 1860s – 1870s
32.	HUNT, Robert, F.R.S. b. Devonport, 1807 d. London, 1887	P	Falmouth, Berkeley Vale 1840 – 45

33. JENKIN (JENKYNS), William b. St Blazey, 1823 d. Penzance, 1860	P	Penzance, North & Queen Sts. 1850s–1860
34. JORDAN, Thomas Brown b. Bristol, 1807 d. Reigate, 1890	A	Falmouth, Polytechnic 1839–40
35. LANYON, George b. Falmouth d. Falmouth	A	Falmouth, Chapel Tce. 1860s–1870s
36. LOBB, Charles Renowden b. Egloshayle, 1841 d. Egloshayle, 1871	P	Wadebridge c. 1860–1871
37. LUKE, Francis b. Scorrier d.	A	Gwennap, Scorrier 1860s
38. MAYELL, Edwin b. St Austell, 1812 d. Liskeard, 1860s	P	Liskeard, Tavern Hill 1850s–1860s
39. MICHELL, William b. St Austell d. St Austell (?)	P	St Austell, Church St. 1846–c. 1870
40. MITCHELL, John b. Truro d. Truro (?)	P	Truro, Pydar St. 1850s–1860s
41. MOODY, James b. Derbyshire, c. 1810–20 d. Redruth	P	Redruth, Fore St. 1859–1880s
42. MOODY, John b. Derbyshire, c. 1840 d. Penzance	P	Penzance, Market Jew St. 1865–1900s
43. MOYLE, Matthew Paul b. Chacewater, 1788 d. Helston, 1880	A	Helston, Cross St. 1850s(+)
44. OKE, William Williams b. Bodmin, 1827 d. Bodmin, 1880s	P	Bodmin, Bore St. 1860s–1880s
45. PADDON, Mr. b. Truro (?) d. Truro (?)	A	Truro 1860s
46. PARKER, Frederick Townley b. Italy, 1832 d. Camborne, 1892	A	Camborne, Rosewarne 1864–1892
47. PHILLPOTTS, Thomas (Rev.) b. Feock, 1807 d. Feock, 1890	A	Feock, Porthgwidden 1860s–1870s
48. PIPER, William b. Devon, 1829 d. Camborne, 1890	P	Camborne, Church St. 1858–1890
49. POLKINGHORNE, William b. St Columb d. St Columb, 1879	A	St Columb, Red Lion 1850s

50. POLKINHORN, Thomas W.   P   Penzance, Chapel Row
        b. Penzance, 1813   1860s
        d. Penzance, c. 1870

51. POOLE, Samuel   P   Truro, River St.
        b. Exeter, 1841   1859–1865
        d. Teignmouth (?), after 1899

52. PRESTON, Robert Hawker Peniel   P   Penzance, various addresses
        b. Sheepscombe, 1838   1860–1933
        d. Penzance, 1933

53. RASHLEIGH, Jonathan   A(?)   Fowey, Menabilly
        b. Fowey, 1820   1850s–1860s
        d. Fowey, 1905

54. RICHARDS, William   P   Penzance, Queen St.
        b. Penzance, 1835   1850s–1880(+)
        d. Penzance, c. 1900 (?)

55. RICKARDS, Robert Francis Bute (Rev.)   A   Constantine, Vicarage
        b. Cape of Good Hope, 1812   1856–1874
        d. Constantine, 1874

56. ROW, Matthew   P   Redruth, Penryn St. and
        b. Redruth (?)   Buller's Row
        d. Redruth   1860s–1870s

57. RULE, John   A   Camborne, Parc Bracket
        b. Camborne, 1801   1850s–1860s
        d. Camborne, 1866

58. STEPHENS, John Counsell   P   Falmouth, High & Church Sts.
        b. ? c. 1815–20   1849–c. 1880
        d.

59. THORN, Harry   P   Bude, The Crescent
        b. Bude, 1838   c. 1860–1876
        d. Bude, 1876

60. THORN, Samuel   P   Bude, The Crescent
        b. Bude, 1853   c. 1863–1898
        d. Bude, 1898

61. TREBILCOCK, James (?)   A   Falmouth, Killigrew St.
        b.   1845(+)
        d.

62. TREBILCOCK, William Barrett   P   St Day (later, Truro)
        b. St Clement, 1834   1860s–1872
        d.

63. TREGASKIS, William (?)   A   Falmouth, Church St.
        b. Redruth, 1832   1860s
        d.

64. TREMBATH, Edwin   P   St Just, Fore St. and Bank
        b. St Just   Square
        d. St Just   1860s–1890s

65. TRESIDDER, John Nicholas   A   Falmouth (and India)
        b. Falmouth, 1817   1850s–1860s(+)
        d. Dulwich, 1899

66. TREVASKIS, William John   P   Leedstown (later, Helston)
        b. Leedstown   1860s–1900(+)
        d. Leedstown

67.	TRULL, James Frederick b. d.	P	Falmouth, Church St. 1861 – 1870s
68.	TRUSCOTT, Charles b. St Stephen in Brannel, 1820 d.	P	Truro and Falmouth, various addresses 1855 – 1883
69.	TRUSCOTT, Walter b. St Stephen in Brannel, 1822 d.	P(?)	Falmouth, Berkeley Place 1864 – 1880s
70.	VEALE, Mr. R. b. d.	A	Falmouth 1860s
71.	VINEY, Mr. b. Plymouth (?) d.	P	Truro, River Street 1850s
72.	WHITFORD, William b. Camborne, 1822 d. Camborne	P	Camborne, Basset Rd. 1860s
73.	WILTON, William Henry b. Penryn d.	P	Penryn, Broad Street 1860s

B: Visiting professionals and amateurs

(Town or locality visited)

74.	COKE, Archibald L. Scotland (?)	VP	Land's End area, Scilly Early 1860s
75.	COLE, J.J. Hornsey Rise, London	VA	'Cliff scenery' 1864 – 65
76.	COX, W.J. Devonport ('Photographer to the Admiralty')	VP	East Cornwall ? 1854 – 55
77.	GUTCH, John Wheeley Gough (b. Bristol, 1809; d. London, 1869) Bristol	VP	Land's End area and The Lizard 1858
78.	HAMPTON, T.A. Plymouth	VP	Liskeard 1856
79.	HEATH, William (b. Plymouth, 1823) Plymouth ('Photographer to the Royal Eye Infirmary')	VP	East Cornwall 1860s
80.	HENDERSON, James 204 Regent St., London	VP	Launceston 1855 – 56
81.	LOBB, Nicholas Blake (b. Truro, 1831; d. Plymouth, 1887) Oxford St., London	VP	Truro, 1854; Boscastle, Tintagel, Delabole, 1859
82.	MANSELL, Thomas L. London ?	VP	Land's End area (?) 1860s
83.	MAY, William Devonport	VP	West Cornwall 1860s
84.	MAYLAND, William (?) London or Cambridge	VP	Truro 1854

85.	MAYOW, H.C. Plymouth ?	VP	East Looe 1855
86.	PALMER, John E. Union St., Plymouth	VP	Truro (branch) 1857−1866
87.	PAUL, Mr. ?	VP(?)	Porthcurno 1859−60
88.	PHILLIPS, Mr. ?	VP	Liskeard 1856
89.	PIPER, W(illiam ?) H. Walworth Rd., London	VP	Truro 1856
90.	TALBOT, William Henry Fox, F.R.S. (b. 1800; d. 1877) Lacock Abbey, Wiltshire	VP	Carclew, 1841; Mount Edgcumbe, 1845
91.	THOMSON, Hugh Plymouth ?	VP	Truro 1854
92.	TOPLISS, Mr. London	VP	Redruth 1856
93.	TRIPE, Linnaeus (Maj.-General) (b. 1822; d. 1902) Devonport ('Government Photographer, Madras Presidency')	VP	East Cornwall Late 1850s
94.	WILSON, George Washington (b. 1823; d. 1893) Aberdeen ('Queen's Photographer in Scotland')	VP	Land's End area 1861
95.	YEO, Richard P. Octagon, Plymouth	VP	Liskeard, 1857; rest of Cornwall (?), 1860s
96.	YEO, Stanley B. (brother of above)	VP	West Cornwall 1860s

Addendum

(97.	LLEWELYN, John Dillwyn (b. 1810; d. 1882) Wales	VA	West Cornwall 1852)

C: Daguerreotype practitioners
(selected from those mentioned above; see also p. 19)

Name	Status	Taken or exhibited, places and dates
DOCTON, Edwin	P(?)	Padstow, 1853
JENKYNS, William	P	Hayle, 1853
MICHELL, William	P	Falmouth, 1846
STEPHENS, John Counsell	P	Redruth (?) and Falmouth, 1849, 1851−52, later(?)
THOMSON, Hugh	VP	Hayle, 1853
TREBILCOCK, J(ames?)	A	Falmouth, 1845−46

APPENDIX II

PRELIMINARY LIST OF PROFESSIONAL PHOTOGRAPHERS IN CORNWALL AND SCILLY,
BY DECADES, 1871—1900

Entries refer to the earliest ascertainable dates. Many of the professionals in Appendix I continued in business long after 1870, their businesses passing to sons, brothers, widows or partners. The list makes no pretension to completeness and is intended as a guide.

First recorded in the decade Jan 1871—Dec 1880

BLIGH, Miss Emma	Fowey	44 RCPS 1876, cat. p. 19.
BURROW, Henry	Truro	K 1873 (with brother J.C.B.).
BURROW, John Charles	Camborne	K 1883, K 1889, K 1893.
GAEL, Edgar	Falmouth	48 RCPS 1880, 37; K 1883.
GRAVES SAWLE, Lady	St Austell	44 RCPS 1876, cat. p. 22.
HAMMER, William Henry	St Austell	K 1873.
JOHN, Thomas Lonser	Callington	K 1873.
JULIAN, Alfred Edmund	St Columb	Cartes of 1870s; K 1889.
LIDDELL, Henry	Bodmin	K 1873, K 1883.
MOOR, J. Walter	Falmouth	48 RCPS 1880, 37.
MOYLE, Simon	Hayle	K 1873.
REYNOLDS, John	Padstow	K 1873.
SANDRY, E.	Camborne	Carte, 1872 (with brother).
SANDRY, William James	Camborne	K 1873; bankrupt, RCG 19.8.81; do. 26.8.81; K 1883, K 1893.
SEARLE, Thomas	Liskeard	K 1873 (died 1893).
SIDDONS, Mr.	Falmouth	c. 1880? partner of J.C. Stephens.
TIMMINS, Joseph	Penryn	K 1873.
TONKIN, Henry	Falmouth	K 1873.
TONKIN, John Carvosso	Scilly	K 1873, K 1883, K 1893.
USHERWOOD, Charles	Truro	(Kenwyn St.) RCG 9.3.1877.
WOODROW, Daniel	Falmouth	K 1873.

First recorded in the decade Jan 1881 — Dec 1890

BAGGOTT, Charles	Falmouth	K 1883.
BEALES, James Henry	Camelford	K 1883, K 1889.
BELLINA, George	Scorrier	By 1883; K 1889, K 1893.
BENNETTS, William John	Camborne	By 1881; Hayle, 1888; K 1893.
BOND, Arthur John Frederick	Bodmin	K 1889, K 1893.
CATER, William Smale	Launceston	K 1889, K 1893.
COATH, John Henry	Liskeard	By 1881; K 1889 (died 1935).
COLENZA, Thomas Henry	Hayle	K 1883.
ELLERY, Edwin Iddol	Truro	K 1883, K 1889, K 1893.
HARRIS, John Alfred	Falmouth	K 1883, K 1889 (died 1892).
HARRISON, William H.	Falmouth	49 RCPS 1881, 21; K 1883, K 1889 (also at Truro, Helston, Redruth)
HAWKEN, William Edward	Lostwithiel	K 1883, K 1889.
JULYAN, Benjamin	St Austell	K 1883.
LIDDICOAT, Sampson	St Columb	K 1889, K 1893.
MARSDEN, William H.	Falmouth	K 1889.

NICHOLLS, John H.	Redruth	K 1883, K 1889.
OPIE, Henry	Redruth	K 1883, K 1889.
ORCHARD, William	St Austell	K 1883 (also Fowey), K 1889.
SAMPSON, P.	St Blazey	K 1883.
SCAMMELL, George	Truro	K 1889.
WAREN, Frederick	Newquay	By 1881; K 1883, K 1889, K 1893.

First recorded in the decade Jan 1891 — Dec 1900

BENNETTO, Wallace	Newquay	K 1893.
BROKENSHIRE, John	Penzance	K 1893.
FLEISCHMANN, L.	Looe	K 1893.
FLEISCHMANN, Shadwell	Polruan	K 1893.
GARLAND, Matthew Pope	Liskeard	K 1893 (son-in-law of Thomas Searle, died 1902).
GOVIER, Samuel John	Chacewater	In 1890s, RIC colln.; K 1906; Fenner 1986, 121.
HARRIS, Miss A.	Chacewater	K 1893.
JANE, Alfred Arthur	Bodmin	K 1893.
Messrs MAJOR & DARKER	Camborne	K 1893 (also at Falmouth, Penzance, St Austell); Fenner 1986, 121.
OATEY, James Edwin	Wadebridge	K 1893.
OLD, Alexander	St Merryn	K 1893.
OSBORNE, William J.	Falmouth	K 1893.
PENGELLY, William	Hayle	Album, c. 1895; K 1903 (grocer).
SMITH, Henry	Helston	K 1893.
TOURTEL, John William	Fowey	K 1893.
TREVORROW, William	St Ives	K 1893.

Fig.130   A Hard Day in My Studio
The interiors of Victorian photographers' studios are not often recorded, least of all in Cornwall; this jumbled scene comes from a family album that probably belonged to W.H. Dunstan's daughter. Dunstan himself, the artist, is worn out after long sessions with babies, lovers, sailors and grandparents. He leans upon his desk, wondering who will tidy up the mess. We must be in a back room at No.9 Berkeley Vale, Falmouth, the date being about 1873. One camera rests upon the chair, right. The camera used to make this image, if not worked by a time release, would have been operated by one of the family (or even by Walter Truscott?).
Carte, paper print, Dunstan's studio, early 1870s.

(Private colln.)

APPENDIX III

TOTALS AND GEOGRAPHICAL DISTRIBUTIONS

With the partial exception of the work of the Historical Group, Royal Photographic Society,[1] which has published about twenty special directories of photographers — mostly town-based and with an emphasis on the period 1840–1910 — there is very little information on the early practitioners as geographical or socio-economic groups. Coverage of English counties, as opposed to that of cities and large towns, is virtually non-existent. It is hoped that the information from Cornwall may inspire other workers to examine the records of their own areas.

Table 1, compiled from the gazetteer entries and *Appendix II,* should be accurate to within 10 per cent; this allows for unrecorded cases. It gives by decades the totals of commercial photographic concerns in Cornwall and Scilly from 1841 to 1900. Businesses that were partnerships, or where there was direct continuity through a relative (spouse, brother, son, son-in-law) as partner or legatee, are reckoned as single concerns. All amateurs and visiting professionals have been omitted.

What the table shows is the very steep increase between 1861 and 1870. This would justify the suggestion that the latter year marks a true horizon, and can be taken, as this book would take it, to form a suitable conclusion to an 'early' period. The 1861–70 increase, a 100 per cent growth over the preceding decade, is linked to the adoption of increased, cost-effective output by the smaller businesses (cartes de visite in place of Ambrotypes, multiple paper prints of views and stereographs); the steady improvement after 1859 in main-line rail communications into Cornwall; and an upturn in the early holiday industry, itself heavily promoted by the railway companies.[2] Growth after 1870 is less well marked. It may reflect a gradual spread of commercial photography into smaller towns and larger villages (Camelford, St Blazey, Scorrier, Chacewater) and also into those new seaside resorts which were getting their first middle-class hotels and summer-period shops (Hayle, Looe, Polruan, Fowey, St Merryn). Without adequate research, one can only hazard this sort of explanation.

154

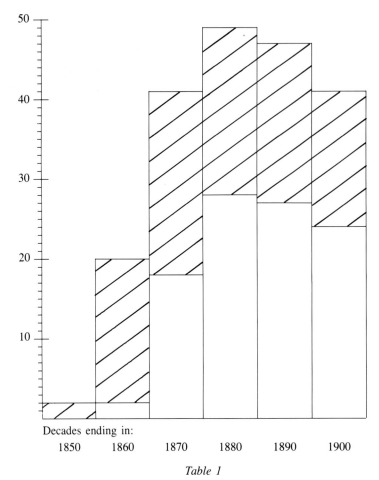

Table 1

Totals, by decades, of professional photographers working in Cornwall and Scilly, 1841–1900. In each column the upper shaded portion indicates businesses started in that decade; the lower plain portion, those continuing from previous decade(s).

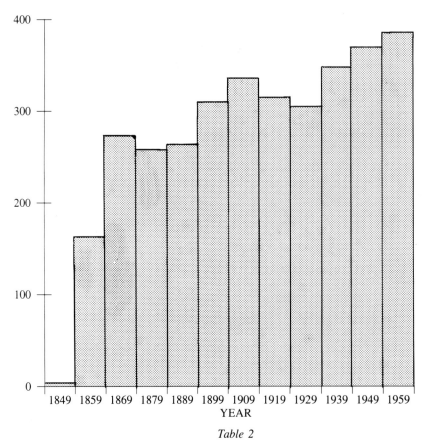

YEAR

Table 2

Totals, at 10-year intervals from 1849 to 1959, of London photographers; from Pritchard, and based on London post office directories.

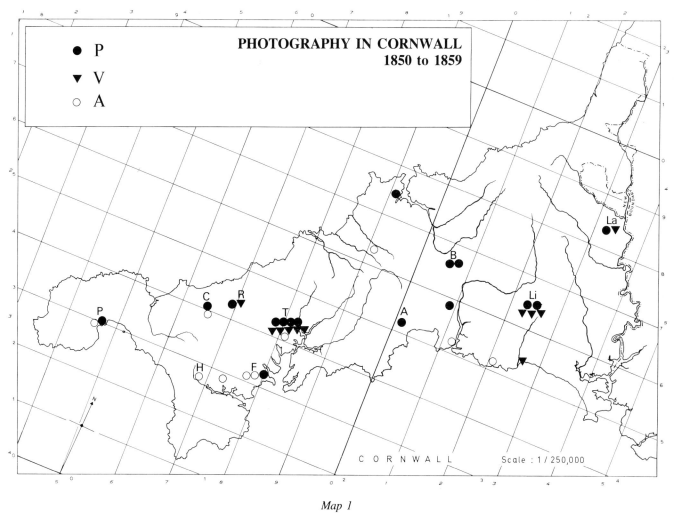

Map 1

Distribution of photographers first recorded between 1850 and 1859 (P, professional; V, visiting professional; A, amateur). Main towns indicated thus − P Penzance, C Camborne, R Redruth, H Helston, F Falmouth, T Truro, A St Austell, B Bodmin, Li Liskeard, and La Launceston.

It is interesting to compare *Table 1* with *Table 2*, which has been borrowed from a directory of London photographers[3] giving totals from 1849 to 1959 at ten-year intervals. Here the overall profile also shows a marked pre-1869 growth, the figure reaching a kind of plateau that in London rose again in the last decade of the century; rather than, as in Cornwall, in the decade 1871−80. Pritchard outlines arguments[4] for seeing a correlation, between the total of photographic studios at any one time and the absolute growth and changing distributional densities of London's population. He offers some support for this in a set of significant distribution maps.[5] This analysis cannot be applied to Cornwall. The levels of *per capita* income were very much lower, giving smaller disposable margins for such luxuries as photographic likenesses; access to non-neighbourhood businesses (e.g., by horse omnibus or inner-city railways) was far less available; and Cornwall's population-growth curve after an 1861 census peak was seriously distorted because of substantial losses through emigration.

The locations maps, *1* to *3,* show at once the very uneven distribution of early photographers west of Plymouth. *Map 1* covers the period 1850−59. At this date there was relatively little hope of a full-time income from photography, and the few professionals were spaced out. The exception is Truro, where four professionals were offering their wares and where short-period visiting photographers found it worthwhile to travel that distance and to rent temporary studios. This is interesting, and tends to confirm the belief that the administrative and financial dominance of Truro, very clear today in a town (or city) whose 'central' character dates on paper only from the 1880s, is probably rooted in the early 1800s; local banks, the legal profession, the convenience of wealthy landed families and a concentration of consumer inputs and outlets may explain this.[6]

Map 2, portraying the same post-1860 increase as *Table 1,* shows several other things. The stimulus afforded by the Polytechnic, beginning with Jordan, Hunt and the first exhibitions in the 1840s and the encouragement of public competition in the 1850s, resulted in a second-stage commercial exploitation. It is clear that amateur photography, in so far as our partial and imperfect records reflect this, grew considerably after 1860; and it makes commonsense to guess that the amateur flourished when he (or she) was in easy reach of a professional who could advise, supply materials, and develop or print.

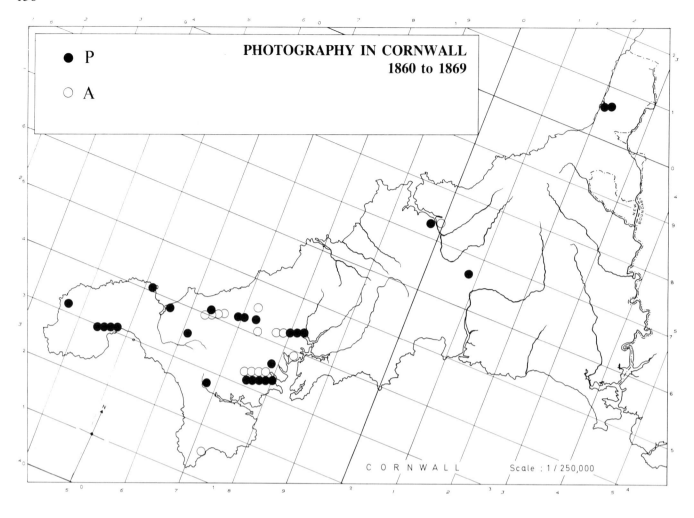

Map 2

Distribution of photographers first recorded between 1860 and 1869 (P, professional; A, amateur). For locations, see Map 1.

The combined *Map 3*, illustrating a twenty-year period, allows further comment. In *Map 2* the former visiting professionals from Plymouth and London no longer figure; after 1860, most of their short-stay portrait business had been taken over by resident local studios. As for the uneven coverage of the county, the pattern of the railway network must be one important factor. With an enormously detailed research programme (invoice-lists and trading ledgers would be needed) it might be possible to demonstrate a kind of reverse flow. A considerable volume of custom, most of it for carte and cabinet portraits, was attracted *from* Cornwall after 1859–60 by photographers in Devonport and Plymouth. Notably true of Liskeard, this affected families from as far west as Penzance. Lastly, in the overall distribution, the weight of emphasis is almost entirely western. Taking the dotted grid line as representing a rough east-west divide across Cornwall, about three times as many symbols of all kinds lie west of that line as lie to the east of it.

The moral ought to be that photography followed money, that in Cornwall money surplus to living requirements was generated mainly through mining and the large infra-structure of the mining industry, and that most of Cornwall's mines lay west of the divide. Well and good; but there may also be a hint that the county's centre of gravity, in intangible as well as statistically demonstrable senses, had shifted westward as early as the middle of the 19th century. In theory, the county town – Assize Courts, Judge's Lodgings, the militia barracks, the 1881 regimental depot – was still Bodmin; until early this century, Cornwall County Council met there. The two older centres that Bodmin itself had replaced (Launceston with its castle and county gaol; Lostwithiel with the Duchy Palace) were both in the east of Cornwall.

The early rise of Truro has already been mentioned. There, from 1850, we can suggest that photographic concerns were not of course subsistence necessities, but merely one of many innovative luxuries, sited where patronage was known to exist. Falmouth's importance also lay in special factors – the deep-water port, docks, international shipping, the vice-consulates held by the Fox family, the coastguard depot, a sporadic naval and military presence and numerous warehouse businesses. The status of Penzance was different. Non-

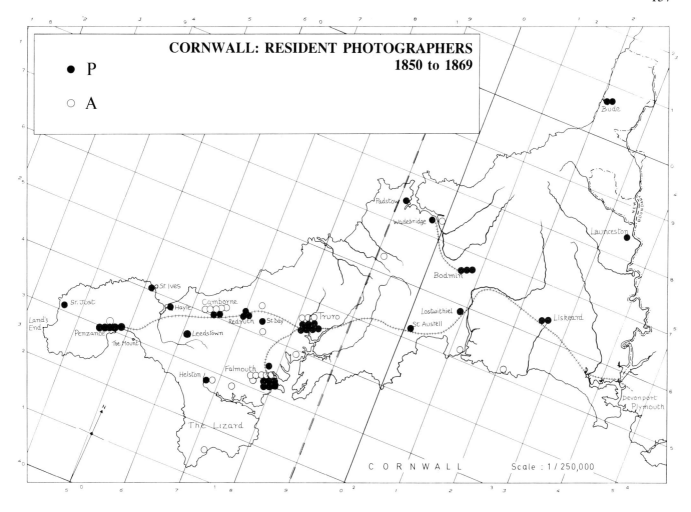

Map 3

Combined distribution of all resident professional and amateur photographers active between 1850 and 1869. The line of the pre-1870 railway network, west from Plymouth, is indicated.

industrial, like Falmouth it owed much of its attraction to a mild climate. It had a high content of retired persons, and such trappings as sub-tropical gardens, a subscription library, new churches and dispensaries, and a growing range of social and learned bodies. It was no accident — looking again at *Map 3* — that the county's major societies, all under Royal patronage, arose in these three towns. We note the Royal Geological Society of Cornwall (Penzance, 1814); Royal Institution of Cornwall (Truro, 1818); and Royal Cornwall Polytechnic Society (Falmouth, 1833).

All these remarks make up no more than a preliminary look at an extremely complex topic. They leave ample room for further social and economic research, now that the broad outline of the material can be drawn. Ultimately, the success or maintenance in profit of any photographic studio lay in its ability to attract custom and to meet competition. As with present-day hairdressers, copyshops or dry-cleaning establishments, there would have been an economic ceiling to the number of photographers any one town could support. Is it worth noting, going back to the individual gazetteer entries, that the few photographers who went under after a short period (like Trebilcock) were those whose clientèle came from the poorer classes; and that conversely a good social or family connection (Preston, Piper), a centre-of-town location (Griffiths, Richards),

or a firm niche in the tourist trade (Gibson, Thorn) could assure relative prosperity in the face of competition? If this is the economic side, social analysis would have to dwell more deeply on individual careers. Many of the photographers had sons; what was the perceived social standing of an early photographer, i.e., on a theoretical scale rising from coal-heavers and barmen, through master-butchers, to dentists and solicitors, and why did so few of the sons follow in their parents' footsteps? At least one photographer was a very rich man (Robert Preston). Others were inherently able (J.C. Burrow was, among other things, a champion marksman at Wimbledon for years) or belonged to notably gifted families (the Beringers). An untapped area of research is that of the amateurs. Many of them must have known each other, have used the same shops and subscribed to the same journals. The Cornish, in their small bustling towns, have always been given to forming little clubs and societies for every conceivable hobby or interest; a town of five thousand might have a hundred such. What were the amateur camera clubs and photographic circles — they exist today — in Victorian Cornwall?

The final message must be that, in its minor and fascinating way, early photography — amateur and professional — became an integral part of Society, and as such is a legitimate field for enquiry. In Cornwall, the picture has been lurking there in the shades for some time, and now the communal conscience of the Royal Institution of Cornwall, custodian for the moment of a major archive of photography, has managed to throw some light on that picture. Photographic history, studied in a growing number of Universities, Polytechnics and schools of art far distant from Cornwall, is a growth area. For the future, this writer would suggest that would-be researchers should leave the well-trodden paths of national and international photography as an art form; leave aside the now thoroughly explored technical and scientific aspects; and concentrate, using the tools of historical research, upon what might be described as the geography, the economics and the sociology of the whole subject. The reward is or should be one of human interest, and of delightful discoveries among pictorial riches that, alas, are vanishing at an alarming rate into junk-shops, flea-markets and even those strongholds of ransom, the London auction houses. As for the question 'Where should one begin?', even our preliminary survey confined to Cornwall and Scilly affirms the answer that many other workers have begun to suspect. There *is* no national picture. There are scores of local pictures, whose sum may amount in the end to a full depiction of photography — art, business, social record, mirror of the past as it really was — in Victorian Britain. The place to start is certainly not London; for the metropolis, one can be choked with too *much* detail. Elucidation must begin at home, a prime attraction to any local historian; and it must be sought the hard way, at town, city or county level.

1. Details from Hon. Secretary of the Group, Royal Photographic Society, The Octagon, Milsom Street, Bath BA1 1DN.
2. Wilson, Roger Burdett, *Go Great Western: A History of G.W.R. Publicity* (David & Charles, Newton Abbot, 1970).
3. Pritchard, Fig.2.
4. *Op.cit.*, 15–17.
5. *Op.cit.*, Fig.5.
6. Best source — Douch, H.L., *The Book of Truro* (Barracuda Books, Chesham, 1977).

APPENDIX IV

THE COMBINATIONS OF PHOTOGRAPHY WITH OTHER OCCUPATIONS

As the individual entries in the gazetteer have shown, many of the early photographers either began in some other career or trade, or practised photography in conjunction with another occupation. Noteworthy is the link between photography and a range of skilled crafts, some of which involved optics or manual dexterity, others of which imply an ability to handle chemicals as applied to glass, metal and other substances.

The list below omits visiting professional photographers, and is confined to Professionals (P) and Amateurs (A) within Cornwall.

Clergymen	A:	Gutteres, Phillpotts, Rickards.
Medical practitioners	A:	Moyle, Tresidder.
Engineers	A:	Gregory.
	P:	Colliver.
Other professions, or managerial	A (all):	Genn, solicitor. Hawke, rope-maker. Paddon, railways. Parker, estate manager. Rule, mine agent. Veale, dockyards.
Art or design teachers:	A:	Geoffroi (?), Gill, Walter Truscott.
practising artists	P:	Griffiths, Hart.
Watch- or clock-makers	A:	Fidelis Beringer, Hocking.
	P:	John Beringer (?), Broad, Hawken, Mayell.
Jeweller	P:	Michell.
Printers, stationers	A:	Tregaskis.
	P:	Griffiths, Higgs.
Gilders, painters, house-decorators	P:	Docton, Row, Trembath, Whitford, Wilton.
Leatherworkers	A:	Lanyon.
	P:	Jenkyns, Richards.
Clerical	A:	Clinton.
Commission agent	P:	Polkinhorn.
General stores	P:	Gibson, Hayman, Higgs.
Draper	P:	Oke.
Grocer	P:	Ashton.
Innkeeper	A:	Polkinghorne.

ABBREVIATIONS

Directories

(Norton	Jane E. Norton, *Guide to the National and Provincial Directories of England and Wales, excluding London, published before 1856* (Roy. Hist. Soc., London, 1950).)
C 1864	Charles Coulson, *Directory of Penzance and its Immediate Neighbourhood* (Cornish, Penzance, 1864).
D 1866	John S. Doidge, *A Directory of Redruth and its Neighbourhood* (Doidge, Redruth, 1866) – with Illogan, Gwennap & Stithians sections, separately paginated.
H 1862	Harrison, Harrod & Co.'s *Postal Directory and Gazetteer of Devonshire and Cornwall* (T. Danks, London, 1862) – Cornwall section, pp. 758–1008.
H 1878	*Harrod's Royal Directory, etc.* (Norwich, London, 1878) – Cornwall section.
K 1856 (&c.)	*Kelly's Directory of Cornwall* (Kelly & Co, London), issues for 1856, 1873, 1883, 1889, 1893, 1897, 1902, 1906 and 1910; pagination sometimes follows on from Devonshire section in two-counties issues.
K Devon 1873	*Kelly's Directory of Devon* (appropriate dates).
Lake 1883	*Lake's Post Office Directory of Truro* (W. Lake, Truro, 1883).
Lake 1902	H.R. Waters, *The Post Office Directory of Falmouth & Neighbourhood* (J.H. Lake & Co., Falmouth, 1902).
Pritchard	Michael Pritchard, *A Directory of London Photographers 1841–1908* (ALMM Books, Bushey, Hertfs., 1986).
P 1823	*Pigot & Co.'s London & Provincial New Commercial Directory for 1822–23* (J. Pigot & Co., London & Manchester, 1823), Cornwall section. (= Norton 36.)
P 1830	The same, for 1830; Cornwall section, pp. 133–172. (= Norton 53.)
P Devon 1830	The same, Devonshire section.
P 1844	*Directory of . . . Cornwall* (50 pp.) (Isaac Slater, late Pigot & Slater, Manchester, 1844). (= Norton 78.)
P 1876	*The Cornwall Calendar & Register for 1876, with, The Devonshire* (ditto; separate pagination) (Percy & Co., London, E.C., 1876).
S 1852	*Slater's Directory of Cornwall* (pp. 1–68; preface dated Dec. 1852) (I. Slater, Manchester, 1852). (= Norton 97.)
W 1847	*William's Commercial Directory of the Principal Market Towns in Cornwall* (J. Williams, Liverpool, 1847). (= Norton 154.)
W Devon 1850	*White's Historical Gazetteer & Directory of Devonshire* (William White, Sheffield, 1850).
W Devon 1879–79	*Ditto,* 2nd edition, Sheffield, 1878–79.
Wa 1864	*Directory and Guide for Falmouth & Penryn and their Vicinities by W. Warn, Falmouth* (Fred. H. Earle, Falmouth, 1864).

Other sources

BC	G.C. Boase & W.P. Courtney, *Bibliotheca Cornubiensis* – 3 vols., A–O, P–Z, Supplement (Longman, Green, Reader & Dyer, London, 1874–1882).
CC	G.C. Boase, *Collectanea Cornubiensia* (Netherton & Worth, Truro, for the author, 1890).
JRIC	*Journal of the Royal Institution of Cornwall,* Truro – Vol. I, 1864–65 (in progress).
LG	*Liskeard Gazette and East Cornwall Advertiser* (Matthews, Liskeard, No. 1, 21 July 1856 – Oct. 1874).
RCG	*Royal Cornwall Gazette and General Advertiser* (Truro, under this title, from 1849 onwards) – now incorporated in WB.

RCPS   *Annual Reports of the Royal Cornwall Polytechnic Society,* Falmouth − No. 1 (for 1833), and in progress.

RRIC   *Reports of the Royal Institution of Cornwall,* Truro − annual from 1818, subsumed in JRIC Vol. I onwards.

WB   *West Briton* (Heard, Truro, from No. 1, 1 June 1810).

BIBLIOGRAPHY

Printed books and articles

Arlott, John (with Rex Cowan and Frank Gibson) *Island Camera − The Isles of Scilly in the photography of the Gibson Family* (David & Charles, Newton Abbot, 1972).

Arnold, H.J.P. *William Henry Fox Talbot − Pioneer of Photography and Man of Science* (Hutchinson Benham, London, 1977).

Barham, T. Fisher *Old Cornwall in Camera* (Glasney Press, Falmouth, 1977).

Buckland, Gail *Fox Talbot and the Invention of Photography* (Scolar Press, 1980).

Burrow, J.C., and Thomas, William *'Mongst Mines and Miners, or, Underground Scenes by Flash-Light* (Camborne Prtg & Staty Co., Camborne, 1893).

Fenner, Robin A. *Devon and Cornwall Illustrated, Through the lens of a Postcard Photographer* (Stannary Press, Callington, 1986).

Fox, Barclay *Barclay Fox's Journal (ed. R.L. Brett)* (Bell & Hyman Ltd., 1979).

Fox, Wilson Lloyd *Historical Synopsis of the Royal Cornwall Polytechnic Society, For 81 Years, 1833−1913* (Lake, Falmouth, 1915). (In two parts − 1833−81, 81 pp., 1882−1913, 80 p. − with separate pagination, but issued as a single publication.)

Gernsheim, Helmut and Alison *Roger Fenton − Photographer of the Crimean War* (Secker & Warburg, 1954).

Gernsheim, Helmut *Incunabula of British Photographic Literature, 1839−1875* (Scolar Press, 1984).

Hunt, Robert *A Popular Treatise on the Art of Photography* (Rd. Griffin & Co., Glasgow, 1841).

King, Ronald *Tresco, England's Island of Flowers* (Constable, London, 1985).

Lanyon, Andrew *The Rooks of Trelawne* (Photographer's Gallery, London, 1976).

Lanyon, Andrew 'A Polperro Fishwife', *History of Photography,* 8.2 (Apr−Jun 1984), 89−98 (= Lanyon 1984a).

Lanyon, Andrew 'The First Cornish Photographs?' *History of Photography,* 8.4 (Oct−Dec 1984), 333−336 (= Lanyon 1984b).

Mathews, Oliver *Early Photographs and Early Photographers − a survey in dictionary form* (Reedminster Publctns, London, 1973).

Noall, Cyril *Botallack* (Barton, Truro, 1972).

Noall, Cyril *The Illustrated Past: Penwith* (Barracuda Books, Buckingham, 1978).

Noall, Cyril *Yesterday's Town − St Ives* (Barracuda Books, 1979).

Osborne, J.A., and Thomas, David H. *Victorian and Edwardian Camborne Through the "Eyes" of the Camera 1850−1920* (Camborne, 1986).

Pearson, Alan *Robert Hunt, F.R.S., 1807−1887* (Federation of Old Cornwall Societies, Penzance, 1976).

Potts, R.A.J. 'Early Cornish Printers, 1740−1850', *JRIC* (n.s.) IV.3 (1963), 264−325.

Stirling, A.J. 'Early Photography: 1839−53', *Journ. Roy. Society of Arts,* 129 (1981), 737−740.

Stirling, A.J. 'The Society of Arts' Photographic Exhibition of 1852', *Journ. Roy. Society of Arts,* 131 (1982), 54−57.

Stevenson, Sara *David Octavius Hill and Robert Adamson − Catalogue of their Calotypes (etc.)* (Nat. Galleries Scotland, Edinburgh, 1981).

Tangye, Michael *Portreath − Some Chapters in its History* (2nd impr., Redruth, 1978).

Trounson, J.H. *Mining in Cornwall 1850–1960, Volume Two* (Moorland Publishing, Ashbourne, n.d. = 1981).

Tong, James Yingpeh *Robert Hunt, A Popular Treatise on the Art of Photography, A Facsimile Edition with Introduction & Notes* (Ohio Univ. Press, Athens, Ohio, USA, 1973).

Watkiss, Reg *Early Photographs, The Land's End Peninsula* (Whites of Alverton, Penzance, 1975) (= Watkiss 1975a.)

Watkiss, Reg *Early Photographs, Penzance and Newlyn* (Dalwood, Penzance, 1975) (= Watkiss 1975b.)

Whitlock, Ralph (ed.) *British Birds from Nature − The Tresco Collection of Early Victorian Paintings . . . by Frances Smith* (Hamlyn, London, 1985).

INDEX

(*Note* This index omits the main Gazetteer entries − the names of 1839−1870 photographers, alphabetically listed in the Contents and in *Appendix I* and cross-referenced; the names and locations in *Appendix II;* and the titles, with names and places, given in the List of Illustrations. Numbers in **bold** refer to the illustrations.)